Simple

MILK STREET

Simple

CHRISTOPHER KIMBALL

WRITING AND EDITING BY

J. M. Hirsch, Michelle Locke and Dawn Yanagihara

RECIPES BY

Wes Martin, Diane Unger, Bianca Borges,
Matthew Card, Courtney Hill, Ari Smolin
and the Cooks at Milk Street

ART DIRECTION BY

Jennifer Baldino Cox

PHOTOGRAPHY BY

Erik Bernstein

FOOD STYLING BY

Erika Joyce

VORACIOUS

LITTLE, BROWN AND COMPANY

NEW YORK BOSTON LONDON

Voracious / Little, Brown and Company
Hachette Book Group
1290 Avenue of the Americas, New York, NY 10104
littlebrown.com

First edition: October 2023

Voracious is an imprint of Little, Brown and Company,
a division of Hachette Book Group, Inc.

The Voracious name and logo are trademarks of
Hachette Book Group, Inc.

The publisher is not responsible for websites (or their content)
that are not owned by the publisher.

The Hachette Speakers Bureau provides a wide range
of authors for speaking events. To find out more, go to
hachettespeakersbureau.com or call (866) 376-6591.

Voracious / Little, Brown and Company books may be purchased
in bulk for business, educational, or promotional
use. For information, please contact your local bookseller
or the Hachette Book Group Special Markets Department
at special.markets@hbgusa.com.

Photography and Props Stylist: Erik Bernstein
Author photograph by Channing Johnson

ISBN: 978-0-316-53855-8
LCCN: 2022949900
10 9 8 7 6 5 4 3 2 1

IM

Print book interior design by Gary Tooth / Empire Design Studio

Printed in China

Contents

Go-to Grains

One Pan

Pasta

Stir-Fried

High Heat

Introduction

Simple doesn't always mean easy. Rather, simple is something so perfectly constructed that every component is essential and in balance. This is particularly true of simple recipes, which should contain only and everything needed for a harmony of tastes and textures. And in achieving that harmony, these recipes offer us learning moments.

The best recipes are, in fact, simple, whether it is a shaved carrot salad, pasta with caramelized onions and pecorino, upside-down pizza, or a pan-roasted pork tenderloin. Along the way, we learn to bloom spices in fat, oven-fry cauliflower, cook pasta directly in the sauce, use stale bread, and make pilafs from barley and bulgur as well as rice.

Simple recipes are reductionist, each step and ingredient integral to the final dish. One does not need to add anything because the recipe is complete as is. A great painter knows when to put down the brush; a great writer conveys the essence of the protagonist's character in as few words as possible.

As a child in Vermont, I spent summers haying. Over time, one learns to pick up a bale in a sweeping motion, lifting up the right knee for support and then, with a smooth flow of momentum, launching the bale onto the hay wagon in an almost effortless arc.

In the kitchen, one learns the same economy of ingredients and technique. Drill down to the essence to extract the full measure of a small handful of ingredients combined in a perfect marriage. Less is more. Good rules for life and excellent guidelines for the kitchen.

The world is complicated, so we celebrate the simple life through cooking. The smallest notion can blossom and bring joy. A handful of ingredients transforms into supper.

Flatbreads and Sandwiches

Shrimp and Avocado Tostadas

Start to finish: 30 minutes
Servings: 4

Tostadas make an easy, satisfying meal, and these can be on the table in about 30 minutes. For ease and speed, we use the oven to crisp the tortillas to make the base. **We broil the shrimp, then toss them while still warm with mayonnaise and lime juice so they better absorb the seasonings.** Garnish the tostadas with chunks of rich, creamy avocado plus quick-pickled red onion for crunch and tang.

½ small red onion, finely chopped

3 tablespoons lime juice, divided,
plus lime wedges to serve

Kosher salt and ground black pepper

Four 6-inch corn tortillas

4 tablespoons extra-virgin olive oil, divided

1 pound large (26/30 per pound)
OR extra-large (21/25 per pound) shrimp,
peeled (tails removed), deveined and patted dry

2 tablespoons mayonnaise

1 ripe avocado, halved, pitted, peeled
and cut into ½-inch cubes

Heat the oven to 400°F with a rack in the upper-middle position. In a small bowl, stir together the onion, 2 tablespoons lime juice and a pinch of salt; set aside. Brush the tortillas on both sides with 1 tablespoon oil, then place in a single layer on a broiler-safe rimmed baking sheet. Bake until golden brown and crisp, 8 to 10 minutes, flipping once halfway through. Transfer to individual plates; reserve the baking sheet. Heat the oven to broil with a rack 4 inches from the element.

Place a wire rack in the reserved baking sheet. In a medium bowl, toss together the shrimp, the remaining 3 tablespoons oil and ½ teaspoon salt. Distribute the shrimp in an even layer on the rack. Broil until lightly charred on the surface and just opaque throughout, 4 to 5 minutes.

In another medium bowl, stir together the mayonnaise, the remaining 1 tablespoon lime juice and ¼ teaspoon pepper. Stir in the warm shrimp. Divide the shrimp among the tortillas. Top with the avocado and pickled onion. Serve with lime wedges.

Optional garnish: Chopped fresh cilantro OR red pepper flakes OR Tajín seasoning OR a combination

Pour-in-the-Pan Pizza with Tomatoes and Mozzarella

Start to finish: 6 hours (35 minutes active)
Servings: 4 to 6

The crust for this pizza borrows from the Milk Street recipe for a light, open-crumbed focaccia, our re-creation of the focaccia we encountered in Bari, Italy. **We make pizza dough with extra water for a batter-like mixture that can simply be poured into the pan.** Instead of making a single large pizza, you could make two 12-inch pies using low-lipped, disk-shaped pizza pans, like the ones used in American-style pizzerias; see the directions facing page.

400 grams (2¾ cups plus 2½ tablespoons)
bread flour

2 teaspoons white sugar

Two ¼-ounce packets instant yeast
(4½ teaspoons)

1½ cups water, 100°F to 110°F

Table salt and ground black pepper

3 tablespoons extra-virgin olive oil, divided,
plus more for oiling your hands

1 pound Campari or cherry tomatoes

6 ounces whole-milk mozzarella cheese,
shredded (3 cups)

1 teaspoon dried oregano

Kosher or flaky sea salt, for sprinkling (optional)

In a stand mixer with the dough hook, mix the flour, sugar and yeast on medium until combined, about 30 seconds. With the mixer running, add the water and mix on medium until a sticky dough forms, about 5 minutes; scrape the bowl and dough hook once during mixing. Turn off the mixer and let rest 10 minutes. Add 2 teaspoons salt and mix on medium for another 5 minutes. The dough will be shiny, wet and elastic.

Coat a large bowl with 1 tablespoon of the oil. Mist a silicone spatula with cooking spray and use it to scrape the dough into the bowl. Flip the dough with the spatula to oil all sides. Cover tightly with plastic wrap and let rise in a warm spot for 4 to 5 hours.

When the dough is ready, generously mist a 13-by-18-inch rimmed baking sheet with cooking spray, then pour 1 tablespoon of the remaining oil onto the center of the baking sheet. Gently scrape the dough onto the center of the sheet and let rest, uncovered, for 20 minutes.

Meanwhile, heat the oven to 500°F with a rack in the lowest position. If using Campari tomatoes, cut them into quarters; if using cherry tomatoes, cut them in half. Place the tomatoes in a large bowl and mash gently with a potato masher. Transfer to a fine-mesh strainer set over a bowl and set aside to drain until ready to use.

After the dough has rested, oil your hands, and, working from the center, gently push it into an even layer to the edges and into the corners of the baking sheet; be careful not to press out all of the air. It's fine if the dough does not completely fill the pan, but it should come close.

Drizzle the tomatoes with the remaining 1 tablespoon oil, then toss. Scatter over the dough, leaving a narrow border. Let rest for another 30 minutes. Scatter the cheese over the dough, then sprinkle with the oregano, pepper and kosher or flaky salt (if using). Bake until the surface of the pizza is golden brown and the bottom is crisped and well browned, 18 to 20 minutes. Slide the pizza from the pan onto a wire rack and cool for a few minutes before slicing.

How to Make Two 12-Inch Round Pizzas

Follow the recipe to make and rise the dough. When the dough is ready, generously mist two 12-inch round pizza pans with cooking spray, then pour 1 tablespoon oil onto the center of each. Scrape half the dough onto the center of each pan. Continue with the recipe, allowing the dough to rest for 20 minutes before pushing it to the edges of the pans and adding toppings. Bake one at a time, reducing the baking time to 12 to 15 minutes.

To Top It Off

Because pour-in-the-pan pizza dough is extremely wet, it's important to use toppings that are dry, or the pie will bake up with a soggy surface. The following are some of our favorite toppings; we suggest using no more than two in addition to the tomatoes and mozzarella. Scatter the ingredient(s) onto the tomato-topped dough just before adding the cheese. If you are using high-sodium toppings, such as olives or capers, you may wish to skip the salt that's sprinkled on before baking.

Sliced pepperoni or salami

Black or green olives, pitted and halved

Roasted red peppers, patted dry and cut into strips

Marinated artichoke hearts, patted dry and cut into chunks

Capers, drained and patted dry

SIMPLE SALSAS

A great sauce may make the dish, but we rarely have time for fussing with finicky recipes such as hollandaise, beurre blanc and other famous French sauces. Which is why when we want to punch up a dish we often turn to salsas.

Salsa is the Spanish word for sauce, and it has come to encompass a range of colorful, flavorful—and simple—toppings that go wonderfully with everything from airy omelets to sturdy stews.

We've picked three of our favorites, starting with an avocado-rich sauce that's a mash-up of Mexican guacamole and Canarian mojo verde; we char a fresh green chili for deep, smoky flavor. We also toast the chilies for a red chili and roasted peanut sauce that is good with tacos, sandwiches and burgers. And Guatemalan chirmol inspired our tomato and charred onion salsa. We simplified by leaving the tomatoes raw but charring the jalapeños and onion wedges for a tangy-sweet condiment we like tucked into tacos or eaten with chips.

RECIPES FROM TOP

| Red Chili and Roasted Peanut Salsa | Tomato and Charred Onion Salsa with Chipotle | Avocado and Poblano Salsa with Toasted Cumin and Almonds |

Avocado and Poblano Salsa with Toasted Cumin and Almonds

Start to finish: 15 minutes
Makes 1½ cups

To make this creamy-rich salsa that melds aspects of Spanish mojo verde with Mexican guacamole, we toast poblano chilies, deepening their flavor and imparting smokiness. The chilies then are blended with bright cilantro and lemon juice as well as avocado, almonds and cumin seeds until thick and spreadable. The salsa is excellent with grilled or roasted chicken, fish or mushrooms, smeared onto quesadillas and sandwiches, or served simply as a dip.

1 large poblano chili, stemmed, seeded and cut lengthwise into quarters

¼ cup slivered almonds

1 teaspoon cumin seeds

3 cups lightly packed fresh cilantro

1 ripe avocado, pitted, peeled and roughly chopped

¼ cup extra-virgin olive oil

1 tablespoon grated lemon zest, plus 3 tablespoons lemon juice

Kosher salt

Heat a 10-inch skillet over medium until droplets of water flicked onto the surface quickly sizzle. Toast the chili, flipping occasionally, until spotty brown on both sides, about 5 minutes. Transfer to a plate and cool. Meanwhile, in the same skillet over medium, toast the almonds, stirring, until fragrant and lightly browned, about 2 minutes; transfer to a blender. In the same skillet over medium, toast the cumin seeds, stirring, until fragrant, about 30 seconds; add to the blender.

Add the chili to the blender along with the cilantro, avocado, oil, lemon zest and juice, and ½ teaspoon salt. With the machine running, stream in 3 tablespoons water and puree until the mixture is thick and smooth, about 2 minutes, scraping the blender jar as needed. Transfer to a bowl, then taste and season with salt. Serve right away.

Optional garnish: Red pepper flakes OR flaky sea salt

Red Chili and Roasted Peanut Salsa

Start to finish: 25 minutes
Makes 1½ cups

Moderately spicy guajillo chilies, which boast complex fruity and smoky flavor, are ubiquitous in Mexican cuisine. **For this salsa, we heat guajillo chilies in a dry skillet with garlic, coaxing warm, toasty notes from both.** Once rehydrated, the chilies are blended with peanuts, honey and lime, yielding a vibrant, earthy sauce. Look for chili pods that are soft and pliable, an indicator of freshness. If you can't find guajillos, dried New Mexico chilies are a fine substitute. Enjoy the sauce drizzled onto tacos or tostadas, or spread onto sandwiches and burgers.

5 large (about 1 ounce) guajillo OR New Mexico chilies, stemmed, seeded and torn into 2-inch pieces

2 medium garlic cloves, smashed and peeled

1½ cups boiling water

¾ cup roasted peanuts

2 tablespoons extra-virgin olive oil

1 tablespoon lime juice

2 teaspoons honey

Kosher salt

2 tablespoons fresh oregano OR 2 teaspoons dried oregano

In a 10-inch skillet over medium-high, toast the chilies and garlic, pressing with a wide metal spatula and flipping halfway through, until fragrant, about 1 minute. Transfer the garlic to a blender; set aside. Put the chilies in a medium bowl and add the boiling water; press down to submerge. Cover and let stand until the chilies have softened, about 10 minutes.

Pour off and discard the soaking water, then add the chilies, peanuts, oil, lime juice, honey, 1 teaspoon salt and ¾ cup fresh water to the blender. Puree until smooth, 1 to 2 minutes, scraping the blender as needed. If desired, add water, 1 tablespoon at a time, to thin the consistency. Add the oregano and pulse until roughly chopped, about 3 pulses. Transfer to a bowl, then taste and season with salt. Serve right away or refrigerate in an airtight container for up to 5 days; bring to room temperature before serving.

Optional garnish: Flaky sea salt OR red pepper flakes OR both

Tomato and Charred Onion Salsa with Chipotle

Start to finish: 1 hour (20 minutes active)
Makes about 2 cups

Guatemalan chirmol is a smoky yet bright mix of charred tomatoes and onions with plenty of fresh herbs. We wanted to create an easy broiler version, but found broiled tomatoes too juicy. **We char jalapeños and red onion wedges under the broiler to mellow their flavors, and leave the tomatoes raw so they remain plump and firm.** The result is a colorful tangy-sweet salsa, delicious with grilled or roasted meats. We also love it spooned over toast, layered in a pita sandwich, tucked into shrimp tacos or scooped up with tortilla chips.

1 medium red onion, root end intact, cut into 8 wedges

2 jalapeño chilies, stemmed, halved and seeded

2 tablespoons extra-virgin olive oil, divided

Kosher salt and ground black pepper

1 pint grape OR cherry tomatoes, chopped

2 cups lightly packed fresh cilantro OR mint OR a combination, finely chopped

1 chipotle chili in adobo sauce, finely chopped

3 tablespoons lime juice

Heat the broiler to high with a rack 4 inches from the element. On a broiler-safe rimmed baking sheet, mound together the onion wedges and jalapeños. Drizzle with 1 tablespoon oil and sprinkle with ½ teaspoon salt; toss to coat. Arrange in an even layer and broil until charred and tender, 10 to 15 minutes, flipping once halfway through. Set aside to cool.

When cool enough to handle, chop the jalapeños; add them to a medium bowl. Trim and discard the root ends from the onion wedges, then chop and add them to the bowl. Stir in the tomatoes, cilantro and chipotle chili, then let stand at room temperature for 30 minutes. Stir in the lime juice and remaining 1 tablespoon oil. Taste and season with salt and pepper. Serve right away or refrigerate in an airtight container for up to 3 days; bring to room temperature before serving.

Ham, Gruyère and Asparagus Tartines

Start to finish: 25 minutes
Servings: 4

In France, a tartine is a slice of bread topped with almost anything—from butter and jam (for breakfast) to cheeses and cured meats (to make open-faced sandwiches). Instead of slices cut from a rustic boule or batard, we use a baguette that has been split open, so these sandwiches are more akin to what the French may call "baguette garnie" or "gondoles." Whatever their name, this is an easy way to throw together a light dinner. **We use average pencil-sized asparagus and cut the spears in half lengthwise so they cook quickly;** if you can find super-slender asparagus, simply leave the spears whole. Serve with a vinaigrette-dressed salad to complete the meal.

10- to 12-ounce baguette

3 tablespoons extra-virgin olive oil, plus more for drizzling

1 medium garlic clove, peeled and halved

3 tablespoons Dijon mustard

6 ounces sliced smoked ham

5 ounces Gruyère cheese, sliced

1 pound asparagus (see headnote), trimmed and halved lengthwise

Ground black pepper

Heat the broiler with a rack about 6 inches from the element. Cut the baguette in half crosswise, then split each half horizontally to create 4 similarly sized pieces. Pull out some of the interior crumb from each piece, slightly hollowing out the centers and creating boat shapes.

Place the bread cut side up on a rimmed baking sheet. Brush with the oil, then rub with the cut sides of the garlic clove; discard the garlic. Spread the mustard on the bread, dividing it evenly, then layer on the ham, tearing the slices as needed to fit. Divide the cheese over the ham, then top with the asparagus, crisscrossing the spears but not creating a solid layer so the cheese is visible underneath; you may not need to use all of the asparagus. Drizzle with additional oil and sprinkle with pepper.

Broil until the edges of the bread are toasted, the cheese is light spotty brown and the asparagus begins to char, about 4 minutes.

Pizzadilla with Tomatoes and Olives

Start to finish: 20 minutes
Makes one 12- to 13-inch pizzadilla

Pizza night gets a speedy overhaul when we skip the hassle of rolling out pizza dough and use at-the-ready flour tortillas instead. You'll need burrito-size flour tortillas, though you could make smaller pizzadillas using standard-size flour tortillas and a 10-inch skillet.

1 cup grape tomatoes, halved

½ medium red onion, thinly sliced

2 tablespoons extra-virgin olive oil, divided

¼ teaspoon red pepper flakes

Kosher salt and ground black pepper

12- to 13-inch (burrito-size) flour tortilla

4 ounces mozzarella OR cheddar cheese OR a combination, shredded (1 cup)

½ cup chopped pitted black olives

Heat the oven to 450°F with a rack in the middle position. In a medium bowl, toss together the tomatoes, onion, 1 tablespoon oil, pepper flakes and a pinch each of salt and pepper.

In a 12-inch oven-safe skillet over medium, heat the remaining 1 tablespoon oil until barely smoking. Add the tortilla and, using a wide metal spatula, press it against the skillet; the edges of the tortilla will form a lip. Remove the pan from the heat. Sprinkle the cheese onto the tortilla, then scatter on the tomato-onion mixture followed by the olives.

Place the skillet in the oven and bake until the tortilla is browned at the edges and the cheese is browned and bubbling, about 10 minutes. Remove the skillet from the oven (the handle will be hot) and slide the pizzadilla onto a cutting board. Cut into wedges.

Optional garnish: Chopped fresh basil

Chorizo and Chimichurri Sandwiches

Start to finish: 30 minutes
Servings: 4

Inspired by Argentinian choripán, this sandwich stars boldly spiced chorizo and chimichurri, Argentina's signature sauce. **Tangy with vinegar and grassy with cilantro (or parsley, or both) chimichurri balances the richness and fattiness of sausage.** It's essential to use Mexican-style chorizo, which is fresh and made with ground pork, as opposed to the Spanish dry-cured or smoked variety; make sure it is link-style chorizo in natural casing. To help the sandwiches remain intact when eaten, we cut a baguette into four sections, then slice through lengthwise on just one side, creating a hinged shape reminiscent of a hot dog bun.

8 tablespoons extra-virgin olive oil, divided

3 tablespoons red wine vinegar

1½ cups lightly packed fresh cilantro OR flat-leaf parsley OR a combination, finely chopped

1 medium garlic clove, finely grated

½ teaspoon red pepper flakes

Kosher salt and ground black pepper

1 baguette, cut into 4 sections, split horizontally, kept hinged on one side

4 links Mexican-style chorizo (see headnote), split horizontally, kept hinged on one side

To make the chimichurri, in a small bowl, whisk together 4 tablespoons oil, the vinegar, cilantro, garlic, pepper flakes and ¼ teaspoon each salt and black pepper; set aside.

Brush 3 tablespoons of the remaining oil onto the insides of the bread. Heat a 12-inch skillet over medium until droplets of water flicked onto the surface sizzle in a few seconds. Toast one bread section at a time, cut side down, until lightly golden, about 1 minute; remove from the pan and set aside.

In the same skillet over medium, heat the remaining 1 tablespoon oil until shimmering. Cook the sausages, cut sides down, until browned, about 4 minutes. Flip the sausages and cook, turning and flipping as needed, until well browned on both sides and the centers reach 160°F, another 4 to 6 minutes.

Place a sausage on each piece of baguette. Stir the chimichurri to recombine, then spoon it onto the sausages. Close the sandwiches and serve.

Optional garnish: Thinly sliced avocado OR sliced tomato OR mayonnaise OR a combination

GIVE MAYO A MAKEOVER

Store-bought mayonnaise is creamy and convenient but doesn't offer much beyond that. Luckily, there's an easy, and equally effortless, fix for that in our lineup of pantry powerhouse ingredients we consider must-haves.

The method couldn't be simpler. Just a little chopping and stirring turns humdrum mayonnaise into a superstar sauce that pairs perfectly with all manner of foods.

We add chopped kimchi (plus a little of the kimchi juice) to make a creamy-spicy dipping sauce that's great with fried potatoes or spooned onto a burger. North African harissa paste combined with lemon and olives gives us a spread that's good in sandwiches and also makes a terrific topping for roasted vegetables. (For a tangy take, substitute Greek yogurt for mayonnaise in this one.) And cilantro, lime and pickled jalapeños combine for a spicy, tangy and yet cooling sauce that's good with tacos or a steaming bowl of chili.

RECIPES FROM TOP

| Kimchi Aioli | Creamy Cilantro-Lime Sauce with Pickled Jalapeños | Harissa Mayonnaise with Olives and Lemon |

Creamy Cilantro-Lime Sauce with Pickled Jalapeños

Start to finish: 20 minutes
Makes about 1 cup

Creamy and cooling but also a little spicy and tangy, this sauce comes together easily. **We use the gentle heat of pickled jalapeños to balance the richness of sour cream and mayonnaise.** It's great anywhere you'd use sour cream as a garnish—drizzled onto tacos or burritos, spooned onto refried beans or dolloped onto a bowlful of chili.

½ cup sour cream

¼ cup mayonnaise

2 tablespoons finely chopped fresh cilantro

1 tablespoon finely chopped pickled jalapeños, plus 1 tablespoon brine

2 teaspoons grated lime zest, plus 2 tablespoons lime juice

¼ teaspoon cayenne pepper

Kosher salt and ground black pepper

In a small bowl, stir together the sour cream, mayonnaise, cilantro, jalapeños with brine, lime zest and juice, and cayenne. Taste and season with salt and black pepper. Use immediately or refrigerate in an airtight container for up to 3 days.

Harissa Mayonnaise with Olives and Lemon

Start to finish: 15 minutes
Makes about 1 cup

This punchy, subtly spicy sauce combines North African flavors. **Briny green olives and lemon add texture and bright contrast to spicy harissa.** Use it as a spread in sandwiches, as an embellishment for a frittata, as a flourish for roasted vegetables or as a dipping sauce (think whole roasted artichokes). For a tangier sauce with a more cooling quality, use whole-milk Greek yogurt in place of the mayonnaise.

¾ cup mayonnaise OR plain whole-milk Greek yogurt

⅓ cup finely chopped pitted green OR black olives OR a combination

1 to 1½ tablespoons harissa paste

1 tablespoon grated lemon zest, plus 3 tablespoons lemon juice

Kosher salt and ground black pepper

In a small bowl, stir together the mayonnaise, olives, harissa and lemon zest and juice. Taste and season with salt and pepper. Use immediately or refrigerate in an airtight container for up to 3 days.

Kimchi Aioli

Start to finish: 20 minutes
Makes about 1 cup

Cabbage kimchi plus grated garlic add loads of kick
to a mayonnaise base, turning it into a terrific East-
meets-West condiment. **In addition to finely chopped
kimchi, we include kimchi juice for tanginess.** How
much liquid is in the jar depends on the brand. If yours
is relatively dry, use a little more rice vinegar instead to
boost the acidity and thin the aioli. Slather this onto a
burger, drizzle it onto roasted or fried potatoes, or offer
it as a dipping sauce for just about anything.

¾ cup mayonnaise

**3 tablespoons finely chopped cabbage kimchi,
plus 1 to 2 tablespoons kimchi juice (see headnote)**

1 medium garlic clove, finely grated

**1 teaspoon unseasoned rice vinegar,
plus more as needed**

Kosher salt and ground black pepper

In a small bowl, stir together the mayonnaise, kimchi
and its juice, garlic and vinegar. Taste and season with
salt, pepper and additional vinegar. Use immediately or
refrigerate in an airtight container for up to 3 days.

Panini with Mortadella, Provolone and Broccoli Rabe

Start to finish: 30 minutes
Serves: 4

Panini offer a tantalizing combination of warm, toasted bread, salty meats and melty cheese. **We add sautéed broccoli rabe to panini for bitter, herbal contrast to the richness of mortadella and provolone.** We spread vinegary crushed red peppers on the bread to add piquancy—sometimes labeled as "hoagie spread," it's sold jarred in most supermarkets. Chopped peperoncini or cherry peppers would be a good substitute.

3 tablespoons extra-virgin olive oil, divided

2 medium garlic cloves, peeled and halved

1-pound bunch broccoli rabe, trimmed and chopped into rough ½-inch pieces

Kosher salt

Four 8-inch crusty rolls or ciabatta rolls

4 tablespoons jarred crushed red peppers (see headnote), divided

8 ounces sliced provolone cheese, preferably aged provolone, slices cut in half

8 ounces sliced mortadella

In a 12-inch skillet over medium-high, heat 1 tablespoon of oil until shimmering. Add the garlic and cook, stirring, until the cloves begin to brown, about 30 seconds. Add the broccoli rabe and ½ teaspoon salt, then cook, stirring, until just starting to soften, about 1 minute. Add ¼ cup water, cover and cook, stirring occasionally, until the stem pieces are tender, 4 to 5 minutes. Remove and discard the garlic, then transfer the rabe to a medium bowl; set aside. Wipe out the skillet and set it aside.

Split each roll horizontally, leaving one side hinged. If the rolls are very thick, pull out and discard some of the crumb so the bread is about ½ inch thick. Spread 1 tablespoon of crushed peppers on the inside of the top half of each roll. Top the other side with the broccoli rabe, dividing it evenly. Lay half of the provolone on the rabe, dividing it evenly. Top the cheese with the mortadella, then finish with the remaining provolone. Close the rolls and press firmly.

In the same skillet over medium, heat 1 tablespoon of the remaining oil until shimmering. Add 2 panini, weight them with a heavy skillet or pot, then cook until the bottoms are nicely toasted, 2 to 3 minutes, adjusting the heat as needed if the bread is browning too quickly. Flip the panini, replace the weight and cook until the second sides are toasted and the cheese begins to melt, 1 to 2 minutes. Transfer to a cutting board. Using the remaining 1 tablespoon oil, toast the remaining 2 panini in the same way. To serve, cut each panini in half on the diagonal.

Skillet Steak with Onion and Sweet Peppers

Start to finish: 40 minutes
Servings: 4

For this easy one-pan dish, inspired by beef fajitas, we double down on the seasonings for bold, layered flavor. To start, we season skirt steak with chili powder and ground cumin, then sear it quickly in a hot skillet. The steak is removed and strips of crunchy-sweet bell pepper and sliced red onion are cooked in the pan juices until tender-crisp. To finish, we return the sliced steak to the mix, allowing it to meld with the vegetables and absorb a second dose of the spices. Serve with warmed tortillas or rice and beans.

4 tablespoons neutral oil, divided

3 teaspoons chili powder, divided

1 teaspoon ground cumin, divided
OR ½ teaspoon granulated garlic, divided OR both

Kosher salt and ground black pepper

1 pound skirt steak OR flank steak, trimmed and cut in half

2 medium red OR orange OR yellow bell peppers, stemmed, seeded and sliced into ½-inch strips

1 medium red onion, halved and sliced about ¼ inch thick

1 tablespoon lime juice, plus lime wedges, to serve

In a wide, shallow dish, stir together 1 tablespoon oil, 2 teaspoons chili powder, ½ teaspoon cumin (and/or ¼ teaspoon granulated garlic), ¾ teaspoon salt and ½ teaspoon pepper. Add the steak and rub the seasonings into all sides.

In a 12-inch skillet over medium-high, heat 2 tablespoons oil until barely smoking. Add the steak, reduce to medium and cook, undisturbed, until well browned, about 1 minute. Flip and cook until well browned on the second sides, another 2 minutes. Transfer to a large plate and wipe out the skillet.

In the same skillet over medium-high, heat the remaining 1 tablespoon oil until shimmering. Add the bell peppers and onion; cook, stirring, until beginning to wilt, about 5 minutes. Add the remaining 1 teaspoon chili powder, the remaining ½ teaspoon cumin (and/or the remaining ¼ teaspoon granulated garlic) and ¼ teaspoon each salt and pepper; cook, stirring, until fragrant, about 1 minute. Remove the pan from the heat.

Transfer the steak to a cutting board and slice it against the grain about ¼ inch thick. Add the steak and accumulated juices to the vegetables in the skillet. Cook over medium-high, stirring and tossing, until the juices have cooked off, 1 to 2 minutes. Off heat, stir in the lime juice, then taste and season with salt and pepper. Serve with lime wedges.

Optional garnish: Chopped fresh cilantro OR sour cream OR pico de gallo OR a combination

Pita Burgers with Crisped Cheese

Start to finish: 40 minutes
Servings: 4

This burger was inspired by the popular folded cheeseburger served at Miznon, an Israeli restaurant with multiple locations. It's seasoned with yellow mustard for spicy tang and dill pickles for brininess. We then fill pita halves with the mixture, forming a thin layer, along with sliced onion and cheese. **Cheese hits the skillet when the sandwiches are pan-fried, crisping and developing flavorful caramelization, and creating an irresistible layer that contrasts deliciously with the juicy patties.** Be sure to use 90 percent lean ground beef; meat that is higher in fat will shrink and the pitas will be greasy.

1 pound 90 percent lean ground beef

¼ cup drained chopped dill pickles OR sweet pickled peppers OR a combination

2 tablespoons yellow mustard

Kosher salt and ground black pepper

Two 8-inch pita breads, cut into half rounds

½ medium red onion, thinly sliced

8 slices sharp cheddar OR American cheese

1 tablespoon neutral oil

In a medium bowl, combine the beef, pickles, mustard, 1 teaspoon salt and ½ teaspoon pepper; mix thoroughly with your hands. Let stand for about 15 minutes to allow the meat to lose some of its chill.

Open each pita half to form a pocket. Fill each half with a quarter of the meat mixture, spreading it to the edges, then lightly pressing on the outside to flatten. Into each pita pocket, tuck a quarter of the onion, followed by 2 cheese slices; it's fine if the cheese peeks out of the pita and if the bread forms cracks. Brush the pita halves on both sides with the oil.

Heat a 12-inch nonstick skillet over medium until droplets of water flicked onto the surface quickly sizzle. Add 2 of the stuffed pita halves and cook until golden brown on the bottoms, about 4 minutes. Using a wide metal spatula, flip and cook, adjusting the heat as needed, until golden brown on the second sides and the exposed cheese is browned and crisp, about 3 minutes. Transfer to a platter or individual plates. Cook the remaining pita halves in the same way.

Chickpea Flour Flatbread

Start to finish: 30 minutes
Makes four 10-inch crepes

Chickpea flour—rather than wheat flour—creates flatbreads with a crisp, light texture, but just as quick and easy to make. They also are gluten-free and delicious hot from the pan or at room temperature. Chickpea flatbreads are known as socca in France, or as farinata in Italy. Some versions are thicker than others, but all are made with chickpea flour and olive oil. Ours are thin and get great flavor from the rich browning they attain in the skillet. To turn our socca into a light meal, offer an olive and roasted pepper relish or spinach, grape and feta salad alongside (see following recipes).

165 grams (1½ cups) chickpea flour

Kosher salt and ground black pepper

1½ cups warm (100°F) water

¼ cup extra-virgin olive oil, plus more to cook

In a large bowl, whisk together the chickpea flour, 1 teaspoon salt and ¼ teaspoon pepper. Pour in half of the water and whisk until smooth. While whisking, slowly pour in the remaining water and whisk until combined. Gently whisk in the oil just until incorporated but small beads of oil remain visible.

In a 10-inch nonstick skillet over medium-high, heat 2 teaspoons oil until shimmering. Pour ¼ of the batter (about ½ cup) into the center of the skillet and tilt so the batter completely covers the surface. Cook until the bottom is well browned, 1½ to 2 minutes. Using a metal spatula, carefully flip and cook until the second side is dark spotty brown, about another minute. Transfer to a wire rack. Repeat with the remaining batter and 2 teaspoons oil for each flatbread.

Cut each flatbread into 4 wedges and serve with one of the following toppings:

Olive and Roasted Pepper Relish: In a medium bowl, stir together 1 cup chopped pitted green olives, ¼ cup drained and chopped roasted red peppers, ¼ cup chopped fresh flat-leaf parsley, 1 tablespoon drained and rinsed capers, 1 finely grated garlic clove and 1 teaspoon red wine vinegar. Let stand for 15 minutes.

Spinach, Grape and Feta Salad: In a large bowl, combine 1 tablespoon minced shallot and 2 teaspoons sherry vinegar; let stand for 10 minutes. Whisk in ½ teaspoon Dijon mustard, a pinch of kosher salt and ⅛ teaspoon ground black pepper. Whisk in 2 table-spoons extra-virgin olive oil. Add 8 cups loosely packed baby spinach, 1 cup halved seedless red grapes and ⅓ cup crumbled feta cheese. Gently toss to combine.

PUT A NEW SPIN ON PIZZA

Store-bought pizza dough is a great time-saver, but the results often don't live up to pizza shop standards. One simple way to turn that situation around is to—literally—turn things around.

Instead of putting dough in a pan and adding toppings, we start by roasting vegetables in the oven until they're beginning to soften and caramelize. We then spread the dough on top, poke a few holes to let steam escape, then slide the whole thing back into the oven to finish baking.

The pizza comes out of the oven with a crisp, golden crust ready to be flipped right side up and finished with herbs or cheese, or both. And the inverted pizzas are big enough to serve six, so no need to shape and bake multiple pies.

We came up with three variations, a sweet-savory combination of onions, anchovies and olives based on pissaladière from the south of France; a tangy-floral pairing of pears and goat cheese; and a rich and savory mix of salami and fennel roasted to jammy softness.

RECIPES FROM TOP

| Inverted Pizza with Pears, Goat Cheese and Pistachios | Inverted Pizza with Olives, Anchovies and Caramelized Onions | Inverted Pizza with Fennel, Taleggio and Salami |

Inverted Pizza with Olives, Anchovies and Caramelized Onions

Start to finish: 45 minutes
Servings: 6

Pissaladière is a classic savory tart from the south of France featuring caramelized onions, savory anchovies and briny black olives—an ideal topping combination for our weeknight-simple inverted pizza. Caramelizing thinly sliced onions on a baking sheet makes quick, hands-off work of the task. Once nicely browned, the topping mixture is covered in store-bought pizza dough, then baked until golden. **After being inverted upright, the browned crust that formed during baking becomes a wonderfully crisp bottom, no pizza stone required.** Fresh thyme and a drizzle of extra-virgin olive oil give the pizza an enticing aroma and shine.

2 medium yellow onions, halved and thinly sliced

3 tablespoons extra-virgin olive oil, divided, plus more to serve

1 tablespoon fresh thyme, chopped

Kosher salt and ground black pepper

2-ounce can oil-packed anchovy fillets (about 10 fillets), drained and roughly chopped

½ cup pitted black olives, roughly chopped

All-purpose flour, for dusting

1½ pounds store-bought refrigerated pizza dough, room temperature

Heat the oven to 450°F with a rack in the lowest position. Line a rimmed baking sheet with kitchen parchment. In a large bowl, toss the onions with 2 tablespoons oil, half of the thyme, ½ teaspoon salt and 1 teaspoon pepper. Spread the onion mixture in an even layer on the prepared baking sheet, then evenly distribute the anchovies and olives over the top. Bake, without stirring, until the onions begin to brown and soften, 20 to 25 minutes.

Meanwhile, on a well-floured counter, use a rolling pin to roll the dough into a 12-by-16-inch rectangle (the same dimensions as the baking sheet); work from the center outward to help ensure the dough is even. If it is resistant or shrinks after rolling, wait 5 to 10 minutes before trying again; if it is very elastic, you may need to give it a few rests. It's fine if the dough rectangle is slightly smaller than the baking sheet.

When the onion mixture is ready, remove the baking sheet from the oven; leave the oven on. Being careful not to touch the hot baking sheet, lay the dough over the onion mixture, gently stretching and tucking in the edges as needed so the dough fills the baking sheet. Brush with the remaining 1 tablespoon oil, then use a fork to poke holes every 2 to 3 inches all the way through the dough. Bake until the surface is well browned, 15 to 17 minutes.

Remove from the oven and immediately invert a wire rack onto the baking sheet. Using potholders or oven mitts, hold the baking sheet and rack together and carefully invert. Lift off the baking sheet, then slowly peel away the parchment. Using a spatula, scrape off any toppings that cling to the parchment and return them to the pizza. Sprinkle with the remaining thyme and drizzle with additional oil.

Optional garnish: Chopped fresh flat-leaf parsley

Inverted Pizza with Pears, Goat Cheese and Pistachios

Start to finish: 45 minutes
Servings: 6

For this inverted pizza, we call on a winning ingredient combination of contrasting flavors: sweet, subtly floral pears and rich, tangy goat cheese. Roasting the pears with shallots balances their sweetness, while pistachios add nutty notes and salty crunch to each bite. Store-bought refrigerated pizza dough makes this pie a breeze to prepare, but for easiest shaping, be sure the dough is at room temperature, not chilled. As a final but optional flourish, sprinkle the savory-sweet pizza with crushed fennel seeds and minced fresh thyme or rosemary.

3 medium ripe but firm pears, stemmed, halved, cored and cut into ¼-inch wedges

2 medium shallots, halved lengthwise and thinly sliced

3 tablespoons extra-virgin olive oil, divided

1 tablespoon honey, plus more to serve

Kosher salt and ground black pepper

All-purpose flour, for dusting

1½ pounds store-bought refrigerated pizza dough, room temperature

4 ounces fresh goat cheese (chèvre) OR blue cheese, crumbled (½ cup)

½ cup roasted salted pistachios, roughly chopped

Heat the oven to 450°F with a rack in the lowest position. Line a rimmed baking sheet with kitchen parchment. In a large bowl, toss together the pears, shallots, 2 tablespoons oil, honey and ½ teaspoon each salt and pepper. Distribute the mixture in an even layer on the prepared baking sheet and bake without stirring until the pears and shallots begin to brown and soften, about 15 minutes.

Meanwhile, on a well-floured counter, use a rolling pin to roll the dough into a 12-by-16-inch rectangle (the same dimensions as the baking sheet); work from the center outward to help ensure the dough is even. If it is resistant or shrinks after rolling, wait 5 to 10 minutes before trying again; if it is very elastic, you may need to give it a few rests. It's fine if the dough rectangle is slightly smaller than the baking sheet.

When the pear mixture is ready, remove the baking sheet from the oven; leave the oven on. Being careful not to touch the hot baking sheet, lay the dough over the pear mixture, gently stretching and tucking in the edges as needed so the dough fills the baking sheet. Brush with the remaining 1 tablespoon oil, then use a fork to poke holes every 2 to 3 inches all the way through the dough. Bake until the surface is well browned, 15 to 17 minutes.

Remove from the oven and immediately invert a wire rack onto the baking sheet. Using potholders or oven mitts, hold the baking sheet and rack together and carefully invert. Lift off the baking sheet, then slowly peel away the parchment. Using a spatula, scrape off any toppings that cling to the parchment and return them to the pizza. Scatter on the goat cheese and sprinkle with the pistachios, then drizzle with additional honey.

Optional garnish: Crushed fennel seeds OR minced fresh thyme OR rosemary OR a combination

Inverted Pizza with Fennel, Taleggio and Salami

Start to finish: 45 minutes
Servings: 6

For this inverted pizza, we employ a mixture of sharp shallots, spiced salami and anise-y fennel. **Roasting the fennel brings out its sweetness, while turning its texture soft and jammy.** Once the topping mixture is cooked, we cover it in store-bought pizza dough, then bake until crisp and golden brown. (So the dough is easy to stretch and shape, be sure it's at room temperature.) After being inverted out of the baking sheet, the pizza is dotted with slices of creamy taleggio (or brie) cheese, which melts and fills the fennel crevices with buttery-tangy richness. The cheese handles more easily when chilled, so slice it straight from the refrigerator.

2 medium fennel bulbs, trimmed, cored and sliced ¼ inch thick

3 medium shallots, halved lengthwise and thinly sliced

3 tablespoons extra-virgin olive oil, divided, plus more to serve

1 tablespoon honey, plus more to serve

Kosher salt and ground black pepper

All-purpose flour, for dusting

2 ounces thinly sliced salami

1½ pounds store-bought refrigerated pizza dough, room temperature

6 ounces taleggio OR brie cheese, cut into ¼-inch slices

Heat the oven to 450°F with a rack in the lowest position. Line a rimmed baking sheet with kitchen parchment. In a large bowl, toss together the fennel, shallots, 2 tablespoons oil, honey, ½ teaspoon salt and 1 teaspoon pepper. Spread the mixture in an even layer on the prepared baking sheet, then evenly distribute the salami over it. Bake, without stirring, until the fennel begins to brown and soften, 15 to 20 minutes.

Meanwhile, on a well-floured counter, use a rolling pin to roll the dough into a 12-by-16-inch rectangle (the same dimensions as the baking sheet); work from the center outward to help ensure the dough is even. If it is resistant or shrinks after rolling, wait 5 to 10 minutes before trying again; if it is very elastic, you may need to give it a few rests. It's fine if the dough rectangle is slightly smaller than the baking sheet.

When the fennel mixture is ready, remove the baking sheet from the oven; leave the oven on. Being careful not to touch the hot baking sheet, lay the dough over the fennel mixture, gently stretching and tucking in the edges as needed so the dough fills the baking sheet. Brush with the remaining 1 tablespoon oil, then use a fork to poke holes every 2 to 3 inches all the way through the dough. Bake until the surface is well browned, 17 to 20 minutes.

Remove from the oven and immediately invert a wire rack onto the baking sheet. Using potholders or oven mitts, hold the baking sheet and rack together and carefully invert. Lift off the baking sheet, then slowly peel away the parchment. Using a spatula, scrape off any toppings that cling to the parchment and return them to the pizza. Evenly distribute the taleggio over the top and drizzle with additional honey and oil.

Optional garnish: Minced fresh rosemary OR finely grated Parmesan cheese OR both

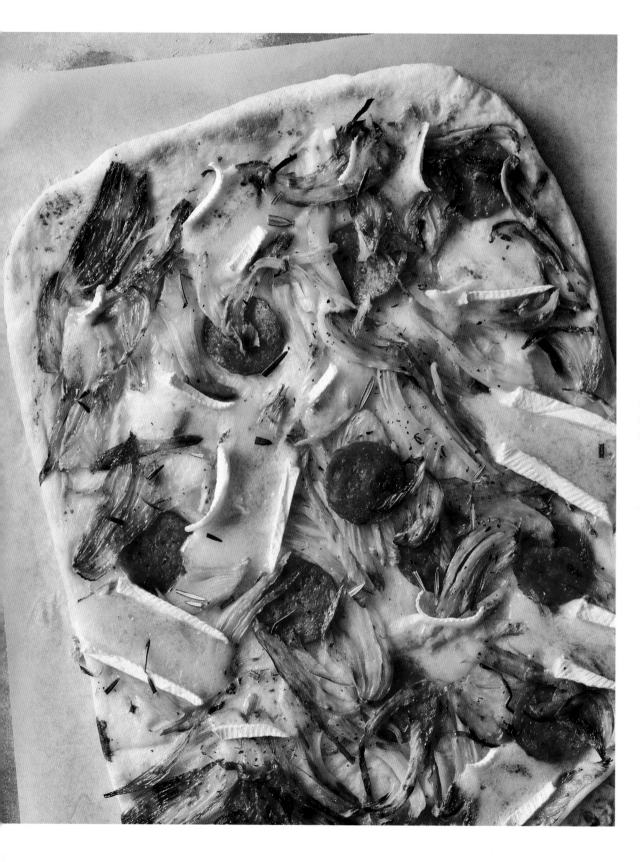

Cuban-Spiced Burgers

Start to finish: 1 hour (20 minutes active)
Servings: 4

The southern Florida tradition of the frita, thin beef patties that began as street food in Havana, inspired the spice mixture we used to add flavor to these burgers. **Partially freezing ground beef before mixing in the spices helps prevent the meat from becoming compacted during mixing and shaping, producing a meatier, more tender burger.** Even with chilling, it's important to use a light touch when handling the beef. This recipe can easily be doubled. For a quick and tangy topping, try our 3-minute spicy sauce (see following recipe).

1½ pounds 85 percent lean ground beef

2 teaspoons smoked paprika

2 teaspoons ground cumin

Kosher salt and ground black pepper

1 tablespoon neutral oil

4 burger buns, toasted

Sliced onion, sliced tomato and/or lettuce, for topping

Line a baking sheet with kitchen parchment. Set the beef on the sheet, then use 2 forks to gently spread the meat. In a small bowl, combine the paprika, cumin, ¾ teaspoons salt and ½ teaspoon pepper. Sprinkle over the beef. Freeze until the meat is very cold and beginning to firm up at the edges, about 20 minutes.

Use a silicone spatula to gently fold the spice mixture into the beef without compacting it; it's fine if the spices are not completely blended. If the beef is still partially frozen, let stand 10 to 15 minutes until slightly softened. Divide the beef into 4 even portions. Shape each into a 4-inch patty about ½ inch thick.

In a 12-inch skillet over medium-high, heat the oil until smoking. Add the patties and cook until well browned, about 5 minutes; flip and continue to cook until the center is 125°F for medium-rare, another 4 to 5 minutes. Transfer to a plate and let rest for 5 minutes. Set each burger on a bun and top as desired.

SPICY SAUCE

Start to finish: 3 minutes
Makes about 1⅓ cups

1 cup mayonnaise

2 tablespoons hot sauce, plus more as needed

2 tablespoons yellow mustard

¼ teaspoon cayenne pepper

In a medium bowl, whisk all ingredients until smooth. Taste and add more hot sauce, if desired. Cover and refrigerate for up to 1 week.

Garlic and Five-Spice Pork Chop Sandwiches

Start to finish: 30 minutes
Servings: 4

We got the idea for these tasty sandwiches from the Macanese street food called "pork chop bun." We use boneless thin-cut pork chops (look for ones about ½ inch thick), pound them even thinner and give them a quick marinade—**we boost bottled teriyaki sauce by adding garlic and five-spice powder.** A broiler makes quick work of cooking the pork. For added flavor and richness, butter the cut sides of the buns before toasting. And if you like, tuck lettuce leaves, pickled red onions or pickled jalapeños into the sandwiches for serving.

¼ cup teriyaki sauce

6 medium garlic cloves, finely grated

½ teaspoon Chinese five-spice powder

Ground black pepper

8 thin-cut boneless pork loin chops
(about 1 pound total; see headnote), trimmed and pounded to ⅛-inch thickness

4 Kaiser rolls OR potato buns, toasted (see headnote)

Mayonnaise, to serve

In a bowl, mix the teriyaki sauce, garlic, five-spice and ½ teaspoon pepper. Add the pork and turn to coat, then set aside. Heat the broiler with a rack about 4 inches from the element. Arrange the pork in a single layer on a rimmed baking sheet. Broil until sizzling and browned at the edges, 4 to 5 minutes, flipping the pieces halfway through. Serve in buns spread with mayonnaise.

Kimchi Grilled Cheese with Ham

Start to finish: 30 minutes
Servings: 4

Spicy, garlicky kimchi ups the umami quotient of the classic grilled cheese. The pairing of cheese and kimchi actually isn't new. Budae jjigae, otherwise known as army base stew, originates with the Korean War. It's a hot pot made with American surplus foods, such as hot dogs, baked beans and instant noodles, along with kimchi and American cheese. These sandwiches aren't quite as lavish, but they're indisputably tasty.

⅓ cup mayonnaise

1 tablespoon kimchi juice, plus 1⅓ cups cabbage kimchi, drained and chopped

8 slices hearty white sandwich bread

8 slices cheddar OR pepper jack OR whole-milk mozzarella cheese

4 slices thinly sliced deli ham OR 4 slices cooked bacon

In a small bowl, stir together the mayonnaise and kimchi brine. Spread evenly over one side of each slice of bread. Flip 4 of the slices to be mayonnaise side down, then top each with 1 slice of cheese, 1 slice of ham (or 1 slice bacon, torn to fit) and a quarter of the kimchi. Top each with a slice of the remaining cheese, then with another slice of bread, mayonnaise side up. Press on the sandwiches to compact the fillings.

Heat a 12-inch nonstick or cast-iron skillet over medium until droplets of water flicked onto the surface quickly sizzle and evaporate. Add 2 of the sandwiches and cook until golden brown on the bottoms, 2 to 3 minutes. Using a wide spatula, flip the sandwiches and cook, pressing down lightly and adjusting the heat as needed, until golden brown on the second sides and the cheese is melted, 2 to 3 minutes. Transfer to a cutting board. Cook the remaining sandwiches in the same way (the second batch may cook faster). Cut each sandwich in half on the diagonal.

Cheese-Crisped Pinto Bean Quesadillas

Start to finish: 40 minutes
Servings: 4

These gooey quesadillas boast double the cheese—some tucked inside the folded tortillas and the rest sprinkled on the outside. As they toast in the oven, the outer layer melts and becomes deliciously crisp. Bonus: **We cook quesadillas on a baking sheet to make a big batch all at once—no need to stand at the stove cooking quesadillas one by one.** To make these vegetarian quesadillas heartier, we include pinto beans (or black beans), which are microwaved with chili powder to infuse them with spice; canned red or green chilies bump up the heat, while lime juice brings an acidic note.

3 tablespoons neutral oil

Two 15½-ounce cans pinto beans
OR black beans, rinsed and drained

1 tablespoon chili powder

Kosher salt and ground black pepper

2 chipotle chilies in adobo sauce, chopped, plus 1 teaspoon adobo sauce OR ¼ cup drained canned green chilies

2 tablespoons lime juice OR cider vinegar

8 ounces pepper jack OR mozzarella cheese OR queso Oaxaca, shredded (2 cups)

Eight 6-inch flour tortillas

Heat the oven to 475°F with a rack in the middle position. Brush the entire surface of a rimmed baking sheet with the oil.

In a large microwave-safe bowl, toss together the beans, chili powder and ¾ teaspoon salt. Cover and microwave on high until hot, 3 to 3½ minutes, stirring once halfway through. Stir in the chipotles with adobo sauce, lime juice and ½ cup cheese. Using a potato masher, mash the mixture until relatively smooth. Taste and season with salt and pepper.

Divide the bean filling evenly among the tortillas and spread it to cover half of each tortilla. Fold the unfilled sides over and gently press to seal. Arrange the filled tortillas on the prepared baking sheet, then flip each one so both sides are coated with oil. Sprinkle the tops of the tortillas with the remaining cheese.

Bake until the cheese is melted and the quesadillas begin to brown and crisp on the bottoms, 7 to 9 minutes. Remove the baking sheet from the oven and, using a wide metal spatula, flip each quesadilla. Bake until browned on the second sides, 2 to 4 minutes. Cool on the baking sheet for about 5 minutes. If desired, cut the quesadillas in half, then serve cheese side up.

Optional garnish: Sour cream OR salsa OR guacamole OR pickled jalapeños OR a combination

Vegetables

Kale Salad with Za'atar, Feta and Pita Crisps

Start to finish: 30 minutes
Servings: 4

For a Mediterranean-inspired salad, **we tenderize sturdy kale by massaging it with salt and letting it rest in the dressing.** Lemon zest and za'atar add tang while spicy-sweet Peppadew peppers bring bright notes. If you can't find them, Italian sweet cherry peppers are a good substitute. Salty feta and just-made pita crisps, which come together quickly while the kale rests, add texture and flavor.

1 large bunch lacinato kale, stemmed
and thinly sliced crosswise (about 12 cups)

1 teaspoon za'atar, plus more to serve

Kosher salt and ground black pepper

4 tablespoons extra-virgin olive oil, divided

2 teaspoons grated lemon zest,
plus 3 tablespoons lemon juice

8-inch pita bread, split into 2 rounds

4 ounces feta cheese, crumbled (1 cup)

½ cup drained Peppadew peppers
OR sweet cherry peppers, sliced into thin rings

In a large bowl, combine the kale, za'atar and ½ teaspoon salt. Using your hands, firmly massage the kale until darkened and the volume has reduced by about half. Add 3 tablespoons oil, the lemon zest and juice, and ¼ teaspoon pepper; toss. Let stand until the kale softens slightly, about 15 minutes.

Meanwhile, brush the pita rounds on both sides with the remaining 1 tablespoon oil. Heat a 12-inch nonstick skillet over medium until a drop of water sizzles and evaporates within a few seconds. Toast 1 pita round until golden brown and crisped, 5 to 7 minutes, flipping once about halfway through; transfer to a wire rack. Toast the remaining pita round in the same way. Cool slightly, then break into bite-size pieces.

Add the feta, Peppadew peppers and pita crisps to the kale mixture; toss. Taste and season with salt and pepper. Transfer to a serving bowl and sprinkle with additional za'atar.

Crispy Chickpea, Cucumber and Mint Salad

Start to finish: 25 minutes
Servings: 4 to 6

A type of savory street snack popular in South Asia, chaat comes in many varieties. All feature a mix of contrasting flavors and textures, from sweet, tart and spicy to creamy and crunchy. Chickpeas fried in oil and seasoned with curry powder bring a layer of deliciousness to this chaat-inspired salad. **We salt cucumber and let it stand to remove excess moisture, keeping the finished salad crisp in texture.** Feel free to swap tomatoes or mango for the cucumber, or use some of each for a variety of color, texture and flavor; you will need a total of 4 cups vegetables and fruit, and the same salting technique works for all three (for ease, they can be salted together).

1 English cucumber, quartered lengthwise and cut crosswise into ¼-inch pieces OR 1½ pounds ripe tomatoes, cored and finely chopped OR 1 ripe mango, peeled, pitted and cut into ¼-inch cubes OR a combination (see headnote)

Kosher salt and ground black pepper

15½-ounce can chickpeas, rinsed, drained and patted dry

2 tablespoons cornstarch

¼ cup neutral oil

2 teaspoons curry powder

1 teaspoon grated lemon zest OR lime zest, plus 2 tablespoons lemon juice OR lime juice

1 cup roughly chopped fresh mint OR cilantro OR a combination

In a colander set over a medium bowl, toss the cucumber with 1 teaspoon salt. Let stand for about 15 minutes, tossing once or twice to encourage the liquid to drain.

Meanwhile, in a medium bowl, toss the chickpeas with the cornstarch. Transfer to a fine-mesh strainer and shake to remove excess cornstarch. In a 10-inch skillet over medium-high, heat the oil until shimmering. Add the chickpeas and cook, stirring occasionally, until golden brown and crisp, about 5 minutes. Add the curry powder and cook, stirring, until fragrant, 30 to 60 seconds. Off heat, stir in ¼ teaspoon each salt and pepper. Transfer the chickpeas to a paper towel-lined plate.

Discard the liquid collected in the bowl, then wipe it out. Add the cucumber to the bowl, along with the lemon zest and juice and mint; toss. Stir in the chickpeas (it's fine if they are slightly warm). Taste and season with salt and pepper.

Optional garnish: Thinly sliced Fresno or jalapeño chili OR plain whole-milk yogurt OR fried wonton strips OR a combination

Butter-Roasted Carrots with Za'atar and Pomegranate Molasses

Start to finish: 40 minutes (20 minutes active)

Servings: 6

Carrots roasted in a moderately hot oven for almost an hour become super-sweet and almost meltingly tender. We start them coated with olive oil but drizzle them with melted butter partway through roasting. The milk solids in the butter caramelize in the oven, adding a rich, nutty fragrance and flavor. Za'atar, a Middle Eastern seed and spice blend, and orange zest and juice bring complexity to the dish. Pistachios and sweet-tart pomegranate molasses are finishing touches that make this dish special. Bunch carrots—the type sold with their greens attached—are especially good here because they're slender and fresh. After halving them, if any of the upper portions are especially thick, cut them in half lengthwise.

2½ pounds long, slender carrots
(see headnote), peeled and halved
crosswise on a sharp diagonal

1 tablespoon extra-virgin olive oil

Kosher salt and ground black pepper

1 orange

4 tablespoons salted butter, melted

2 teaspoons za'atar OR ground coriander
OR Aleppo pepper, divided

2 tablespoons raw OR roasted pistachios,
finely chopped

2 teaspoons pomegranate molasses

Heat the oven to 350°F with a rack in the middle position. On a rimmed baking sheet, toss the carrots with the oil, ¾ teaspoon salt and ¼ teaspoon pepper, then distribute evenly. Roast for 30 minutes. Meanwhile, grate 1 teaspoon zest from the orange, then cut the orange into quarters.

Drizzle the carrots with the butter and sprinkle with the za'atar and zest. Toss, then redistribute evenly. Place the orange quarters cut sides up on the baking sheet. Roast until a skewer inserted into the largest carrot meets no resistance, another 15 to 20 minutes, stirring once about halfway through.

Squeeze the juice from 1 orange quarter over the carrots. Using a wide metal spatula, transfer to a platter, scraping up any browned bits. Taste the carrots and season with salt and pepper. Sprinkle with the pistachios and drizzle with the pomegranate molasses. Serve the remaining orange quarters on the side.

Escarole and Fennel Salad with Capers and Golden Raisins

Start to finish: 20 minutes
Servings: 4

We combine pleasantly bitter greens with crisp, anise-y fennel and a punchy vinaigrette for a light, leafy salad with a terrific contrast of flavors and textures. Capers bring brininess to the vinaigrette, while golden raisins add a touch of chewy sweetness. We first soak the raisins and shallot in vinegar to plump the fruit and mellow the allium's bite. Escarole or frisée are a great choice for the greens, as their frilly leaves catch and hold the capers and raisins. If your fennel bulb still has the fronds attached, trim them off and chop for a colorful garnish.

⅓ cup golden raisins

1 small shallot, halved and thinly sliced

2½ tablespoons white balsamic vinegar OR white wine vinegar

Kosher salt and ground black pepper

1 medium fennel bulb, trimmed, halved lengthwise and cored

3 tablespoons extra-virgin olive oil

2 tablespoons drained capers, roughly chopped

1 medium head escarole, tough outer leaves removed and discarded OR 2 small heads frisée OR a combination, torn into bite-size pieces

In a large bowl, stir together the raisins, shallot, vinegar and ¼ teaspoon each salt and pepper. Let stand, stirring occasionally, to plump the raisins and lightly pickle the shallot, about 15 minutes.

Meanwhile, use a mandoline or sharp chef's knife to slice the fennel ¹/₁₆ inch thick. To do so with the mandoline, hold each fennel half by the base and slice crosswise as far as is safe; discard the base. Set aside.

Into the bowl with the raisins and shallots, stir in the oil and capers. Add the fennel and escarole, then toss. Taste and season with salt and pepper.

Optional garnish: Chopped fennel fronds OR fresh tarragon OR fresh dill

Shredded Carrot Salad with Cumin and Cashews

Start to finish: 20 minutes
Servings: 4

This recipe transforms ho-hum carrots into a delicious, eye-catching salad. **The key is to shred carrots, which releases their sugars and aromas, creating an earthy sweetness.** Use the large holes on a box grater or a food processor fitted with the medium shredding disk. **We add a final layer of flavor to the finished dish with a tarka, made by blooming spices and/or aromatics in hot fat to release their fragrance and flavor.** Cilantro lends herbaceousness, while jalapeños bring a kick of heat. For less heat, remove the seeds from the chilies.

1 pound medium carrots, peeled and shredded (see headnote)

2 jalapeño chilies, stemmed and thinly sliced

2 tablespoons lemon juice

Kosher salt and ground black pepper

3 tablespoons neutral oil

2 teaspoons cumin seeds OR brown mustard seeds OR a combination

½ cup roughly chopped unsalted OR salted cashews

½ cup roughly chopped fresh cilantro OR mint

In a large bowl, toss together the carrots, two-thirds of the chilies, lemon juice and ¼ teaspoon salt; set aside.

To make the tarka, in an 8-inch skillet over medium-high, combine the oil and cumin seeds. Cook, swirling the pan, until the seeds begin to sizzle, 30 to 60 seconds. Add the cashews, then cook, stirring often, until fragrant and once again beginning to sizzle, about 1 minute.

Pour the tarka over the carrot mixture and toss. Cool slightly, then add the cilantro and toss again. Taste and season with salt and pepper. Serve sprinkled with the remaining chilies.

SHAVE FOR FLAVOR

We love vegetable salads—but not when we have to gnaw our way through tough vegetables. Enter the close shave.

Using either a sharp vegetable peeler (we prefer a Y-style peeler, but any variety works) or a mandoline, we slice raw vegetables into almost paper-thin shavings. This creates tender strips from otherwise sturdy vegetables, such as carrots and radishes. In addition, the shavings have ample surface area, perfect for absorbing dressings and seasonings.

We shave carrots and zucchini lengthwise one side at a time, rotating as we go and stopping when we hit the cores, which we discard. For smaller vegetables, such as radishes and Brussels sprouts, we use the stem end as a handle when slicing to keep fingertips safe.

For particularly tough vegetables, such as carrots, we sometimes also microwave the shavings on high until wilted, but still crisp-tender, 3 to 5 minutes. This not only softens them, it also helps them absorb more dressing as they cool.

RECIPES FROM TOP

| Orange, Arugula and Shaved Radish Salad | Shaved Carrot Salad with Toasted Cumin and Cilantro Vinaigrette | Shaved Zucchini and Chicken Salad with Lemon and Almonds |

Shaved Carrot Salad with Toasted Cumin and Cilantro Vinaigrette

Start to finish: 30 minutes (10 minutes active)
Servings: 4

This carrot salad makes a beautiful presentation and, because it requires hardly any knifework, is a breeze to prepare. **Shaving the carrots with a vegetable peeler creates lots of surface area to which the dressing can cling while also tenderizing the carrot.** Choose large, thick carrots because they're easier to shave than slender ones, and stop shaving when you reach the core, which can be very tough. When microwaving the carrot ribbons, take care not to overcook them; they should wilt but remain tender-crisp. This is a great accompaniment to roasted pork or chicken.

½ cup roughly chopped fresh cilantro stems, plus ½ cup lightly packed cilantro leaves, reserved separately

1 jalapeño OR serrano chili, stemmed and seeded

¼ cup extra-virgin olive oil

2 tablespoons lime juice

2 teaspoons honey

Kosher salt and ground black pepper

4 or 5 large carrots (about 1½ pounds; see headnote), peeled

1½ teaspoons cumin seeds, lightly crushed

In a blender, combine the cilantro stems, jalapeño, oil, lime juice, honey and ¼ teaspoon each salt and pepper. Process until mostly smooth, scraping the blender jar as needed, about 1 minute; set aside.

Using a Y-style peeler, shave the carrots from top to bottom into long, wide ribbons, rotating as you go. Stop shaving when you reach the core; discard the cores. In a large, microwave-safe bowl, toss the carrot ribbons with 1 teaspoon salt. Cover and microwave on high until wilted but still tender-crisp, 1½ to 2 minutes, stirring halfway through. Drain in a colander, then return them to the bowl.

Add the dressing to the carrots, then toss. Taste and season with salt and pepper. Let stand for 15 minutes, tossing once or twice. Meanwhile, in an 8-inch skillet over medium, toast the cumin seeds, stirring often, until fragrant, about 3 minutes. Transfer to a small bowl; set aside to cool. Add the cilantro leaves and cumin seeds to the carrots; toss. Taste and season with salt and pepper.

Optional garnish: Toasted sunflower seeds

Orange, Arugula and Shaved Radish Salad

Start to finish: 40 minutes (25 minutes active)
Servings: 4

Bright and refreshing, this salad combines thinly shaved radishes with juicy oranges and peppery arugula (or watercress), all tossed with a tangy-sweet vinaigrette. **We let the salad stand for about 15 minutes before serving so the radish slices soften and absorb the flavorful vinaigrette.** The recipe calls for red radishes, but use any variety you like. A mandoline makes fast work of thinly slicing the radishes; keep the green tops attached so you can hold onto them like a handle. When peeling the oranges, be sure to remove the white pith, which tastes bitter.

3 medium oranges

3 tablespoons unseasoned rice vinegar

1 tablespoon neutral oil

2 teaspoons honey

Kosher salt and ground black pepper

1-pound bunch red radishes
(with greens attached), root ends trimmed

5-ounce container baby arugula OR 1 bunch
watercress, stemmed and roughly chopped
(about 6 cups)

Grate the zest from 1 orange into a large bowl, then
squeeze in the juice. Add the vinegar, oil, honey, ¼ teaspoon salt and ⅛ teaspoon pepper. Whisk to combine,
then set aside.

Using a sharp knife, slice about ½ inch off the top
and bottom of the remaining 2 oranges. One at a time,
stand an orange on a cut end and cut from top to
bottom following the contours of the fruit to remove the
peel and white pith. Cut the oranges in half lengthwise.
Lay each half cut side down, then cut crosswise into
½-inch slices. Add to the vinaigrette.

Adjust the blade of your mandoline to slice ¹/₁₆ inch
thick. Hold each radish by the greens and slice on the
mandoline as far as is safe; discard the greens. Add
the slices to the bowl with the oranges; toss. Let stand
for about 15 minutes. Add the arugula and toss again.
Taste and season with salt and pepper.

Optional garnish: Toasted sliced almonds OR toasted
sesame seeds

Shaved Zucchini and Chicken Salad with Lemon and Almonds

Start to finish: 35 minutes
Servings: 4

This unusual salad was inspired by a dish we tasted at
Trattoria Masuelli San Marco in Milan, Italy. **Crunchy
celery and salty fried almonds balance smooth, mild
shaved zucchini and shredded chicken.** We like the
richness of Spanish Marcona almonds that have been
fried and salted, but toasted regular blanched almonds
work, too. For easy prep, use the meat from a store-
bought rotisserie chicken; an average-size bird yields
about 3 cups, the amount needed for this recipe.

¼ cup extra-virgin olive oil

½ teaspoon ground allspice

2 teaspoons grated lemon zest, plus
¼ cup lemon juice

Kosher salt and ground black pepper

Two 8- to 10-ounce zucchini, trimmed

½ cup Marcona almonds OR toasted whole blanched
almonds, roughly chopped (see headnote)

2 medium celery stalks, thinly sliced on the diagonal

3 cups shredded cooked chicken (see headnote)

In a large bowl, whisk together the oil, allspice, lemon
zest and juice and ½ teaspoon each salt and pepper;
set aside.

Using a Y-style peeler, shave the zucchini from top
to bottom into long, wide ribbons, rotating as you go.
Stop shaving when you reach the core; discard the
cores. Add the zucchini, almonds, celery and chicken
to the dressing, then toss. Taste and season with salt
and pepper. Let stand at room temperature for about
15 minutes before serving.

Optional garnish: Roughly chopped or torn fresh
flat-leaf parsley

Harissa Potato Salad
with Mint and Lemon

Start to finish: 50 minutes
Servings: 4 to 6

Harissa—a chili paste from North Africa that is a Milk Street pantry staple—brings earthy spice, heat and bold flavor to an otherwise basic potato salad. Harissa varies in spiciness brand to brand, so start with 2 tablespoons and taste, then add more if you like. **Before tossing the potatoes with the mayonnaise, we combine them while warm with lemon zest, lemon juice and black pepper so they better absorb the seasonings.** Fresh mint balances the heat, while red onion brings a refreshing bite.

2 pounds russet potatoes, peeled
and cut into ¾-inch pieces

Kosher salt and ground black pepper

1 tablespoon grated lemon zest,
plus 4 tablespoons lemon juice, divided

⅓ cup mayonnaise

2 to 2½ tablespoons harissa paste

1 small red onion, halved and thinly sliced
OR 3 medium radishes, halved and thinly sliced

¾ cup lightly packed fresh mint OR cilantro
OR a combination, roughly chopped

In a large saucepan, combine the potatoes and 1½ tablespoons salt, then add enough water to cover by 1 inch. Bring to a boil over medium-high, then reduce to medium and simmer, uncovered and stirring occasionally, until a skewer inserted into the potatoes meets no resistance, 8 to 10 minutes.

Drain the potatoes in a colander, then transfer to a large bowl. Add the lemon zest, 2 tablespoons lemon juice and ½ teaspoon pepper; toss. Cool to room temperature, about 20 minutes, stirring occasionally. Meanwhile, in a small bowl, stir together the mayonnaise, harissa and the remaining 2 tablespoons lemon juice.

Into the cooled potatoes, stir in the onion and mayonnaise mixture, followed by the mint. Taste and season with salt and pepper.

Lentil Salad with Arugula and Pickled Sweet Peppers

Start to finish: 40 minutes
Servings: 4 to 6

French lentils du Puy hold their shape and are meaty and firm even when fully cooked, so they're great in salads. We balance mild lentils with tangy, sharp and sweet notes from vinegar, Dijon mustard, peppery arugula and pickled sweet peppers. **We steep shallots in vinegar to soften their bite.** We like Peppadew peppers, although sweet cherry peppers work nicely, too. Serve the salad at room temperature as a side dish or light vegetarian main.

1 cup lentils du Puy, rinsed and drained

Kosher salt and ground black pepper

2 tablespoons cider vinegar OR white wine vinegar

2 medium shallots, sliced into thin rings

¼ cup extra-virgin olive oil, plus more to serve

1 tablespoon Dijon mustard

½ cup drained Peppadew peppers OR sweet cherry peppers, patted dry and sliced into ¼-inch rings

2 cups lightly packed baby arugula

In a large saucepan, combine the lentils, ½ teaspoon salt and 4 cups water. Bring to a simmer over medium-high, then reduce to medium and cook, uncovered and stirring occasionally, until the lentils are tender, about 25 minutes. Drain and cool completely, tossing occasionally.

Meanwhile, in a large bowl, stir together the vinegar and shallots; let stand for 10 minutes. Stir in the oil, mustard and sweet peppers. Add the lentils and toss, then toss in the arugula. Taste and season with salt and black pepper. Serve drizzled with additional oil.

Beet Salad with Horseradish Dressing and Caraway Breadcrumbs

Start to finish: 1 hour (15 minutes active)
Servings: 4

We make salad interesting by packing it with contrasting textures—crisp breadcrumbs, creamy dressing and tender beets. We love the buttery-soft bite and earthy-sweet flavor of just-roasted beets, but pre-cooked ones are a great time-saving alternative. If desired, substitute two 8.8-ounce packages of refrigerated, cooked red beets, drained and cut into ½-inch wedges. As for the horseradish, we prefer the prepared vinegar-based variety found in the refrigerated section of the grocery store, which has fewer additives. The vibrant salad pairs wonderfully with roast beef, pork or salmon.

1 pound medium red OR golden beets, peeled and cut into ½-inch wedges (see headnote)

2 tablespoons extra-virgin olive oil, divided

Kosher salt and ground black pepper

¼ cup sour cream

2 tablespoons prepared horseradish (see headnote)

1 tablespoon lemon juice

2 ounces light OR dark rye bread OR pumpernickel bread, torn into 1-inch pieces (about 1½ cups)

1 teaspoon caraway seeds

Heat the oven to 425°F with a rack in the middle position. Cut an 18-inch square of extra-wide foil and place it on a rimmed baking sheet. Place the beets in the center of the foil. Drizzle with 1 tablespoon oil and sprinkle with ½ teaspoon each salt and pepper; toss. Enclose the beets in the foil and tightly crimp the edges. Roast until a skewer inserted into the beets meets no resistance, 40 to 45 minutes; be careful of escaping steam when opening the packet.

Meanwhile, in a small bowl, stir together the sour cream, horseradish, lemon juice and ¼ teaspoon each salt and pepper; set aside. In a food processor, pulse the bread until coarsely ground, 10 to 12 pulses; you should have about ¾ cup breadcrumbs. In a 10-inch skillet over medium, stir together the breadcrumbs, caraway and the remaining 1 tablespoon oil; cook, stirring, until the breadcrumbs are crisp and dry, 4 to 5 minutes. Transfer to a plate and cool to room temperature.

On a platter, arrange the warm or room-temperature beets in an even layer, leaving behind any liquid in the packet. Drizzle with the dressing, then sprinkle with the breadcrumbs.

Optional garnish: Chopped fresh flat-leaf parsley OR dill OR both

VERSATILE VINAIGRETTES

Classic French vinaigrette often is defined as a 3:1 ratio of oil to vinegar seasoned with a bit of salt and pepper. But truthfully, a dressing can be just about anything you drizzle on or toss with something else.

In the Middle East, it's tahini and lemon juice on chopped tomatoes and cucumber. In Morocco, roasted vegetables are dressed with chermoula, a bold puree of parsley, cilantro, olive oil and lemon. In Greece, citrus juice often serves as the acid.

Our takes include a dressing that starts by browning walnuts in butter—it takes just minutes but delivers rich and savory depth. For a bright and tangy dressing, we blend lime zest and juice with toasted sesame oil; honey and some pepper add sweet kick. And since Greece is where we learned to mix things up dressing-wise, we've got a salty-tangy version inspired by the flavors of the Greek islands that features orange and lemon juice and chopped green olives.

RECIPES FROM TOP

| Browned Butter Vinaigrette with Walnuts and Herbs | Citrus Vinaigrette with Green Olives and Garlic | Sesame-Lime Vinaigrette |

Browned Butter Vinaigrette with Walnuts and Herbs

Start to finish: 20 minutes
Makes about ½ cup

Toasting walnuts while browning the butter gives this warm vinaigrette an intense nuttiness and luxurious richness. Garlic, rosemary and lemon zest add layers of bright, herbal flavor and fragrance. This is perfect spooned onto roasted vegetables such as asparagus, green beans, carrots, broccoli, cauliflower or Brussels sprouts. Or drizzle it onto seared scallops or delicate fish such as cod or flounder.

**4 tablespoons salted butter,
cut into 4 pieces**

½ cup walnuts, chopped

1 medium garlic clove, minced

1 tablespoon finely chopped fresh rosemary

**1 teaspoon grated lemon zest, plus
3 tablespoons lemon juice**

**¼ cup lightly packed fresh flat-leaf parsley,
finely chopped**

Kosher salt and ground black pepper

In a 10-inch skillet over medium, heat the butter and walnuts, stirring occasionally, until the butter is browned and the mixture smells nutty, 3 to 4 minutes. Off heat, whisk in the garlic, rosemary, lemon zest and juice, parsley and ¼ teaspoon each salt and pepper. Use while warm.

Sesame-Lime Vinaigrette

Start to finish: 20 minutes
Makes about ½ cup

To make this bright, citrusy vinaigrette, we first steep a minced shallot in lime juice to tame its allium bite. Sesame flavor is layered in, with oil providing deep, rich notes and toasted ground seeds bringing subtle bitterness and earthy notes. The seeds also give the dressing body. To coarsely grind the seeds, pulse them a few times in a spice grinder. Drizzle onto steamed baby bok choy, asparagus or snow peas. It's also good with roasted carrots or cauliflower.

**2 teaspoons grated lime zest,
plus ¼ cup lime juice**

1 large shallot, minced

¼ cup neutral oil

2 teaspoons toasted sesame oil

**2 tablespoons sesame seeds, toasted
and coarsely ground**

1 tablespoon honey

½ teaspoon red pepper flakes

Kosher salt

In a small bowl, stir together the lime juice and shallot; let stand for 15 minutes. Whisk in the lime zest, both oils, sesame seeds, honey, pepper flakes and ¼ teaspoon salt.

Citrus Vinaigrette with Green Olives and Garlic

Start to finish: 15 minutes
Makes about ½ cup

Briny olives, savory garlic and sunny-sweet orange zest and juice give this vinaigrette Mediterranean spirit. **The garlic gets a brief soak in lemon juice for more mellow flavor.** This dressing is best with sturdy bitter greens, such as frisée, radicchio and escarole, that hold their own against the big, bold flavor of the dressing and also catch the fine bits of olives. We also love to drizzle this over cannellini beans or a salad of oranges and fennel.

1 small garlic clove, finely grated

1 tablespoon lemon juice

⅓ cup extra-virgin olive oil

1 teaspoon grated orange zest,
plus 2 tablespoons orange juice

Kosher salt and ground black pepper

2 tablespoons finely chopped pitted green olives

In a small bowl, stir together the garlic and lemon juice; let stand 10 minutes. Add the oil, orange zest and juice, and ¼ teaspoon each salt and pepper; whisk to combine. Stir in the olives.

Braised Collard Greens with Cumin, Garlic and Sweet-Tart Raisins

Start to finish: 45 minutes
Servings: 4 to 6

This side dish uses every part of the collard greens, with the stems and leaves added at different times so both cook perfectly. First, we cook the tougher stems with onion until soft and starting to caramelize. Next, we add the leaves, simmering them low and slow so they become silky and tender. Cumin seeds lend warmth and crunch. The dish is finished with golden raisins quick-pickled in vinegar, bringing a sweet-tart punch. Use white balsamic for gentler acidity or cider vinegar for more acidic notes. Drizzle the collards with pomegranate molasses for a touch of sweetness and sprinkle with Aleppo pepper for gentle heat.

⅓ cup golden raisins

1½ tablespoons white balsamic vinegar
OR 1 tablespoon cider vinegar

Kosher salt and ground black pepper

¼ cup extra-virgin olive oil

1 medium red onion, halved and thinly sliced

2 bunches collard greens, stems chopped, leaves chopped into rough 1-inch pieces, reserved separately

4 medium garlic cloves, thinly sliced

2 teaspoons cumin seeds

In a small bowl, stir together the raisins, vinegar and a pinch of salt; set aside. In a large Dutch oven over medium, heat the oil until shimmering. Add the onion, collard stems, garlic, cumin seeds and ½ teaspoon salt. Cook, stirring occasionally, until the onion and collard stems are softened and the onion is beginning to brown, 18 to 20 minutes.

Add the collard leaves and ½ cup water, then bring to a simmer over medium. Cover and cook, stirring occasionally, until the leaves are wilted, about 2 minutes. Stir, then re-cover, reduce to medium-low and simmer, stirring occasionally, until the leaves are tender and only a little liquid remains, about 15 minutes. Off heat, stir in the raisins and pickling liquid. Taste and season with salt and pepper.

Optional garnish: Pomegranate molasses OR Aleppo pepper OR red pepper flakes OR a combination

Tomato Salad with Peanuts, Cilantro and Chipotle-Sesame Dressing

Start to finish: 35 minutes
Servings: 4 to 6

To create this toothsome tomato salad, we took inspiration from Mexican salsa macha, which is made with dried chilies, garlic, nuts and seeds that are fried in oil, then pureed. We skipped the blender and deconstructed the salsa, adding the ingredients directly to the salad—the fried peanuts and sesame seeds add texture that contrast beautifully against meaty tomatoes. **Salting the tomatoes and letting them stand deepens their flavor and softens them slightly for extra succulence and juiciness.** For an especially colorful salad, use heirloom tomatoes of different hues.

2 tablespoons neutral oil

¼ cup roasted peanuts

2 tablespoons sesame seeds
OR 1 medium garlic clove, thinly sliced OR both

1 chipotle chili in adobo sauce, minced,
plus 1 teaspoon adobo sauce

3 tablespoons cider vinegar

Kosher salt and ground black pepper

2 pounds ripe tomatoes, cored and
cut into ½-inch wedges (see headnote)

1½ cups lightly packed fresh cilantro
OR basil OR flat-leaf parsley OR a combination,
torn if large

In a small saucepan over medium, combine the oil and peanuts. Cook, stirring occasionally, until fragrant and browned, 4 to 6 minutes. Using a slotted spoon, transfer the peanuts to a paper towel-lined plate.

To the same saucepan over medium, add the sesame seeds. Cook, stirring, until lightly golden, about 2 minutes. Remove from the heat, then stir in the chipotle and adobo sauce, vinegar and ¼ teaspoon each salt and pepper. Cool to room temperature. Meanwhile, in a serving bowl, toss the tomatoes with ½ teaspoon salt; let stand for about 10 minutes. Chop the peanuts.

Spoon the chipotle-sesame mixture over the tomatoes. Add the cilantro and peanuts, then stir gently. Taste and season with salt and pepper.

Optional garnish: Flaky salt OR crumbled cotija cheese OR both

Broccolini with Miso Caesar Dressing

Start to finish: 30 minutes
Servings: 4 to 6

This spin on Caesar dressing uses mayonnaise as a base. It's rich in umami because of the Parmesan (or anchovies), and a couple tablespoons of white miso adds incredible depth of flavor, loads of complexity and a subtle sweetness. A splash of olive oil and garlic, its bite tempered by a quick steep in tangy lemon juice, complete the dressing. We use this on blanched Broccolini, but you could substitute 1 large head romaine lettuce, torn into bite-size pieces, then finish the salad with crunchy croutons.

2 tablespoons lemon juice

1 medium garlic clove, finely grated

½ cup mayonnaise

½ ounce Parmesan cheese, finely grated (¼ cup) OR 2 oil-packed anchovy fillets, patted dry and mashed to a paste

2 tablespoons white miso

2 tablespoons extra-virgin olive oil

Kosher salt and ground black pepper

2 pounds Broccolini, trimmed

In a small bowl, stir together the lemon juice and garlic. Let stand for 10 minutes. Add the mayonnaise, Parmesan, miso and oil; whisk until well combined. Taste and season with salt and pepper.

In a large pot, bring 2 quarts water to a boil. Add 1 tablespoon salt and the Broccolini; cook, stirring occasionally, until bright green and tender-crisp, 6 to 8 minutes. Drain in a colander, shaking to remove excess water, then transfer to a platter. Drizzle with three-fourths of the dressing. Sprinkle with additional pepper and serve with the remaining dressing on the side.

Optional garnish: Shaved Parmesan cheese OR red pepper flakes OR hot sauce OR toasted breadcrumbs

Mango Salad with Toasted Coconut and Cashews

Start to finish: 45 minutes (30 minutes active)
Servings: 4

This bright, tropical salad gets a zingy boost from red onion pickled quickly in lime juice. Combined with ripe, juicy mangoes, the result is a balanced tangle of tangy and sweet flavors, as well as contrasting soft and crisp textures. Toasted coconut and cashews contribute crunch, while mint adds cool, fresh notes. Don't worry if the mango slices are uneven—a loose, thrown-together look is part of the salad's charm. This is great paired with grilled fish or shrimp, as well as pork or chicken.

⅓ cup unsweetened wide-flake coconut

⅓ cup roasted cashews, roughly chopped

1 small red onion, halved and thinly sliced

1 teaspoon grated lime zest, plus
3 tablespoons lime juice

Kosher salt and ground black pepper

2 tablespoons extra-virgin olive oil

Two 14- to 16-ounce ripe mangoes, peeled, pitted and thinly sliced

½ cup lightly packed fresh mint OR cilantro OR a combination, torn

In an 8-inch skillet over medium, toast the coconut and cashews, stirring, until golden brown and fragrant, 2 to 3 minutes. Transfer to a plate and cool to room temperature. Meanwhile, in a large bowl, stir together the onion, lime zest and juice and ¼ teaspoon salt; let stand for 15 minutes.

To the onion mixture, stir in the oil and ¼ teaspoon each salt and pepper. Add the mangoes and mint, then toss. Taste and season with salt and pepper. Transfer to a platter and sprinkle with the coconut and cashews.

Optional garnish: Flaky sea salt OR thinly sliced Fresno or jalapeño chilies OR both

Brussels Sprouts with Apples and Bacon

Start to finish: 30 minutes
Servings: 4 to 6

Thinly sliced Brussels sprouts, apples and shallot cook quickly and absorb flavors beautifully, and we cook the ingredients in stages to create layered texture and taste. Two of the three sliced apples hit the skillet several minutes ahead of the remaining apple and vegetables; this gives the fruit time to soften and for their flavors to concentrate. A food processor fitted with a slicing disk makes for fast and easy prep, but feel free to use a sharp chef's knife instead.

3 tablespoons cider vinegar

2 tablespoons extra-virgin olive oil

2 teaspoons whole-grain mustard OR Dijon mustard

Kosher salt and ground black pepper

3 crisp, sweet apples, such as Honeycrisp or Gala, unpeeled, quartered and cored

1 pound Brussels sprouts, trimmed

1 medium shallot, halved lengthwise

4 ounces bacon, chopped

In a small bowl, whisk together the vinegar, oil, mustard, ½ teaspoon salt and ¼ teaspoon pepper; set aside.

In a food processor with a slicing disk, slice 2 of the apples; transfer to a small bowl. Using the same slicing disk, slice the remaining apple, the sprouts and shallot; set the mixture aside separately from the first 2 sliced apples.

In a 12-inch skillet over medium, cook the bacon, stirring, until browned, 5 to 6 minutes. Using a slotted spoon, transfer the bacon to a paper towel-lined plate; set aside.

To the fat remaining in the skillet, add the 2 sliced apples; cook over medium, stirring occasionally, until softened, 4 to 5 minutes. Add the sprouts mixture and cook, stirring occasionally, until the sprouts are tender-crisp, 5 to 6 minutes. Off heat, toss in the dressing and bacon. Taste and season with salt and pepper.

QUICK PICKLES

Onion, garlic, shallot—these kitchen-staple alliums get lots of use in our cooking, adding savoriness, a little funk, sharpness and even a little sweetness to dishes of all sorts. But sometimes, when raw, they add too much pungency and overwhelm other ingredients. To solve this problem, we quick-pickle the allium in question, which tames its fieriness without altering its freshness.

The method couldn't be simpler. We steep the sliced or chopped allium, sometimes including fresh chilies, in an acid (vinegar or citrus juice) plus seasonings for 15 to 30 minutes. The flavors mellow and meld, while the textures remain crisp. The quick pickle—both the allium and liquid—is then ready to use, either as an ingredient or garnish.

Our trio of sides featuring quick-pickled allium includes a slaw inspired by pikliz, the spicy relish from Haiti. It features salted sliced cabbage, red onion and habanero chilies pickled in vinegar and sugar. Peruvian ceviche gave us the idea for sweet potatoes paired with chilies and onion steeped in lime juice. And Polish mizeria gave rise to our cucumber salad featuring vinegar-pickled onions.

RECIPES FROM TOP

| Coconut-Lime Sweet Potatoes | Cucumber Salad with Sour Cream and Dill | Cabbage Slaw with Habanero and Allspice |

Cabbage Slaw with Habanero and Allspice

Start to finish: 40 minutes (10 minutes active)
Servings: 4 to 6

This piquant slaw was inspired by pikliz, the fiery Haitian pickled relish that accompanies meats and fried foods to balance the richness. **We toss thinly sliced cabbage with salt and let it stand for about 30 minutes to soften and draw out the water.** At the same time, we quick-pickle red onion and habanero chilies in vinegar and sugar to tame their bite, then combine them with the drained cabbage. The chilies bring heat and fruity notes, while allspice adds warmth and savory-sweetness. Serve right away or refrigerate it for up to five days. Serve with rice and beans or grilled pork, chicken or fish.

1 pound green OR red cabbage, cored and thinly sliced (about 5 cups)

Kosher salt and ground black pepper

½ medium red onion, thinly sliced

1 or 2 habanero chilies, stemmed, halved, seeded and thinly sliced

¼ cup white vinegar

2 tablespoons white sugar

1 tablespoon neutral oil

½ teaspoon ground allspice

In a large colander set over a large bowl, toss the cabbage with 1 tablespoon salt. Let stand until the cabbage softens slightly, about 30 minutes, tossing once or twice to encourage the liquid to drain. Meanwhile, in a small bowl, stir together the onion, chilies, vinegar, ½ teaspoon salt and ¼ teaspoon pepper; let stand until the cabbage is ready.

Discard the liquid in the large bowl, then transfer the cabbage to the bowl. Add the sugar, oil and allspice to the onion mixture; stir until the sugar dissolves, then add the mixture to the cabbage. Toss, then taste and season with salt and pepper.

Optional garnish: Fresh flat-leaf parsley leaves OR fresh cilantro leaves

Coconut-Lime Sweet Potatoes

Start to finish: 30 minutes
Servings: 4 to 6

The idea for this recipe came from Peruvian ceviche, which often is served with a side of boiled sweet potato. We skip the fish and let the potato take center stage, seasoning it like ceviche with lime, red onion, chilies and cilantro, plus coconut milk for richness. **No stovetop cooking is needed; to streamline prep, the sweet potatoes are steamed in the microwave. Be sure to toss them with the dressing while warm so they absorb all the flavors.** If you like, garnish with crushed corn nuts, a nod to the toasted, salted Andean corn kernels known as canchitas that often are sprinkled over ceviche.

1 teaspoon grated lime zest, plus ¼ cup lime juice

Kosher salt and ground black pepper

¼ medium red onion, thinly sliced

2 Fresno OR serrano chilies, stemmed, seeded and sliced into thin half rings

2 pounds orange-fleshed sweet potatoes, peeled and cut into ¾- to 1-inch chunks

¼ cup coconut milk

¼ cup lightly packed fresh cilantro, roughly chopped, plus more to serve

In a small bowl, whisk together the lime zest and juice and ¼ teaspoon salt. Stir in the onion and chilies; let stand for about 15 minutes.

Meanwhile, in a large microwave-safe bowl, combine the sweet potatoes and 3 tablespoons water. Cover and microwave on high until a skewer inserted into the largest piece meets no resistance, about 10 minutes, stirring once halfway through. Immediately drain the sweet potatoes in a colander and return the potatoes to the bowl.

To the warm potatoes, add the onion-chili mixture and any liquid, the coconut milk and cilantro; toss gently. Taste and season with salt and pepper. Serve at room temperature or cover and refrigerate until chilled, about 1 hour. Sprinkle with additional cilantro just before serving.

Optional garnish: Crushed corn nuts OR chopped roasted peanuts

Cucumber Salad with Sour Cream and Dill

Start to finish: 45 minutes (15 minutes active)
Servings: 4 to 6

To create this creamy, crunchy dish, we looked to the Polish salad known as mizeria, which features cucumbers, sour cream, dill and sometimes red onion. Though it's not traditional, we also added prepared horseradish for a spicy kick. **Be sure to salt the cucumbers first and let them stand for 15 minutes, then squeeze them before dressing to remove excess moisture. This produces a crisp texture and a drier surface to which the dressing and seasonings can adhere.** Cool and refreshing, this makes a great accompaniment to seared or roasted salmon or crisp-crusted chicken or pork cutlets.

2 English cucumbers, peeled, halved lengthwise and cut on the diagonal into ¼-inch slices

Kosher salt and ground black pepper

½ medium red onion, thinly sliced

¼ cup white vinegar

½ cup sour cream

¼ cup prepared horseradish

1 cup lightly packed fresh dill, roughly chopped

In a large colander set over a large bowl, toss the cucumbers with 1 teaspoon salt. In a small bowl, stir together the onion, vinegar and ¼ teaspoon salt. Let both the cucumbers and the onion mixture stand for 15 minutes; occasionally toss the cucumbers to encourage the liquid to drain.

In a medium bowl, stir together the sour cream and horseradish. Using your hands, firmly squeeze the cucumbers to remove as much water as possible; discard the liquid. Add the cucumbers to the sour cream mixture and stir. Drain the onion in the now-empty colander, then add it to the cucumber mixture; discard the liquid. Stir in the dill. Taste and season with salt and pepper. Serve immediately or cover, refrigerate for about 1 hour and serve chilled.

Hungarian Paprika-Braised Potatoes

Start to finish: 30 minutes
Servings: 6

In Zákányszék, a village in southern Hungary, home cook Piroska Tanácsné taught us paprikás kumpli—a simple, traditional side of paprika-braised potatoes, often served with sausage. For our take, **we cook potatoes in a vibrant paprika- and cumin-seasoned broth instead of plain water.** As the potatoes simmer, the spice-rich liquid reduces to yield a deeply flavorful sauce. Seek out fresh, good-quality paprika, and in particular look for brands produced in Hungary. If yours has been in the pantry for a while, it may have lost its kick (it should be bright red, not dull brown, and full of fragrance).

2 tablespoons lard or grapeseed
or other neutral oil

1 large yellow onion, finely chopped

Kosher salt and ground black pepper

2½ pounds medium (2-inch) red potatoes
OR Yukon Gold potatoes, peeled,
quartered lengthwise

3½ tablespoons sweet paprika

2 teaspoons caraway seeds, lightly crushed

1 teaspoon ground cumin

¼ teaspoon cayenne pepper

In a large Dutch oven over medium, melt the lard. Add the onion and ½ teaspoon salt; cook, stirring often, until well browned, about 10 minutes. Stir in the potatoes, then the paprika, caraway, cumin, cayenne and 1 teaspoon salt, followed by 2 cups water. Bring to a simmer over medium-high, then cover, reduce to low and simmer until a skewer inserted into the potatoes meets just a little resistance, 15 to 18 minutes.

Uncover and increase to medium-high; cook, stirring gently to avoid breaking up the potatoes, until the liquid is saucy and reduced and a skewer inserted into the potatoes meets no resistance, about 10 minutes. Remove the pot from the heat, cover and let stand to allow the potatoes to absorb some liquid, about 5 minutes. Taste and season with salt and pepper.

Optional garnish: Chopped fresh dill

Roasted Acorn Squash with Orange–Pumpkin Seed Vinaigrette

Start to finish: 45 minutes (10 minutes active)
Servings: 4

We roast acorn squash in a hot oven for deeply caramelized flavor, velvety texture and skin tender enough to eat, no need for peeling. While the squash is cooking, we whirl a simple vinaigrette in the blender to drizzle on at the end. It includes olive oil, sherry vinegar and orange zest and juice; the acids keep the flavors bright and balance the richness of the oil. Toasted pumpkin seeds blended into the dressing add a nutty flavor while also lending creaminess. This is the perfect side dish for fall and winter meals.

2-pound acorn squash, halved lengthwise and seeded

3 tablespoons extra-virgin olive oil, divided

Kosher salt and ground black pepper

⅓ cup plus 2 tablespoons pumpkin seeds, toasted

⅓ cup lightly packed fresh flat-leaf parsley, plus finely chopped parsley to serve

1 tablespoon grated orange zest, plus ¼ cup orange juice

2 tablespoons sherry vinegar OR cider vinegar

1 tablespoon honey

Heat the oven to 450°F with a rack in the middle position. On a rimmed baking sheet, rub the cut sides of the squash halves with 1 tablespoon oil, then sprinkle with ½ teaspoon salt and ¼ teaspoon pepper. Place the halves cut sides down and roast until a skewer inserted into the squash meets no resistance, 30 to 35 minutes.

Meanwhile, in a blender, combine the remaining 2 tablespoons oil, ⅓ cup pumpkin seeds, the parsley, orange zest and juice, vinegar, honey and ¼ teaspoon each salt and pepper. Blend on high until smooth, about 1 minute, scraping the jar as needed.

Transfer the squash to a cutting board and cut each half in half lengthwise. Place skin side down on a platter, then drizzle with the vinaigrette. Sprinkle with the remaining 2 tablespoons pumpkin seeds and additional parsley.

Optional garnish: Lime wedges OR red pepper flakes OR both

Black-Eyed Pea and Tomato Salad

Start to finish: 1 hour (20 minutes active)
Servings: 4

This simple salad of earthy-sweet black-eyed peas, crisp vegetables and fragrant herbs stars a smooth, rich garlicky dressing. **We simmer a whole head of garlic with the beans, softening and mellowing its flavor, to make the dressing, and we add it to black-eyed peas while they're still warm, allowing them to absorb ample flavor as they cool.** It's important to gently incorporate the ingredients; aggressive stirring will turn the black-eyed peas to mush.

1 head garlic, top third cut off
and discarded

8 ounces (1½ cups) dried black-eyed peas,
rinsed and drained

1 pint cherry OR grape tomatoes, halved

3 tablespoons white wine vinegar
OR red wine vinegar

3 tablespoons extra-virgin olive oil,
plus more to serve

Kosher salt and ground black pepper

2 medium celery stalks, chopped

1 cup lightly packed fresh flat-leaf parsley
OR basil, roughly chopped

In a large saucepan, combine the garlic head and black-eyed peas. Add 6 cups water and bring to a boil over medium-high. Boil for 5 minutes, then reduce to medium-low and simmer, uncovered and stirring occasionally, until the peas are fully tender but still hold their shape, 20 to 25 minutes. Meanwhile, in a medium bowl, toss the tomatoes with ½ teaspoon salt; set aside.

When the peas are done, drain them in a colander. Using tongs, remove the garlic head and squeeze the cloves into a small bowl; discard the skins. Using a fork, mash the garlic cloves until mostly smooth. Stir in the vinegar, oil and ¼ teaspoon pepper.

Transfer the still-warm peas to the tomatoes, then add the dressing and gently stir to combine. Stir in the celery and parsley, then taste and season with salt and pepper. Serve warm or at room temperature, drizzled with additional oil.

Potato, Poblano and Sweet Corn Hash

Start to finish: 30 minutes
Servings: 4

**This hearty hash is weeknight-quick thanks to
potatoes that are parcooked in the microwave.**
Smoky bacon, spicy poblano chili and sweet corn
bring layers of contrasting texture and flavor. Dried
Mexican oregano adds earthy, citrusy notes and is
available in most well-stocked supermarkets, but
standard Mediterranean oregano works well, too.
Top with runny-yolk fried eggs and one or some of
the optional garnishes listed below.

1 pound Yukon Gold OR red potatoes,
unpeeled, cut into ½-inch cubes

Kosher salt and ground black pepper

8 ounces bacon, chopped

1 tablespoon neutral oil

1 medium red OR yellow onion, chopped

1 medium poblano chili OR green bell pepper,
stemmed, seeded and chopped

2 cups fresh corn kernels (from about 2 ears)
OR frozen corn kernels, thawed

1 teaspoon dried oregano, preferably
Mexican oregano

In a medium microwave-safe bowl, toss the potatoes
with ½ teaspoon salt and ¼ cup water. Cover and
microwave on high until tender, 5 to 6 minutes, stirring
once halfway through. Pour off and discard any water
in the bowl.

In a 12-inch nonstick skillet over medium-high, cook
the bacon, stirring occasionally, until lightly browned,
5 to 6 minutes. Using a slotted spoon, transfer to a
paper towel-lined plate; set aside. Pour off and discard
all but 1 tablespoon fat from the skillet, then return
the pan to medium-high. Add the potatoes and cook,
stirring occasionally, until browned, 4 to 5 minutes.
Transfer the potatoes to the plate with the bacon.

In the same skillet over medium, heat the oil until
shimmering. Add the onion, poblano, ¼ teaspoon salt
and ½ teaspoon pepper; cook, stirring occasionally
until beginning to brown, 2 to 3 minutes. Add ½ cup
water, cover and cook, stirring occasionally, until the
liquid has reduced by about half, about 2 minutes. Add
the corn and oregano; cook, uncovered and stirring
occasionally, until the corn is tender-crisp, about
2 minutes. Return the potatoes and bacon to the pan;
cook, stirring, until warmed through, 1 to 2 minutes.
Taste and season with salt and pepper.

Optional garnish: Crumbled cotija or queso fresco
cheese OR chopped fresh cilantro OR diced avocado
OR hot sauce OR a combination

SEAR AND STEAM FOR CRISP-TENDER VEGETABLES

The intense, dry heat of skillet-charring does a good job of searing vegetables. Unfortunately, the exteriors of the vegetables often burn before the interiors have time to turn tender. Our solution? Sear and steam.

We start by briefly searing vegetables with a bit of fat in a hot skillet to develop browning and flavor. We then add a scant amount of water and cover the pan. The liquid produces a burst of steam that tenderizes the vegetables in just a few short minutes; the moisture evaporates by the time the dish is done so the flavors are bold and concentrated, not thin and dilute.

Timing varies by vegetable, but this technique works on everything from green beans and asparagus to cauliflower and broccoli.

RECIPES FROM TOP

| Broccoli with Smoked Paprika and Toasted Garlic Breadcrumbs | Asparagus in Black Bean–Garlic Sauce | Green Beans with Chipotle Chili and Peanuts |

Broccoli with Smoked Paprika and Toasted Garlic Breadcrumbs

Start to finish: 20 minutes
Servings: 4

In this texture-packed dish, a combination of browned garlic, smoky paprika and crisp breadcrumbs—inspired by the Catalan sauce picada—enhances skillet-cooked broccoli. **After being seared in a hot pan, the broccoli is combined with water, quickly covered and steamed until tender-crisp.** Added just before serving, a good dose of fresh thyme and a splash of woodsy-sweet sherry vinegar bring bright, fresh notes.

4 tablespoons extra-virgin olive oil, divided

⅓ cup panko breadcrumbs

3 medium garlic cloves, minced

½ teaspoon smoked paprika

1 pound broccoli crowns, cut into 1- to 1½-inch florets

Kosher salt and ground black pepper

1 tablespoon fresh thyme, chopped

1 tablespoon sherry vinegar

In a 12-inch skillet over medium, heat 2 tablespoons oil until shimmering. Add the panko and cook, stirring occasionally, until lightly golden, about 2 minutes. Stir in the garlic and smoked paprika; cook until the panko is deep golden brown and the garlic no longer is raw, about 1 minute. Transfer to a small bowl and set aside; wipe out the skillet.

In the same skillet over medium-high, heat the remaining 2 tablespoons oil until barely smoking. Add the broccoli and stir to coat, then sprinkle with ¼ teaspoon salt and ½ teaspoon pepper and distribute in an even layer. Cook, stirring only a few times, until lightly charred, about 4 minutes. Add ¼ cup water, then immediately cover. Reduce to medium and cook, occasionally shaking the pan, until the water has cooked off and the broccoli is tender-crisp, about 4 minutes.

Off heat, stir in the thyme and vinegar. Taste and season with salt and pepper. Transfer to a serving dish and sprinkle with the panko mixture.

Optional garnish: Toasted sliced or slivered almonds OR shaved manchego cheese OR both

Asparagus in Black Bean–Garlic Sauce

Start to finish: 20 minutes
Servings: 4

Spicy-sweet and rich with umami, this easy asparagus dish uses prepared black bean–garlic sauce. The widely available seasoning base can be found in the international aisle of most supermarkets. Paired with red pepper flakes, honey and Shaoxing wine (or dry sherry), it makes a flavor-packed glaze for earthy asparagus. **We char then steam the asparagus for the perfect tender-crisp bite.** A final flourish of thinly sliced scallions contributes zingy crunch and brightness.

2 tablespoons black bean–garlic sauce

¼ to ½ teaspoon red pepper flakes

1 tablespoon honey

2 tablespoons Shaoxing wine OR dry sherry

2 tablespoons neutral oil

1 pound asparagus, trimmed and cut on the diagonal into 2-inch lengths

Kosher salt and ground black pepper

3 scallions, thinly sliced

In a small bowl, whisk together the black bean sauce, pepper flakes, honey and Shaoxing wine; set aside. In a 12-inch skillet over medium-high, heat the oil until barely smoking. Add the asparagus and stir to coat, then sprinkle with ½ teaspoon pepper and distribute in an even layer. Cook, stirring only a few times, until the asparagus is lightly charred, about 4 minutes.

Stir in the black bean mixture and ¼ cup water, then immediately cover. Reduce to medium and cook, occasionally shaking the pan, until the asparagus is tender-crisp, about 2 minutes. Uncover, increase to medium-high and cook, stirring, until the sauce thickens and clings to the asparagus, 1 to 2 minutes. Taste and season with salt and black pepper, then transfer to a serving dish and sprinkle with the scallions.

Optional garnish: Toasted sesame seeds

Green Beans with Chipotle Chili and Peanuts

Start to finish: 20 minutes
Servings: 4

Inspired by the smoky, nutty notes of Mexican salsa macha, this green bean dish employs our sear-and-steam technique. **We sear the beans in a hot skillet until charred, then add water and a tight-fitting lid, allowing them to steam through. The result is deep flavor from browning and a pleasing tender-crisp texture.** Sesame seeds and peanuts add plenty of crunch, while chipotle chili in adobo and fresh lime juice contribute smokiness and bright, citrusy flavor.

4 tablespoons extra-virgin olive oil, divided

3 medium garlic cloves, thinly sliced

½ cup roasted peanuts, chopped

2 tablespoons sesame seeds

1 pound green beans, trimmed

Kosher salt and ground black pepper

1 chipotle chili in adobo sauce, minced

2 tablespoons lime juice

In a 12-inch skillet over medium, combine 2 tablespoons oil and the garlic. Cook, stirring, until the garlic begins to brown, about 1 minute. Add the peanuts and sesame seeds; cook, stirring, until the mixture is golden brown, about 1 minute. Transfer to a small bowl and set aside; wipe out the skillet.

In the same skillet over medium-high, heat the remaining 2 tablespoons oil until barely smoking. Add the green beans and stir to coat, then sprinkle with ¼ teaspoon salt and ½ teaspoon pepper and distribute in an even layer. Cook, stirring only a few times, until the beans are lightly charred, about 4 minutes. Add ¼ cup water, then immediately cover. Reduce to medium and cook, occasionally shaking the pan, until the water has cooked off and the beans are tender-crisp, about 3 minutes.

Off heat, stir in the chipotle chili and lime juice. Taste and season with salt and pepper. Transfer to a serving dish and sprinkle with the peanut-sesame mixture.

Mustard-Roasted Cauliflower with Dill

Start to finish: 30 minutes
Servings: 4

We use a preheated baking sheet to quickly maximize the caramelization of roasted cauliflower and bring out sweet, nutty flavors. Before they go on to the searing-hot sheet, the florets are tossed in a mix of whole-grain and Dijon mustards spiked with honey and lemon for spicy, tangy contrast.

⅓ cup whole-grain mustard

2 tablespoons Dijon mustard

2 tablespoons extra-virgin olive oil

2 teaspoons grated lemon zest, plus 1 tablespoon lemon juice

1 teaspoon honey

Kosher salt

2-pound head cauliflower, trimmed, cored and cut into 1½-inch florets

Chopped fresh dill, to serve

Heat the oven to 500°F with a rimmed baking sheet on the middle rack.

In a large bowl, whisk together the mustards, oil, lemon zest and juice, honey and ¼ teaspoon salt. Add the cauliflower and toss to coat.

Quickly remove the hot baking sheet from the oven and empty the cauliflower onto it, scraping the bowl; distribute the florets in an even layer. Roast until well browned and tender, 15 to 20 minutes, stirring halfway through. Taste and season with salt. Serve sprinkled with dill.

Garam Masala–Spiced Smashed Potatoes

Start to finish: 1¼ hours (20 minutes active)
Servings: 4 to 6

Crisp on the outside and creamy inside, these smashed potatoes feature garam masala, an Indian spice blend that often contains fennel and cumin. We also add whole fennel and cumin seeds for texture. **To boost flavor, we make a tarka, or a fat and spice infusion, by blooming the spices in butter on the stovetop.** Cooking the potatoes is a two-step process: First they're simmered until tender, then tossed with the tarka. After they're "smashed," the potatoes are finished in a blisteringly hot 500°F oven until deliciously browned and crisped.

2½ pounds small (1- to 1½-inch) Yukon Gold
OR fingerling potatoes, unpeeled

Kosher salt and ground black pepper

6 tablespoons salted butter

1½ teaspoons garam masala

1½ teaspoons fennel seeds

1 teaspoon cumin seeds

4 scallions, thinly sliced on
the diagonal OR ½ cup
lightly packed fresh
cilantro, roughly
chopped

In a large pot, combine the potatoes, 3 tablespoons salt and 2 quarts water. Bring to a boil and cook, stirring occasionally, until a skewer inserted into the largest potato meets no resistance, about 25 minutes. Meanwhile, heat the oven to 500°F with a rack in the middle position.

Drain the potatoes in a colander; set aside. Wipe out the pot, then set it over medium. Add the butter and heat, stirring, until foamy and melted. Add the garam masala, fennel seeds, cumin seeds and ½ teaspoon pepper. Cook, stirring, until fragrant and the seeds begin to crackle, about 1 minute. Remove the pot from the heat, add the potatoes and stir to coat.

Empty the potatoes and spiced butter onto a rimmed baking sheet. Using the bottom of a dry measuring cup or ramekin, press down on each potato so it is slightly flattened and splits open but remains intact. Roast without turning them until browned and crisp, 35 to 40 minutes. Serve sprinkled with the scallions.

Optional garnish: Lime wedges OR thinly sliced jalapeño chilies OR a combination

Tahini-Roasted Sweet Potatoes with Za'atar

Start to finish: 50 minutes (20 minutes active)
Servings: 4

Two Middle Eastern pantry staples, tahini and za'atar, the seed and spice blend, boost the flavor of sweet potatoes. First we coat the potato wedges with tahini, za'atar and cornstarch, then roast them in a hot oven until golden brown and meltingly tender. **The cornstarch helps bind the fatty tahini and produce a deliciously crisp coating.** For the finishing sauce, we stir more tahini and za'atar into creamy yogurt, then add lime juice for a refreshing tang.

⅓ cup plus 3 tablespoons tahini, divided

2 tablespoons extra-virgin olive oil

2 tablespoons cornstarch

1 tablespoon plus 1 teaspoon za'atar, divided

Kosher salt and ground black pepper

2 pounds orange-fleshed sweet potatoes, peeled and cut into 1- to 1½-inch wedges

¾ cup plain whole-milk yogurt

1 teaspoon grated lime zest OR lemon zest, plus 2 tablespoons lime juice OR lemon juice

Heat the oven to 450°F with a rack in the lower-middle position. Line a rimmed baking sheet with kitchen parchment. In a small bowl, whisk together the ⅓ cup tahini and oil; set aside.

In a large bowl, whisk together the cornstarch, 1 tablespoon za'atar, 1 teaspoon salt and ½ teaspoon pepper. Add the sweet potatoes and toss to coat. Pour in the tahini mixture and rub the mixture into the potatoes; reserve the small bowl. Distribute in an even layer on the prepared baking sheet.

Roast until the potatoes are lightly browned on the bottom, about 15 minutes, rotating the baking sheet about halfway through. Remove from the oven and, using a thin metal spatula, flip each wedge. Roast until golden brown and a skewer inserted into the potatoes meets no resistance, about another 15 minutes, once again flipping the wedges and rotating the sheet halfway through.

Meanwhile, in the reserved bowl, whisk together the yogurt, lime zest and juice, the remaining 3 tablespoons tahini, the remaining 1 teaspoon za'atar and ¼ teaspoon each salt and pepper. Transfer the potatoes to a platter. Serve with the yogurt-lime sauce.

Optional garnish: Ground sumac OR Aleppo pepper OR chopped fresh flat-leaf parsley OR a combination

Hot-Oil Brussels Sprouts with Ginger and Sesame

Start to finish: 25 minutes
Servings: 4

Earthy and subtly sweet with pleasant hints of bitterness, shredded raw Brussels sprouts make excellent slaw-style salads. **We massage shredded sprouts with rice vinegar and soy sauce, tenderizing the sprouts and tempering their cabbage-like qualities.** We add fresh ginger and chilies, then **we draw fragrance and flavor from aromatics by pouring a mixture of sizzling hot oil and sesame seeds on top.** The sprouts are lightly cooked, each bite imbued with nutty, toasty notes.

1 pound Brussels sprouts, trimmed

3 tablespoons unseasoned rice vinegar

2 tablespoons soy sauce, plus more as needed

Kosher salt and ground black pepper

1 tablespoon finely grated fresh ginger

1 or 2 Fresno OR serrano OR jalapeño chilies, stemmed and thinly sliced OR 2 scallions, thinly sliced OR both

3 tablespoons neutral oil

2 tablespoons sesame seeds

In a food processor fitted with the medium (3mm) slicing disk, slice the sprouts, emptying into a large bowl as needed. Add the vinegar, soy and ¼ teaspoon each salt and pepper. Using your hands, massage the sprouts until they wilt, 10 to 20 seconds. Let stand for 10 minutes. Transfer the mixture to a serving bowl. Distribute the ginger and chilies evenly over the top; do not stir or toss.

In an 8-inch skillet over medium-high, combine the oil and sesame seeds. Cook, stirring occasionally, until golden brown, 1 to 2 minutes. Drizzle the oil-seed mixture onto the sprouts and aromatics, then immediately toss. Taste and season with additional soy sauce and pepper.

Optional garnish: Chopped fresh cilantro

Go-to Grains

Carrot Rice with Cumin and Bay

Start to finish: 35 minutes (10 minutes active)
Servings: 4 to 6

For this easy, colorful side, we took inspiration from Indian carrot rice. **We shred the carrots on a box grater before cooking to rupture cell walls and release natural sugars, allowing the vegetable's sweet flavors to permeate the grains.** Whole cumin seeds balance the sweetness with their warm, earthy notes. Indian carrot rice traditionally is made with curry leaves, which impart toasted allium notes with hints of citrus. But they can be difficult to find, so we swapped in bay leaves. Though bay is different in flavor, their nuances of menthol and eucalyptus work well in this dish.

2 tablespoons extra-virgin olive oil

2 medium shallots, thinly sliced

Kosher salt and ground black pepper

2 teaspoons cumin seeds

2 bay leaves

2 cups basmati OR other long-grain white rice, rinsed and drained

1 medium carrot, peeled and grated on the large holes of a box grater

½ cup roasted pistachios, chopped OR golden raisins OR a combination

In a large saucepan over medium, heat the oil until shimmering. Add the shallots and ½ teaspoon salt, then cook, stirring occasionally, until golden brown, 4 to 5 minutes. Add the cumin, bay, ½ teaspoon salt and 1 teaspoon pepper; cook, stirring, until fragrant, about 30 seconds. Add the rice and carrot, tossing to coat, then add 2½ cups water. Bring to a simmer over medium-high, then cover, reduce to low and cook without stirring until the rice is tender and the water is mostly absorbed, 15 to 20 minutes.

Remove the pan from the heat. Uncover, drape a kitchen towel over the pan and re-cover. Let stand for 10 minutes. Remove and discard the bay, then fluff with a fork. Taste and season with salt and pepper. Transfer to a serving dish and sprinkle with pistachios.

Lemon Quinoa with Toasted Mustard Seeds and Peanuts

Start to finish: 30 minutes
Servings: 4

Spicy, tangy and nutty, this recipe was inspired by lemon rice, a traditional South Indian dish, but we swap out the usual white rice for nutrient-rich quinoa. **Peanuts, mustard seeds (or cumin seeds) and turmeric are first cooked in hot oil, a technique called blooming, or tempering, to release their fragrance and flavor.** A portion of this mixture is reserved for garnish, then the quinoa is cooked in the remaining nut-spice mixture so it's infused with seasoning and aroma. Adding lemon juice at the very end keeps the flavors bright. This is an excellent side to grilled or roasted chicken or seafood; it's also an excellent base for a grain bowl.

¼ cup extra-virgin olive oil

½ cup roasted peanuts OR cashews, roughly chopped

1 tablespoon brown OR yellow mustard seeds OR cumin seeds OR a combination

½ teaspoon ground turmeric

Kosher salt and ground black pepper

1 cup white quinoa, rinsed and drained

2 tablespoons lemon juice

In a medium saucepan over medium, heat the oil until shimmering. Add the peanuts, mustard seeds, turmeric, 1 teaspoon salt and ¼ teaspoon pepper. Cook, stirring occasionally, until fragrant and the peanuts begin to brown, 1 to 2 minutes. Transfer ¼ cup of the peanut mixture to a small bowl; set aside for garnish.

Add the quinoa to the remaining peanut mixture in the saucepan, then cook, stirring, until the mixture begins to crackle, about 30 seconds. Add 2 cups water and bring to a simmer over medium-high, then cover, reduce to medium-low and cook, without stirring, until the quinoa has absorbed the water, about 15 minutes.

Remove from the heat and let stand, covered, for 10 minutes. Drizzle with the lemon juice, then fluff with a fork. Transfer to a serving dish and spoon on the reserved nut mixture.

Optional garnish: Chopped fresh cilantro OR red pepper flakes OR both

Pistachio-Orange Bulgur Salad with Mint

Start to finish: 30 minutes
Servings: 4

A fresh orange does double duty in this colorful side dish: Grated zest gives a flavor boost to quick-pickled red onions, which provide a bright, tangy contrast to the nutty bulgur, while the chopped fruit adds sweetness and juiciness. We use red wine vinegar in the pickling liquid to tame the onion. Pistachios bring crunch and mint lends freshness. Feel free to swap in other nuts, such as pecans or almonds. We call for coarse bulgur rather than finely ground (the type used in tabbouleh) because the coarse variety holds up well when cooked. Serve alongside hearty braises and roasted meats.

1 cup coarse bulgur

Kosher salt and ground black pepper

½ small red onion, halved and thinly sliced

3 tablespoons red wine vinegar

1 medium orange

3 tablespoons extra-virgin olive oil

⅓ cup roughly chopped pistachios OR pecans OR sliced almonds

½ cup lightly packed fresh mint OR cilantro, roughly chopped

In a medium saucepan, combine the bulgur, ½ teaspoon salt and 1½ cups water. Bring to a boil over medium-high, then cover, reduce to medium-low and cook without stirring until the liquid has been absorbed, 15 to 18 minutes. Remove from the heat and let stand, covered, for 5 minutes.

Meanwhile, in a large bowl, stir together the onion, vinegar, ½ teaspoon salt and ¼ teaspoon pepper. Grate 1 tablespoon zest from the orange, then stir it into the onion-vinegar mixture. Using a sharp knife, slice about ½ inch off the top and bottom of the orange. Stand the orange on a cut end and cut from top to bottom following the contours of the fruit to remove the peel and white pith. Quarter the orange lengthwise, then thinly slice crosswise.

Using a fork, fluff the bulgur and add to the bowl. Stir in the oil, then fold in the orange pieces. Cool slightly, about 10 minutes, then stir in the pistachios and mint. Taste and season with salt and pepper.

BAKE A BETTER POLENTA

The endless stirring at the stove called for by traditional recipes can leave polenta feeling fussy. And the results, weighed down by too much butter and cheese, often don't reward your efforts. But in a tiny hilltop town in Northern Italy we learned a better, easier, way.

Maria Teresa Marino, whose family has a centuries old grain mill in a village about two hours south of Milan, showed us how to let the corn shine by making polenta with just water, coarsely ground corn-meal and salt, and doing the majority of the cooking in the gentle heat of a moderate oven.

We've built on this approach, finishing with just a touch of butter and cheese and creating complementary toppings of roasted or charred vegetables and fruits.

RECIPES FROM TOP

| Polenta with Roasted Tomatoes and Gorgonzola | Polenta with Charred Corn and Taleggio | Polenta with Roasted Stone Fruit, Mascarpone and Rosemary |

Polenta with Roasted Tomatoes and Gorgonzola

Start to finish: 1½ hours (15 minutes active)
Servings: 4

Cooking polenta in the even heat of the oven instead of on the stovetop means virtually no stirring. And while the polenta cooks gently on the lower rack, cherry (or grape) tomatoes and shallots roast on the upper rack, their textures softening and flavors becoming sweet and concentrated. Crumbled Gorgonzola cheese adds saltiness and pungency that contrast the sweetness of the roasted vegetables as well as rich creaminess.

1 cup coarse stoneground yellow cornmeal

Kosher salt and ground black pepper

2 pints cherry OR grape tomatoes

4 medium shallots, cut into ½-inch wedges, layers separated

1 tablespoon extra-virgin olive oil

1 large thyme sprig, plus 2 teaspoons chopped fresh thyme

2 tablespoons salted butter, cut into 2 pieces

2 ounces Gorgonzola cheese, crumbled (½ cup)

Heat the oven to 375°F with racks in the upper- and lower-middle positions. In a small Dutch oven or medium oven-safe saucepan (about 3-quart capacity), whisk together the cornmeal, 1½ teaspoons salt and 5½ cups water. Bring to a gentle simmer over medium-high, stirring often, then place uncovered in the oven on the lower rack and cook for 1 hour.

Meanwhile, in a 9-by-13-inch baking dish, toss together the tomatoes, shallots, oil, thyme sprig, ½ teaspoon salt and ¼ teaspoon black pepper. Roast on the upper rack until the tomatoes have burst and are juicy, about 1 hour, stirring once about halfway through. Remove from the oven, then remove and discard the thyme. Cover with foil and set aside.

After the polenta has cooked for 1 hour, remove the pot from the oven. Add the butter and whisk until melted, then return the pot, uncovered, to the oven; cook until the granules are tender and the polenta is thick and creamy, another 10 to 30 minutes. Remove from the oven, whisk until smooth and let stand for 5 to 10 minutes. Taste and season with salt and pepper. Whisk in additional water, if needed, to thin.

Serve the polenta topped with the Gorgonzola, roasted tomatoes, chopped thyme and additional black pepper.

Optional garnish: Red pepper flakes

Polenta with Charred Corn and Taleggio

Start to finish: 1½ hours (15 minutes active)
Servings: 4

We deliver a double dose of sweet corn flavor in this almost effortless oven-baked polenta. **Once the polenta is done, we fire up the broiler and char corn kernels to make a topping that echoes the flavor of the polenta.** Plump, tender kernels cut from fresh cobs are best, but frozen works, too. If using frozen, before broiling, be sure to thaw it and pat it dry. Salty, creamy cheese and bold, pungent fresh oregano complement the natural sugars of the corn.

1 cup coarse stoneground yellow cornmeal

Kosher salt and ground black pepper

2 tablespoons salted butter, cut into 2 pieces

3 cups fresh corn kernels (from about 4 ears) OR 3 cups frozen corn, thawed and patted dry

2 tablespoons balsamic vinegar OR sherry vinegar

1 tablespoon extra-virgin olive oil

4 ounces taleggio cheese OR brie OR camembert cheese, cut into ¼-inch slices

2 tablespoons fresh oregano, chopped

Heat the oven to 375°F with a rack in the lower-middle position. In a small Dutch oven or medium oven-safe saucepan (about 3-quart capacity), whisk together the cornmeal, 1½ teaspoons salt and 5½ cups water. Bring to a gentle simmer over medium-high, stirring often, then place uncovered in the oven and cook for 1 hour.

Remove the pot from the oven. Add the butter and whisk until smooth, then return the pan, uncovered, to the oven; cook until the granules are tender and the polenta is thick and creamy, another 10 to 30 minutes. Remove from the oven, whisk until smooth and let stand for 5 to 10 minutes.

While the polenta rests, heat the broiler with a rack about 6 inches from the element. On a broiler-safe rimmed baking sheet, toss together the corn, vinegar, oil and ½ teaspoon salt, then distribute in an even layer. Broil until the kernels darken and begin to pop, about 2 minutes, stirring once about halfway through.

Taste the polenta and season with salt and pepper. Whisk in additional water, if needed, to thin. Serve the polenta topped with the taleggio, corn, oregano and additional pepper.

Optional garnish: Calabrian chili paste OR red pepper flakes

Polenta with Roasted Stone Fruit, Mascarpone and Rosemary

Start to finish: 1½ hours (20 minutes active)
Servings: 4

Cooking polenta in the oven is hands off-easy, freeing you to prep a sweet and savory fruit topping. We really love juicy, ripe stone fruit—peaches, nectarines, plums, cherries or a combination. And when fresh figs are available, they're excellent in place of the stone fruit. This is a perfect dish for breakfast or brunch.

1 cup coarse stoneground yellow cornmeal

Kosher salt and ground black pepper

2 tablespoons salted butter, cut into 2 pieces

1½ pounds peaches OR cherries OR nectarines OR plums OR a combination, halved, pitted and cut into 1-inch wedges

1 tablespoon extra-virgin olive oil

1 teaspoon white sugar

½ cup mascarpone cheese OR whole-milk ricotta cheese

1 tablespoon fresh rosemary, finely chopped

Heat the oven to 375°F with a rack in the lower-middle position. In a small Dutch oven or medium oven-safe saucepan (about 3-quart capacity), whisk together the cornmeal, 1½ teaspoons salt and 5½ cups water. Bring to a gentle simmer over medium-high, stirring often, then place uncovered in the oven and cook for 1 hour.

Remove the pot from the oven. Add the butter and whisk until smooth, then return the pot, uncovered, to the oven; cook until the granules are tender and the polenta is thick and creamy, another 10 to 30 minutes. Remove from the oven, whisk until smooth and let stand for 5 to 10 minutes.

While the polenta rests, heat the broiler with a rack about 6 inches from the element. On a broiler-safe rimmed baking sheet, toss together the fruit, oil, sugar and a pinch of salt, then distribute in an even layer. Broil until the fruit begins to char and soften, 4 to 6 minutes.

Taste the polenta and season with salt and pepper. Whisk in additional water, if needed, to thin. Serve the polenta topped with the mascarpone, fruit, rosemary and additional black pepper.

Optional garnish: Honey OR red pepper flakes OR shaved Parmesan cheese OR a combination

Shortcut Paella

Start to finish: 45 minutes
Servings: 4

Think of this as a pared-down paella. It features two classic Spanish ingredients: chorizo and smoked paprika. **To bump up the tomato flavor, we brown tomato paste along with the chorizo, garlic and paprika, then stir in rice and green beans so they absorb the bold seasonings and meaty goodness.** If you like, brighten the dish with a garnish of chopped parsley, roasted red pepper strips or a squeeze of lemon—or all three. Be sure to use dry-cured Spanish chorizo, not Mexican chorizo, which is a fresh sausage.

4 ounces Spanish chorizo, casings removed, halved lengthwise and thinly sliced crosswise

6 large garlic cloves, thinly sliced

2 teaspoons smoked paprika

¼ cup tomato paste

1½ cups Arborio rice

12 ounces green beans, trimmed and cut into 1-inch lengths

Kosher salt and ground black pepper

In a Dutch oven over medium, cook the chorizo, stirring occasionally, until it releases some of its oil and starts to brown, 5 to 8 minutes. Add the garlic and paprika; cook, stirring, until fragrant, about 1 minute. Add the tomato paste and cook, stirring often, until the paste begins to brown, about 2 minutes.

Stir in the rice, then add the green beans, 1 teaspoon salt, ¼ teaspoon pepper and 6 cups water. Bring to a simmer over medium-high, then reduce to medium-low and cook, uncovered and stirring occasionally, until the rice is tender and creamy and the water is mostly absorbed, 15 to 20 minutes. If a creamier texture is desired, stir in additional water. Off heat, taste and season with salt and pepper.

Optional garnish: Lemon wedges OR chopped fresh flat-leaf parsley OR roasted red peppers, cut into strips OR a combination

Ginger Beef with Rice and Peas

Start to finish: 1 hour (15 minutes active)
Servings: 4

Satisfyingly chewy short-grain rice and soy-seasoned beef is a classic Japanese pairing. This version of gyu soboro gohan cooks rice and ground beef separately to keep the tastes and textures distinct, then combines the two at the end. **We layer the seasonings for flavor complexity, adding soy sauce and mirin (a subtly sweet rice cooking wine) to the rice as it cooks and adding more of each, plus fresh ginger, to the beef after sautéing.** With a steamed or stir-fried vegetable alongside, this rice dish is hearty enough to be a light main.

1¾ cups Japanese-style short-grain white rice, rinsed well and drained

3 tablespoons soy sauce, divided

3 tablespoons mirin, divided

Kosher salt and ground white OR black pepper

¾ cup thawed frozen peas

2 teaspoons neutral oil

8 ounces 90 percent lean ground beef

4 teaspoons finely grated fresh ginger

In a medium saucepan, stir together the rice, 2 tablespoons soy, 2 tablespoons mirin, 2 cups water and ¼ teaspoon salt. Let stand for about 30 minutes.

Place the saucepan over medium-high, scatter the peas over the rice and bring to a boil. Cover, reduce to low and cook until the rice has absorbed the liquid, 12 to 15 minutes. Meanwhile, in a 10-inch skillet over medium-high, heat the oil until shimmering. Add the beef and ¼ teaspoon pepper; cook, stirring and breaking the beef up into small bits, until no longer pink, about 2 minutes. Remove from heat, stir in the ginger, the remaining 1 tablespoon soy sauce and the remaining 1 tablespoon mirin; set aside.

When the rice is done, remove the pan from the heat. Uncover and, working quickly, scatter the beef mixture, including its juices, over the rice; do not stir. Cover and let stand for 10 minutes. Uncover and, using a fork, fluff the rice, stirring to incorporate the beef. Taste and season with salt and pepper.

Optional garnish: Thinly sliced scallions OR toasted sesame seeds OR both

Spiced Beef, Bulgur and Tomato Pilaf

Start to finish: 40 minutes (20 minutes active)
Servings: 4 to 6

Bulgur, made by cracking, cooking then drying whole-grain wheat, stars in this Middle Eastern-style pilaf. **To bring out the grains' nutty taste, we first toast them in a dry pan. Then we brown tomato paste with onion, which boosts the umami and sweetness and builds layers of flavor.** This is especially delicious topped with Greek yogurt seasoned with grated garlic, chopped fresh mint or parsley and a squeeze of lemon juice. Be sure to use coarse bulgur here, rather than finely ground; the hearty texture of coarse bulgur holds up well when cooked for a pilaf.

8 ounces 80 percent lean ground beef
OR ground lamb

2 medium garlic cloves, minced, divided

1 teaspoon ground cumin OR sweet paprika
OR both

Kosher salt and ground black pepper

1 cup coarse bulgur

2 tablespoons extra-virgin olive oil

1 medium red onion, chopped

6-ounce can (⅔ cup) tomato paste

In a medium bowl, stir together the beef, half of the garlic, the cumin, 1 teaspoon salt and ½ teaspoon pepper; set aside. In a medium saucepan over medium, toast the bulgur, stirring occasionally, until lightly browned and fragrant, about 5 minutes. Transfer to a small bowl; set aside.

In the same saucepan over low, combine the oil, onion, tomato paste, the remaining garlic and ½ teaspoon salt. Cook, stirring, until the paste browns and slightly sticks to the pan, about 5 minutes. Add the beef mixture and cook, breaking the meat into small bits, until no longer pink, about 5 minutes. Stir in the bulgur and 1 cup water. Cover, increase to medium-low and cook without stirring until the liquid has been absorbed, 15 to 18 minutes.

Remove the pan from the heat and let stand, covered, for 5 minutes. Using a fork, fluff the bulgur mixture. Taste and season with salt and pepper.

Optional garnish: Greek yogurt OR chopped fresh mint OR flat-leaf parsley OR lemon wedges OR a combination

Bacon and Barley Pilaf with Celery Root

Start to finish: 1 hour
Servings: 4

We give barley pilaf-style treatment in this recipe, which adds earthy celery root, sweet leeks and salty-smoky bacon. **To tie everything together, the barley is tossed with a tangy mustard vinaigrette, which the grains absorb beautifully. Toasting barley before simmering is the key to enhancing the grain's naturally nutty taste.** Be sure to use pearled barley, which has been polished, or "pearled," to remove the outer husk and bran layers; this reduces the cooking time. Serve this hearty, autumnal dish warm or at room temperature, garnished with fresh dill if you like.

1 tablespoon Dijon mustard

1 teaspoon cider vinegar

1 tablespoon extra-virgin olive oil

1 cup pearled barley

4 ounces bacon OR pancetta, chopped

1 medium leek, white and light green parts thinly sliced, rinsed and drained OR 2 medium shallots, finely chopped

8 ounces celery root, peeled and cut into ½-inch pieces

Kosher salt and ground black pepper

In a small bowl, whisk together the mustard, vinegar, oil and 1 tablespoon water; set aside. In a medium saucepan over medium-high, toast the barley, stirring occasionally, until lightly browned and fragrant, 3 to 4 minutes. Transfer to another small bowl; set aside.

In the same saucepan over medium-low, cook the bacon, stirring occasionally, until browned and crisp, 5 to 7 minutes. Add the leek, then cook, stirring occasionally, until softened, about 2 minutes. Add the celery root and ¼ cup water, then scrape up the browned bits. Stir in the barley, 2¾ cups water and ½ teaspoon each salt and pepper. Bring to a simmer over medium-high, stirring occasionally, then cover, reduce to low and cook without stirring until the water is absorbed and the barley and celery root are tender, about 40 minutes.

Off heat, use a fork to fluff the mixture, then gently stir in the vinaigrette. Taste and season with salt and pepper. Serve warm or at room temperature.

Optional garnish: Chopped fresh dill

Brown Rice and Mushroom Risotto with Miso and Scallions

Start to finish: 1 hour 10 minutes
Servings: 4 to 6

We've given Italian risotto Japanese flair in a few ways. **We swapped out the traditional Arborio rice for short-grain brown rice, which we first toast to bring out its nutty taste. We also replaced the usual wine with sake, which lends subtly sweet, mellow flavor, and the Parmesan with white miso for umami and salty savoriness.** Cooked with earthy mushrooms, this hearty dish makes a satisfying main course that happens to be vegan.

1 cup short-grain brown rice

2 tablespoons neutral oil

1 bunch scallions, white parts minced, green parts thinly sliced, reserved separately

8 ounces cremini mushrooms, thinly sliced OR shiitake mushrooms (stemmed), thinly sliced OR a combination

Kosher salt and ground black pepper

3 tablespoons white miso

¼ cup sake OR dry white wine

In a large saucepan over medium, toast the rice, stirring, until fragrant and nutty, about 2 minutes. Transfer to a small bowl; set aside. In the same saucepan over medium-high, heat the oil until shimmering. Add the scallion whites, mushrooms, ½ teaspoon salt and 1 teaspoon pepper. Cook, stirring occasionally, until the mushrooms are soft and the moisture they release has mostly evaporated, 4 to 5 minutes.

Add the miso and cook, stirring, until it starts to brown and stick to the bottom of the pan, about 2 minutes. Add the sake and cook, scraping up any browned bits, until slightly thickened, about 2 minutes. Stir in the rice, then add 3 cups water. Bring to a simmer over medium-high, then reduce to low, cover and cook, stirring occasionally and briskly, until the rice is creamy and the grains are tender but with a little chewiness, 50 to 55 minutes; if at any point, the rice looks dry, stir in ¼ to ½ cup water and continue to cook.

Off heat, taste and season with salt and pepper. Serve sprinkled with the scallion greens.

Optional garnish: Toasted sesame oil OR toasted sesame seeds OR furikake OR shichimi togarashi

TOAST YOUR GRAINS

Toasting dry grains caramelizes some of their starches, drawing out sweet, nutty flavors and enhancing their aroma. The process works on all kinds of grains and takes just a few minutes and a dry pan.

We toast bulgur for our salad based on Armenian eetch and pair it with browned tomato paste for a double shot of caramelized flavor.

Barley gets a quick toast for our dish inspired by Korean boribap, a mix of rice and barley. The toasted barley has a deeper flavor and stands up well to the savory mushrooms, sesame oil and spicy kimchi that make up the dish.

And quinoa (technically a seed but treated as a grain) also benefits from a touch of toast. The quinoa for our fruity-spicy salad is toasted first, then dressed while still warm so it better absorbs the flavors.

RECIPES FROM TOP

| Toasted Bulgur with Tomato and Mint | Quinoa Salad with Pineapple, Cilantro and Lime | Toasted Barley with Shiitake Mushrooms and Kimchi |

Toasted Bulgur with Tomato and Mint

Start to finish: 40 minutes
Servings: 4

The Armenian bulgur salad called eetch is reminiscent of tabbouleh, but it's grain-centric rather than herb-forward. It inspired this tomatoey bulgur side. We build flavor into the dish in a couple ways. **We toast the bulgur—make sure to use coarse bulgur, not fine—to accentuate its sweet, wheaty notes. Then we brown the tomato paste for deeper color and greater flavor intensity.** To make this more substantial, we like to stir blanched green beans into the finished bulgur and finish it with any or all of the optional garnishes.

1½ cups coarse bulgur

3 tablespoons extra-virgin olive oil

1 medium red bell pepper OR
2 medium wax peppers, stemmed, seeded and finely chopped

3 medium garlic cloves, minced

Kosher salt and ground black pepper

¼ cup tomato paste

1 teaspoon Aleppo pepper OR sweet paprika

¾ cup lightly packed fresh mint OR fresh flat-leaf parsley OR a combination, finely chopped

In a medium saucepan over medium, toast the bulgur, stirring occasionally, until lightly browned and fragrant, about 5 minutes. Transfer to a small bowl and set aside.

In the same pan over medium-high, heat the oil until shimmering. Add the bell pepper, garlic, ¾ teaspoon salt and ½ teaspoon black pepper; cook, stirring occasionally, until tender, about 2 minutes. Add the tomato paste and Aleppo pepper, then cook, stirring, until the paste browns and slightly sticks to the pan, 1 to 3 minutes. Stir in the bulgur, then add 2¼ cups water. Bring to a boil, then cover, reduce to medium-low and cook

without stirring until the bulgur has absorbed the liquid, 15 to 18 minutes. Remove from the heat and let stand, covered, for 5 minutes.

Transfer the bulgur to a wide, shallow bowl and cool until warm, about 5 minutes. Stir in the mint, then taste and season with salt and black pepper. Serve warm or at room temperature.

Optional garnish: Pomegranate molasses OR finely chopped walnuts OR crumbled feta cheese OR a combination

Toasted Barley with Shiitake Mushrooms and Kimchi

Start to finish: 1¼ hours (20 minutes active)
Servings: 4 to 6

This umami-packed barley dish was inspired by Korean boribap, a mix of rice and barley that's steamed and served with banchan (small plates) and soup. **We first toast the barley, which brings out a richness and depth of flavor in the grain so it holds its own amidst meaty mushrooms, aromatic sesame oil and tangy, fiery kimchi.** If your kimchi is dryish and doesn't have 2 tablespoons of juice for stirring into the barley, use 1 tablespoon water plus 1 tablespoon soy sauce instead. Topping this with runny-yolked fried eggs will transform the barley into a satisfying meal.

1 cup pearled barley

2 tablespoons neutral oil

8 ounces shiitake mushrooms, stemmed, caps sliced about ¼ inch thick

Kosher salt and ground black pepper

1 tablespoon gochujang

1½ teaspoons finely grated fresh ginger

1 cup cabbage kimchi, chopped, plus 2 tablespoons kimchi juice

1½ teaspoons toasted sesame oil

In a large saucepan over medium-high, toast the barley, stirring occasionally, until lightly browned, 4 to 5 minutes. Transfer to a small bowl; set aside.

In the same pan over medium-high, heat the neutral oil until shimmering. Add the mushrooms and ¼ teaspoon salt; cook, stirring occasionally, until softened and lightly browned, about 3 minutes. Return the barley to the pan, add the gochujang and ginger and stir until incorporated. Add 2¾ cups water, scraping up any browned bits. Bring to a boil, then reduce to low, cover and simmer, stirring occasionally, until the barley has absorbed the liquid and is tender, 40 to 45 minutes. Remove from the heat, drape a kitchen towel across the pan and re-cover. Let stand for about 10 minutes.

Using a fork, fluff the barley mixture. Add the kimchi plus kimchi juice and the sesame oil; stir until well combined and the barley has absorbed the liquid. Taste and season with salt and pepper.

Optional garnish: Cucumber matchsticks OR toasted sesame seeds OR crumbled nori snacks OR thinly sliced scallions OR a combination

Quinoa Salad with Pineapple, Cilantro and Lime

Start to finish: 1¼ hours (20 minutes active)
Servings: 4

This quinoa salad combines tropical fruit, citrusy lime and spicy fresh chilies (feel free to use a sweet bell pepper instead). **We dry-toast the quinoa—which is actually a seed, not a grain—to give it fragrant, nutty notes, and dress it while warm to help it absorb flavor.** To tame the onion's bite, we steep the slices in lime juice while the quinoa cooks. If mango is more to your liking, use an equal amount in place of the pineapple. Serve the salad at room temperature or chilled; if chilled, wait to add the cilantro until the last minute.

½ medium red onion, thinly sliced

2 Fresno chilies, stemmed, seeded and thinly sliced OR 1 small red or orange bell pepper, stemmed, seeded and finely chopped

1 teaspoon grated lime zest, plus 3 tablespoons lime juice, divided

1 cup quinoa, preferably rainbow (tricolor) quinoa, rinsed and drained

Kosher salt and ground black pepper

2 cups chopped fresh pineapple OR thawed frozen pineapple chunks

2 tablespoons extra-virgin olive oil

¾ cup lightly packed fresh cilantro, roughly chopped

In a large bowl, combine the onion, chilies and lime juice; set aside while you cook the quinoa. In a medium saucepan over medium-high, toast the quinoa, stirring occasionally, until crackling, about 3 minutes. Stir in 2 cups water and ½ teaspoon salt and bring to a boil. Cover, reduce to low and simmer, without stirring, until the liquid is absorbed, 13 to 15 minutes. Remove from the heat and let stand, covered, for about 10 minutes.

While the quinoa rests, stir the pineapple, oil and ¼ teaspoon salt into the onion mixture. When the quinoa is done, use a fork to fluff it, then add it to the onion-pineapple mixture and toss. Cool until barely warm to the touch, 20 to 30 minutes, tossing a few times. Stir in the lime zest and cilantro. Taste and season with salt and pepper.

Optional garnish: Toasted unsweetened coconut OR chopped roasted cashews

Rice and Chickpeas with Caramelized Onions

Start to finish: 40 minutes
Servings: 4

This recipe was loosely inspired by Middle Eastern mujaddara, which transforms a few humble ingredients—grains, lentils and onions—into a hearty and satisfying dish. Our version swaps out the traditional lentils for canned chickpeas, though canned lentils also work well. **We briefly heat cumin and allspice in oil to bloom the flavors, then add the rice and legumes so they absorb the seasonings as they simmer.** At the same time, we caramelize onions in a skillet, then serve them atop the finished dish; the sweet onions provide a nice contrast to the fragrant rice and earthy chickpeas.

3 tablespoons extra-virgin olive oil, divided

2 large yellow onions, halved
and thinly sliced

Kosher salt and ground black pepper

1 teaspoon ground cumin

½ teaspoon ground allspice

15½-ounce can chickpeas OR
15-ounce can lentils, rinsed and drained

1 cup basmati OR other long-grain
white rice, rinsed and drained

¼ cup chopped fresh flat-leaf parsley

In a 12-inch skillet over medium, stir together 2 tablespoons oil, the onions and ½ teaspoon salt. Cover and cook, stirring occasionally, until the onions are jammy, about 12 minutes. Reduce to low and cook, uncovered and stirring occasionally, until caramelized, about 5 minutes. Remove from the heat.

Meanwhile, in a medium saucepan over medium, combine the remaining 1 tablespoon oil, the cumin, allspice and ¼ teaspoon pepper. Cook, stirring, until fragrant, about 1 minute. Stir in the chickpeas, rice, 1 teaspoon salt and 1½ cups water. Bring to a simmer, then cover, reduce to medium-low and cook without stirring until the liquid is absorbed, 15 to 17 minutes.

Remove the pan from the heat and let stand, covered, for 10 minutes. Using a fork, fluff the rice mixture. Taste and season with salt and pepper. Transfer to a serving dish, top with the onions and garnish with the parsley.

Optional garnish: Toasted slivered almonds OR pomegranate seeds OR pomegranate molasses OR plain Greek yogurt OR a combination

Farro with Feta, Olives and Herbs

Start to finish: 45 minutes (20 minutes active)
Servings: 4

We coax caramel-y, nutty notes from dried farro by toasting it on the stovetop until fragrant. Once fully cooked, the still-warm grains then are tossed with dressing, allowing them to absorb flavor as they cool. Crunchy celery and chewy farro provide texture, while feta and olives add pops of bold, briny flavor. Any meaty green olive is good, but plump Castelvetrano olives are particularly nice. Don't use whole-grain farro, which won't cook through in the time indicated. Pearled farro, from which the bran has been removed, is faster-cooking than its whole-grain counterpart. If the front of the package doesn't clearly indicate, check the ingredient list.

1½ cups pearled farro

Kosher salt and ground black pepper

¼ cup extra-virgin olive oil,
plus more to serve

3 tablespoons red wine vinegar
OR white wine vinegar

1 cup pitted green olives, roughly chopped,
plus 1 tablespoon olive brine

2 medium celery stalks, thinly sliced
OR ½ English cucumber, halved lengthwise
and thinly sliced OR a combination

½ cup lightly packed fresh flat-leaf parsley
OR mint OR basil OR dill OR a combination,
roughly chopped

3 ounces feta cheese, crumbled (¾ cup)

In a large saucepan over medium, toast the farro, stirring, until lightly browned and fragrant, about 3 minutes. Stir in 6 cups water and 1 teaspoon salt. Bring to a simmer over medium-high, then reduce to medium and simmer, uncovered, stirring once or twice, until the farro is tender with a little chew, about 20 minutes. Meanwhile, in a large bowl, whisk together the oil, vinegar, olive brine and ¼ teaspoon each salt and pepper; set aside.

When the farro is done, drain well in a colander. Add the still-warm farro to the dressing and toss. Let stand until cooled to room temperature, stirring once or twice, about 10 minutes.

Add the olives, celery and parsley; toss to combine. Add the feta and gently toss once more. Taste and season with salt and pepper, then drizzle with additional olive oil.

Black Pepper–Garlic Chicken Fried Rice

Start to finish: 30 minutes
Servings: 4 to 6

A classic Filipino preparation, adobo usually is made with pork or chicken seasoned with soy sauce, abundant garlic, vinegar and black pepper. Here, we created a chicken fried rice that features those flavors. If you like, serve this topped with fried eggs. **For the best texture, use cooked rice that's been refrigerated until firm; just-cooked rice will turn mushy.** To make enough rice for this recipe, in a large saucepan, combine 2 cups water and 1½ cups long-grain white rice (preferably jasmine), rinsed and drained. Bring to a simmer over medium-high, then reduce to low, cover and cook for 15 to 18 minutes. Let stand, covered, for 10 minutes, then transfer to a wide, shallow bowl. Cool to room temperature, then cover and refrigerate until well chilled.

3 tablespoons plus 1 teaspoon neutral oil, divided

6 medium garlic cloves, minced

1 bunch scallions, thinly sliced, white and green parts reserved separately

12 ounces boneless, skinless chicken thighs, trimmed and cut into 1-inch pieces

¼ cup soy sauce

3 tablespoons white vinegar OR unseasoned rice vinegar

4 cups cooked and chilled long-grain white rice, preferably jasmine rice (see headnote)

Kosher salt and ground black pepper

In a 12-inch nonstick skillet over medium, combine 3 tablespoons oil, the garlic and scallion whites; cook, stirring, until the garlic is golden brown, about 1 minute. Add the chicken, soy sauce and vinegar. Cook, stirring occasionally, until the liquid has evaporated and the chicken is browned in spots, about 7 minutes.

Drizzle the chicken mixture with the remaining 1 teaspoon oil. Add the rice, ¼ teaspoon salt and 1 teaspoon pepper, breaking up any clumps. Increase to medium-high and cook, stirring occasionally, until the rice is sizzling and heated through, 3 to 4 minutes. Serve sprinkled with the scallion greens and additional pepper.

Optional garnish: Thinly sliced Fresno or jalapeño chilies

Coconut Rice with Lemon Grass and Cashews

Start to finish: 35 minutes
Servings: 4 to 6

This dish gets a double dose of coconut: The rice is cooked in coconut water, then garnished with toasted shredded coconut. We use coconut water, not coconut milk, to cook rice because it's lighter and brighter. Turmeric lends an earthy flavor and golden hue, while lemon grass, fresh ginger or makrut lime leaves brings subtle citrusy notes. Serve the rice with everything from grilled pork to steamed fish to stir-fried greens.

2 tablespoons chopped unsalted OR salted cashews

2 tablespoons unsweetened shredded coconut

1½ cups jasmine OR other long-grain white rice, rinsed and drained

2 cups unsweetened coconut water

1 lemon grass stalk, trimmed to the bottom 6 inches, dry outer layers discarded, bruised OR 1-inch piece fresh ginger, peeled, halved crosswise and bruised OR 2 makrut lime leaves OR a combination

¾ teaspoon ground turmeric

Kosher salt and ground black pepper

In a medium saucepan over medium, toast the cashews and coconut, stirring often, until golden brown and aromatic, about 3 minutes. Transfer to a small bowl; set aside.

In the same saucepan, combine the rice, coconut water, lemon grass, turmeric, 1¼ teaspoons salt and ¼ teaspoon pepper. Bring to a simmer over medium-high, then cover, reduce to low and cook without stirring until the rice has absorbed the liquid, 12 to 15 minutes.

Remove from the heat and let stand, covered, for 10 minutes. Fluff the rice with a fork. Remove and discard the lemon grass. Taste and season with salt and pepper. Serve sprinkled with the cashews and coconut.

Optional garnish: Chopped fresh cilantro OR lime wedges OR both

Caramelized Onion Bulgur with Greens and Pomegranate Molasses

Start to finish: 1 hour (30 minutes active)
Servings: 4

Inspired by a dish we had in Galilee, this recipe combines hearty bulgur with silky greens and bittersweet caramelized onions. **Instead of slowly caramelizing the onions to a jammy consistency, we cook them over higher heat so they retain some crispy texture. We season the dish with baharat and allspice, cooking them briefly in oil to bloom the flavors.** Baharat is a Middle Eastern blend of black pepper, cardamom and other warm spices, though you can substitute cumin plus cinnamon instead. We toast coarse, not fine, bulgur in the spices to enhance the grains' nutty taste and infuse them with the seasonings. Pomegranate molasses brings a sweet, tart pop to the finished dish.

4 tablespoons extra-virgin olive oil, divided

2 medium yellow onions, halved and thinly sliced

Kosher salt and ground black pepper

1 cup coarse bulgur

1½ teaspoons baharat (see headnote)
OR 2 teaspoons ground cumin plus
¼ teaspoon ground cinnamon

½ teaspoon ground allspice

1 bunch collard greens OR lacinato kale
OR curly kale, stemmed and chopped

Pomegranate molasses, to serve

In a 12-inch skillet over medium-high, heat 3 tablespoons oil until shimmering. Add the onions and cook, stirring occasionally at the start then more frequently once beginning to brown, until deeply caramelized and crisped, 10 to 15 minutes; reduce the heat if the onions brown too quickly. Transfer to a paper towel-lined plate and sprinkle with a pinch of salt; set aside.

In the same skillet over medium, toast the bulgur, stirring occasionally, until lightly browned and fragrant, 2 to 3 minutes. Add the remaining 1 tablespoon oil, the baharat, allspice and ½ teaspoon pepper; cook, stirring, until fragrant, about 1 minute. Add the greens 1 large handful at a time, stirring to slightly wilt before adding more. Add 2 cups water and 1 teaspoon salt, then scrape up the browned bits. Bring to a simmer over medium-high, then cover, reduce to medium-low and cook without stirring until the liquid has been absorbed, about 15 minutes.

Remove the skillet from the heat and let stand, covered, for 10 minutes. Using a fork, fluff the bulgur mixture, then stir in half of the caramelized onions. Taste and season with salt and pepper. Transfer to a serving dish, top with the remaining onions and drizzle with pomegranate molasses.

Optional garnish: Pomegranate seeds OR thinly sliced scallions OR both

EASY RICE BOWLS

Making a bowl of rice checks the boxes of easy and filling. Making it taste good requires just a bit more effort—and some help from our umami toolbox.

Browned tomato paste, one of our favorite flavor boosters, elevates a beef topping based on Lebanese hashweh. We also get the most out of fresh dill by mincing the stems and cooking them into the meat mixture; the chopped leaves are sprinkled on at the end.

Kimchi, a spicy fermented cabbage, and gochujang, a fermented pepper paste, are staples of the Korean kitchen and add punch to our bibimbap-inspired bowl, serving as the base of a sauce as well as a finishing drizzle.

And for the ultimate bowl of comfort, we turn to Japanese oyako donburi, which is chicken and egg cooked in a kind of omelet and served over hot rice. The combination of rich, savory flavors blends beautifully with the mild, starchy rice.

RECIPES FROM TOP

| Baharat-Spiced Beef and Butter-Toasted Pine Nut Rice Bowls | Japanese-Style Chicken and Egg Rice Bowls | Stir-Fried Zucchini and Kimchi Rice Bowls |

Stir-Fried Zucchini and Kimchi Rice Bowls

Start to finish: 30 minutes
Servings: 4

Korean bibimbap, a meal-in-a-bowl of rice topped with various vegetables plus meat and/or seafood, then finished with an egg, gave us the idea for these rice bowls. Stir-fried zucchini is tender but almost meaty in texture, and kimchi brings a jolt of spice and garlic. **Gochujang, an umami-packed fermented pepper paste and a core ingredient in the Korean kitchen, is a go-to seasoning at Milk Street. It serves as the base for the sauce that seasons the zucchini and is drizzled on as a finishing touch.** Sticky, pleasantly chewy short-grain rice is best. We like to top each bowl with a runny-yolked fried egg.

2 to 3 tablespoons gochujang

1 tablespoon kimchi brine, plus
1 cup cabbage kimchi, drained and chopped

1 tablespoon toasted sesame oil

2 tablespoons neutral oil

1½ pounds medium zucchini OR summer squash, quartered lengthwise and cut crosswise into 1- to 1½-inch lengths

Kosher salt and ground black pepper

1 teaspoon finely grated fresh ginger

3 scallions, thinly sliced on the diagonal

About 6 cups freshly cooked rice, preferably short grain

In a small bowl, whisk together the gochujang, kimchi brine, sesame oil and 2 tablespoons water. Measure 2 tablespoons of this mixture into another small bowl and set aside. Into the remaining mixture, whisk in 3 tablespoons water and set near the stovetop for stir-frying.

In a 12-inch nonstick skillet over medium-high, heat the neutral oil until barely smoking. Add the zucchini and ½ teaspoon salt, then cook, stirring occasionally, until golden brown, 5 to 7 minutes. Add the ginger and gochujang mixture reserved for stir-frying; cook, stirring, until the zucchini has absorbed the sauce, 2 to 4 minutes. Off heat, taste and season with salt and pepper.

Divide the rice among 4 serving bowls. Spoon on the zucchini mixture, then top with the kimchi. Sprinkle with the scallions and drizzle with the reserved gochujang mixture.

Optional garnish: Red pepper flakes OR toasted sesame seeds

Japanese-Style Chicken and Egg Rice Bowls

Start to finish: 25 minutes
Servings: 4

Oyako donburi—chicken and egg cooked with onion and seasonings to make an omelet-like mixture served on top of steaming-hot rice—is Japanese comfort food. For this simplified version, **we use low-sodium chicken broth in place of the customary dashi, a stock made of seaweed and shaved dried bonito.** If you're able to find instant dashi in the supermarket, give it a try. It requires only water to brew or dissolve the granules and lends the omelet a smoky, umami-rich flavor that's uniquely Japanese. Short-grain rice is the best type to use for these rice bowls.

4 large eggs

1 pound boneless, skinless chicken thighs, trimmed, halved crosswise and thinly sliced on the diagonal

1 small yellow OR red onion, halved and thinly sliced

½ cup low-sodium chicken broth OR dashi (see headnote)

¼ cup soy sauce, plus more to serve

3 tablespoons mirin

About 6 cups freshly cooked rice, preferably short grain

Ground black OR white pepper

In a medium bowl, whisk the eggs; set aside. In a 12-inch skillet, combine the chicken, onion, broth, soy sauce and mirin. Bring to a vigorous simmer over medium-high and cook, stirring occasionally, until the onion is softened, the chicken is cooked through and about ¼ inch of liquid remains in the pan, 8 to 11 minutes.

Pour the egg in an even layer over the chicken mixture. Cover, reduce to medium and cook without stirring until the eggs are just barely set, 2 to 4 minutes. Remove the pan from the heat.

Divide the rice among 4 serving bowls, then spoon on the chicken-egg mixture, dividing it evenly. Sprinkle with pepper and serve with soy sauce on the side.

Optional garnish: Torn watercress OR thinly sliced scallions OR shichimi togarashi OR a combination

Baharat-Spiced Beef and Butter-Toasted Pine Nut Rice Bowls

Start to finish: 25 minutes
Servings: 4

These rice bowls are inspired by hashweh, a classic Lebanese meat and rice dish that's garnished with toasted nuts. **Tomato paste is a secret weapon here— cooking it until caramelized builds on its umami richness and adds great depth of flavor.** Dill does its part, too. We mince the stems and cook them into the meat mixture; the leaves, chopped and sprinkled onto the bowls, add freshness. Baharat is a Middle Eastern spice blend that's savory yet sweet, with lots of warm, earthy notes. If not available, a mixture of

cumin and cinnamon is a fine substitute. Ground lamb is excellent in place of the beef.

4 tablespoons salted butter, cut into 4 pieces

¼ cup pine nuts OR sliced almonds

1 pound 85 or 90 percent lean ground beef OR ground lamb OR a combination

2½ teaspoons baharat OR 2 teaspoons ground cumin plus ¼ teaspoon ground cinnamon

Kosher salt and ground black pepper

3 tablespoons tomato paste

1 tablespoon minced fresh dill stems, plus ½ cup roughly chopped leaves, divided

About 6 cups freshly cooked rice

In a 12-inch skillet over medium, melt the butter. Add the pine nuts and cook, stirring, until lightly browned, 1½ to 2 minutes. Using a slotted spoon, transfer the nuts to a small bowl; set aside.

Return the skillet to medium-high and add the beef, baharat, ¾ teaspoon salt and ½ teaspoon pepper. Cook, breaking the meat into small bits, until little pink remains, 3 to 4 minutes. Add the tomato paste and dill stems; cook, stirring, until the mixture is browned and begins to stick to the pan, about 3 minutes. Stir in ¾ cup water and cook, stirring and scraping up any browned bits, until the mixture is saucy, about 2 minutes. Off heat, taste and season with salt and pepper.

Divide the rice among 4 serving bowls. Spoon on the beef mixture, then sprinkle with the pine nuts and chopped dill.

Optional garnish: Plain whole-milk yogurt OR ground sumac OR lemon wedges OR a combination

Farro and Brussels Sprouts Salad with Manchego

Start to finish: 40 minutes (20 minutes active)
Servings: 4

A type of ancient wheat, farro boasts a wonderfully tender-chewy texture that pairs well with tangy-sweet raisins and earthy Brussels sprouts. **First, we toast the farro in a little olive oil to bring out its nutty taste. While the grains simmer in water, we soak raisins and chopped onion in vinegar to soften and plump the fruit and mellow the onion. Then the mixture is combined with the warm farro so the grains soak up the flavors as they cool.** Shaved manchego (or Parmesan) cheese adds a contrasting salty note. Serve room-temperature alongside roast chicken or as a meatless main topped with a soft poached egg.

½ cup pearled farro

3 tablespoons extra-virgin olive oil, divided, plus more to serve

Kosher salt and ground black pepper

¼ cup white balsamic vinegar
OR white wine vinegar

⅓ cup raisins OR dried cherries

½ small red onion, finely chopped

12 ounces Brussels sprouts, trimmed

1 ounce manchego OR Parmesan cheese, shaved with a vegetable peeler

In a large saucepan over medium, combine the farro and 1 tablespoon oil. Toast, stirring occasionally, until lightly browned and fragrant, about 3 minutes. Stir in 2 cups water and ½ teaspoon salt. Bring to a simmer over medium-high, then reduce to medium and simmer, uncovered and stirring occasionally, until tender with a little chew, 25 to 30 minutes.

Meanwhile, in a large bowl, stir together the vinegar, raisins, onion and ¼ teaspoon each salt and pepper; set aside. When the farro is done, drain in a colander if needed. Add the still-warm farro to the vinegar mixture and toss. Let stand until cooled to room temperature, tossing once or twice.

Working in batches if needed, in a food processor with a slicing disk, slice the sprouts and add to the farro mixture. Add the remaining 2 tablespoons oil, ¼ teaspoon salt and ½ teaspoon pepper; toss to combine. Taste and season with salt and pepper. Serve topped with the cheese and drizzled with additional oil.

Optional garnish: Chopped toasted walnuts OR hazelnuts

Rice Salad with Asparagus and Dill

Start to finish: 45 minutes (15 minutes active)
Servings: 4

Light, bright and perfect for spring, this rice salad is chock-full of tender-crisp asparagus and fragrant dill. **The dressing includes sliced scallions, which we mellow by soaking in vinegar before whisking in the olive oil and mustard. Be sure to dress the salad while warm so the rice and asparagus absorb the flavors.** To quickly slice asparagus, trim off the woody ends, then retie the bunch with a rubber band and cut the spears all at once. **After removing the cooked rice from the stovetop, we scatter the asparagus on top and allow the residual heat to gently steam it.** Serve alongside roast lamb or chicken, or top with canned tuna or hard-cooked eggs for a simple supper.

1 cup basmati OR jasmine OR other
long-grain white rice, rinsed and drained

Kosher salt and ground black pepper

4 scallions, thinly sliced, white and green parts
reserved separately

1½ tablespoons white balsamic OR
red wine vinegar

1 pound thin asparagus, trimmed and sliced
about ¼ inch thick (see headnote)

2 tablespoons extra-virgin olive oil

1½ tablespoons Dijon mustard

1 cup lightly packed fresh dill OR mint
OR flat-leaf parsley, roughly chopped

In a large saucepan, combine the rice, 1 teaspoon salt and 1½ cups water. Bring to a simmer over medium-high, then cover, reduce to low and cook without stirring until the rice has absorbed the liquid, 12 to 15 minutes. Meanwhile, in a large bowl, stir together the scallion whites, vinegar, a pinch of salt and ¼ teaspoon pepper; set aside.

When the rice is done, remove the pan from the heat. Quickly uncover, scatter the asparagus in an even layer on top (do not stir) and re-cover. Let stand for 10 minutes. Using a fork, fluff the rice mixture, stirring in the asparagus.

Meanwhile, whisk the oil and mustard into the scallion-vinegar mixture. Add the rice mixture to the dressing and toss. Let stand until cooled to room temperature, stirring once or twice, about 15 minutes. Stir in the scallion greens and dill, then taste and season with salt and pepper.

Optional garnish: Toasted sliced almonds

Rosemary-Tomato Rice and Beans

Start to finish: 30 minutes
Servings: 4

We reduce tomato juices to boost their flavor in this **Italian version of rice and beans,** which uses Arborio rice for a satisfyingly creamy consistency. The only knife work required is slicing a couple of garlic cloves, so the prep goes quickly and dinner can be on the table in about half an hour. Roman beans also are known as borlotti or cranberry beans; if they're not available, pinto beans, which have a similar texture, are a fine substitute.

¾ cup Arborio rice

Kosher salt and ground black pepper

2 tablespoons extra-virgin olive oil

2 medium garlic cloves, thinly sliced

½ teaspoon red pepper flakes

1 large rosemary sprig

28-ounce can whole peeled tomatoes, drained, juices reserved, tomatoes crushed by hand and reserved separately

15½-ounce can Roman beans OR pinto beans, rinsed and drained

In a medium saucepan, combine the rice, ½ teaspoon salt and 1¼ cups water. Bring to a boil over medium-high, stirring, then cover, reduce to low and cook, stirring occasionally, until the rice is creamy and al dente, 20 to 22 minutes.

Meanwhile, in a 12-inch skillet over medium, cook the oil, garlic, pepper flakes and rosemary sprig, stirring, until the garlic begins to brown, about 2 minutes. Add the tomato juices and bring to a simmer, then cook, stirring often, until a spatula leaves a trail when drawn through the mixture, 6 to 8 minutes. Add the tomatoes and beans; cook, stirring occasionally, until heated through, about 5 minutes.

When the rice is done, stir in the tomato-bean mixture. Taste and season with salt and black pepper, then remove and discard the rosemary sprig.

Optional garnish: Finely grated Parmesan cheese

One Pan

Tex-Mex Migas with Chorizo

Start to finish: 20 minutes
Servings: 4

Tex-Mex migas is a breakfast and brunch staple of scrambled eggs mixed with tortilla chips, sautéed aromatics (such as onion and chilies) and, typically, cheese. **We fold chips into eggs at the end of cooking for addictive, crunchy-chewy texture. To keep the eggs tender and fluffy, we cook them over direct heat for just 1 minute, then let them finish with residual heat as we stir in the chips.** Spicy, tangy chorizo sausage makes a deluxe version of migas. Be sure to use fresh Mexican-style chorizo, not dry-cured Spanish chorizo. Migas loves garnishes. The recipe calls for diced or sliced avocado and pickled jalapeños, but you could offer salsa, Mexican crema (or sour cream), additional cheese or whatever suits you. Warm tortillas offered alongside can be used to make migas tacos, and refried beans also are a great accompaniment.

8 large eggs

2 ounces pepper jack cheese, shredded (½ cup)

Kosher salt and ground black pepper

8 ounces Mexican-style chorizo (see headnote), casings removed, chorizo crumbled

2 tablespoons neutral oil

3 tablespoons pickled jalapeños, roughly chopped, plus more to serve

1 ripe tomato, cored and chopped

1 cup good-quality tortilla chips (about 1 ounce), lightly crushed

In a large bowl, whisk the eggs until foamy. Whisk in the cheese and ¼ teaspoon pepper; set aside. In a 12-inch nonstick skillet, combine the chorizo and oil. Cook over medium-high, stirring often and breaking up the chorizo, until sizzling, 1 to 2 minutes. Add the pickled jalapeños and tomato; cook, stirring occasionally, until the moisture from the tomato has evaporated and the chorizo is browned, 3 to 5 minutes.

Pour the egg mixture into the center of the skillet and cook, using a silicone spatula to stir continuously, pushing the egg mixture toward the middle as the edges begin to set, until the eggs are mostly set but still shiny, about 1 minute. Remove the pan from the heat, add the tortilla chips and fold just until combined. Taste and season with salt and pepper. Serve garnished with additional pickled jalapeños and avocado.

Optional garnish: Diced or sliced avocado **OR** chopped fresh cilantro **OR** both

Sea Scallops with Browned Butter, Capers and Lemon

Start to finish: 25 minutes
Servings: 4

Sea scallops get the piccata treatment in this quick supper. We pair sweet, briny scallops with nutty browned butter, salty capers and puckery lemon. **And we use the lemon juice to deglaze the pan after cooking the scallops to create a sauce that is both rich and bright.** When shopping, look for U15 dry sea scallops—the sizing indicates there are fewer than 15 scallops per pound. "Dry" indicates that the shellfish has not been treated with sodium tripolyphosphate (STPP), a preservative that forces water retention and that has a bleaching effect. In fact, bright white color is a tell-tale sign of the presence of STPP, as untreated scallops have a pale coral or ivory hue. And at the seafood counter, dry scallops should not be sitting in a pool of milky liquid. Serve with crusty bread and a leafy salad dressed with a bright vinaigrette.

1 to 1¼ pounds dry sea scallops (see headnote), side tendons removed and discarded, patted dry

Kosher salt and ground black pepper

2 tablespoons extra-virgin olive oil

4 tablespoons salted butter, cut into 4 pieces

¼ cup drained capers

2 scallions, thinly sliced on the diagonal, whites and greens reserved separately

1 teaspoon grated lemon zest, plus 1 tablespoon lemon juice, plus lemon wedges to serve

Place the scallops on a paper towel-lined plate. Season lightly on all sides with salt; set aside. In a 12-inch nonstick skillet over medium-high, heat the oil until barely smoking. Quickly pat the scallops dry once again and place in the pan, a flat side down, spacing them evenly apart. Cook without disturbing until golden brown on the bottoms and they release easily from the pan, 2 to 4 minutes. Flip each scallop, then add the butter, capers and scallion whites, swirling the pan to incorporate.

Cook, spooning some of the hot butter over the scallops, until the butter smells nutty and the scallops are opaque throughout, 2 to 3 minutes. Remove the pan from the heat and, using tongs, transfer the scallops to a serving plate. To the skillet, add the lemon zest and juice; stir to combine. Taste and season with salt and pepper, then pour the sauce over the scallops. Sprinkle with the scallion greens.

Parmesan-Garlic Crisped Bread with Spicy Greens

Start to finish: 35 minutes
Servings: 4

Pancotto, also known as pane cotto, translates as "cooked bread," a reference to the stale bread that is torn into pieces and cooked similar to pappa al pomodoro, the much-loved Tuscan tomato-bread soup. In Italy, we learned there is no one way to make pancotto. In fact, the version we learned near Naples was hardly a soup, and more like a soft, forkable, egg-free stuffing. For our adaptation, we start with fresh bread and toast the pieces in garlic-infused oil for chewy crispness. **Following the lead of Italian cooks, we sauté lightly crushed garlic cloves in olive oil then discard them, which yields subtle but not overwhelming garlic flavor.** We pair the bread with escarole, a type of chicory that boasts a pleasant bitterness and a leafiness that becomes silky with heat. We cooked the bread and greens separately, brought the two together at the end and finished with another drizzle of olive oil.

¾ cup extra-virgin olive oil, divided, plus more to serve

6 medium garlic cloves, smashed and peeled

8 ounces crusty white bread, cut into ½-inch cubes (about 6 cups)

1 ounce Parmesan cheese, finely grated (½ cup), plus more to serve

½ cup low-sodium chicken broth or vegetable broth

1 teaspoon red pepper flakes

3 large heads escarole (2½ to 3 pounds total), bruised outer leaves discarded, torn into rough 1-inch pieces (about 16 cups)

Kosher salt and ground black pepper

In a large Dutch oven over medium-low, combine ½ cup oil and the garlic. Cook, stirring often, until the garlic is lightly browned, about 2 minutes. Using a slotted spoon, remove and discard the garlic. Add the bread to the pot and toss to coat with the oil. Cook over medium, stirring, until the bread is well browned and crisp, 5 to 7 minutes. Remove from the heat and transfer the bread to a large bowl; reserve the pot. Add the Parmesan and toss to combine; set aside.

In the same pot over medium-high, bring the broth and pepper flakes to a simmer. Add the escarole a couple handfuls at a time, stirring to wilt the leaves before adding more. After all the escarole has been added, cook, uncovered and stirring often, until the escarole is tender and most of the liquid has evaporated, about 10 minutes.

Off heat, drizzle in the remaining ¼ cup oil, then return the toasted bread to the pot and stir to combine. Taste and season with salt and black pepper. Serve sprinkled with additional cheese.

Basque-Style Leek and Potato Soup

Start to finish: 1¼ hours
Servings: 4

For our version of porrusalda, a rustic leek and potato soup from Spain's Basque Country, **we sear the cut side of a garlic head to create caramelization that adds complexity; the flavor boost means we can use just water for our cooking liquid.** Carrots are classic in porrusalda; parsnips are not, but we like their nutty notes and earthiness. Use whichever you prefer, or even a mix. Leeks' many layers trap dirt and sand, so be sure to thoroughly wash the sliced leeks, then drain them well in a colander so excess water doesn't cause steaming, which will delay browning. Serve drizzled with olive oil, and with warm, crusty bread.

3 tablespoons extra-virgin olive oil,
plus more to serve

1 head garlic, top third cut off
and discarded

4 medium leeks, white and light green
parts, halved lengthwise, thinly sliced,
rinsed and drained (4 cups)

4 bay leaves

Kosher salt and ground black pepper

1½ pounds Yukon Gold potatoes, unpeeled,
cut into 1- to 1½-inch chunks

3 medium carrots OR parsnips, OR a combination,
peeled and sliced into ¼-inch rounds

2 teaspoons lemon juice

In a large pot over medium-high, heat the oil until shimmering. Add the garlic head cut side down and cook undisturbed until well browned, 2 to 4 minutes. Transfer the garlic to a small plate, then add the leeks, bay and ½ teaspoon salt to the pot. Cook, stirring occasionally, until the leeks are lightly browned, about 6 minutes.

Add the potatoes, ½ teaspoon each salt and pepper, then continue to cook, stirring occasionally, until the potatoes begin to brown and stick to the pot, about 4 minutes. Add 6 cups water and bring to a boil. Stir in the carrots and garlic head, reduce to medium-low and cook, at a gentle simmer, uncovered and stirring occasionally. Cook until a skewer inserted into the head of garlic and potatoes meets no resistance, 35 to 45 minutes

Remove and discard the bay. Using tongs, remove the garlic head and squeeze the cloves into a small bowl. Mash the garlic to a smooth paste, then stir into the soup and cook, stirring occasionally, for about 5 minutes. Off heat, add the lemon juice, then taste and season with salt and pepper. Serve the soup drizzled with additional oil.

Cauliflower and Chickpea Tagine

Start to finish: 30 minutes
Servings: 4 to 6

A tagine is a shallow Moroccan earthenware pot with a conical lid. The term also refers to the stew cooked in the vessel. We use the more common Dutch oven to simmer a cauliflower and chickpea "tagine," and we add complex flavor in just one-stroke with ras el hanout, a Moroccan blend of warm and pungent spices. **Tomato paste cooked until it begins to brown gives us a quick and umami-rich base for our cooking liquid.** If ras el hanout isn't available, a simple mixture of ground cumin and cinnamon also delivers a delicious, richly aromatic dish. Serve with couscous or flatbread.

2 tablespoons extra-virgin olive oil,
plus more to serve

1 medium yellow onion, chopped

¼ cup tomato paste

2- to 2½-pound head cauliflower, trimmed
and cut into ½- to 1-inch florets

2 tablespoons ras el hanout OR
1 tablespoon ground cumin, plus
½ teaspoon ground cinnamon

Kosher salt and ground black pepper

15½-ounce can chickpeas, rinsed
and drained

2 tablespoons lemon juice

In a large Dutch oven over medium-high, heat the oil until shimmering. Add the onion and cook, stirring occasionally, until softened and beginning to brown, 5 to 7 minutes. Add the tomato paste and cook, stirring, until beginning to brown, about 1 minute. Pour in 2 cups water and scrape up the browned bits, then stir in the cauliflower, ras el hanout and ½ teaspoon each salt and pepper. Bring to a simmer, cover and cook, stirring occasionally, until the cauliflower is crisp-tender, 5 to 6 minutes.

Stir in the chickpeas, re-cover and cook until the cauliflower is fully tender, about another 5 minutes. Off-heat, stir in the lemon juice, then taste and season with salt and pepper. Serve drizzled with additional oil and sprinkled with mint.

Optional garnish: Torn fresh mint

Sautéed Corn with Miso, Butter and Scallions

Start to finish: 30 minutes
Servings: 4

To balance the sweetness of corn, we draw on the fermented, savory and lightly sweet flavors of miso to add depth. Plump, tender kernels cut from the cob are our first choice, but out of season an equal amount of frozen corn kernels that have been thawed and patted dry will work; they'll just take a few minutes longer to brown. The optional furikake garnish adds even more layers of savory-sweet flavor (furikake is a Japanese condiment often sprinkled onto rice). Alternatively, add a little heat plus notes of sesame and citrus by sprinkling on some shichimi togarashi, or Japanese seven-spice blend.

¼ cup sake

3 tablespoons white miso

2 tablespoons salted butter, cut into
1-tablespoon pieces

4 cups fresh corn kernels (from about 5 ears corn)

1 bunch scallions, white parts thinly sliced,
green parts cut into 1-inch lengths, reserved
separately

2 teaspoons finely grated fresh ginger

Ground white or black pepper

In a small bowl, whisk together the sake and miso until no lumps remain. Set aside. In a 12-inch nonstick skillet over medium, melt the butter. Add the corn and scallion whites, then cook, stirring often, until the corn begins to brown, about 5 minutes.

Add the ginger and cook, stirring, just until fragrant, about 30 seconds, then stir in the miso mixture and the scallion greens. Off heat, taste and season with pepper.

Optional garnish: Furikake **OR** shichimi togarashi

Garlicky White Bean Soup with Broccoli Rabe and Parmesan

Start to finish: 1 hour
Servings: 4 to 6

This quick soup stars hearty greens and creamy white beans. **Browned garlic and tomato paste, as well as an optional Parmesan rind, enhance store-bought broth, adding depth, umami and richness. Poaching a whole head of garlic in broth mellows its flavor;** the result is reminiscent of roasted garlic. We squeeze out the softened cloves and mash them with some beans to mix into the broth, adding body to the soup. Warm crusty bread is the perfect accompaniment.

3 tablespoons extra-virgin olive oil,
divided, plus more to serve

1 head garlic, top third cut off and discarded

2 tablespoons tomato paste

Two 15½-ounce cans cannellini
OR great northern beans, rinsed and drained

Kosher salt and ground black pepper

1 quart low-sodium chicken broth
OR vegetable broth

1-inch piece Parmesan rind (optional),
plus finely grated Parmesan cheese, to serve

1-pound bunch broccoli rabe, trimmed
and roughly chopped OR 1 large head
escarole, chopped

In a large pot over medium, heat 2 tablespoons oil until shimmering. Add the garlic head cut side down and cook until well browned, 2 to 3 minutes. Transfer to a small plate; set aside.

To the same pot over medium, add the tomato paste and cook, stirring, until it browns and slightly sticks, 2 to 3 minutes. Stir in the beans, 3 cups water and ½ teaspoon each salt and pepper, scraping up any browned bits. Return the garlic to the pot, then add the broth and Parmesan rind (if using). Bring to a simmer over medium-high, then reduce to medium, cover partially, and cook, stirring, until a skewer inserted into the largest garlic clove meets no resistance, 25 to 30 minutes.

Using tongs, remove the garlic head and squeeze the cloves onto a large plate; discard the skins. Using a slotted spoon, transfer about ½ cup beans to the plate with the garlic. Drizzle the garlic and beans with the remaining 1 tablespoon oil, then use a fork to mash them to a smooth paste.

Stir the garlic-bean mixture into the pot. Add the rabe and simmer, stirring, until tender, 5 to 6 minutes. Off heat, remove and discard the Parmesan rind (if used). Taste and season with salt and pepper. Serve sprinkled with grated Parmesan and drizzled with additional oil.

Optional garnish: Red pepper flakes

COOK PASTA IN THE SAUCE

Pasta already is fast and simple. But we've made it even faster and simpler. When we don't feel like hauling out two pots and boiling water, we simply cook our pasta directly in the sauce for one-pot ease.

And it's not just efficient. It's also more flavorful. Cooked directly in the sauce, pasta absorbs more flavor, so every bite is more satisfying.

We start the sauce by browning aromatics in a large pan, add seasonings and a bit of butter or oil. We then stir in any remaining ingredients, along with some water and the pasta.

This works for all manner of pasta shapes and just requires a little adjustment to the liquid added. For instance, we add more water for fresh tomatoes, less for canned tomatoes with juices.

RECIPES FROM TOP

| Capellini with Smoked Paprika and Olives | Orecchiette with Cherry Tomatoes and Mozzarella | Tomato Masala Pasta with Chicken |

Capellini with Smoked Paprika and Olives

Start to finish: 30 minutes
Servings: 4 to 6

This garlicky one-pot pasta takes inspiration from Catalan fideua, a paella-like dish made with short, thin noodles. Smoked paprika adds earthy heat, while sherry contributes sweet, fruity notes—both balanced by the briny olives. **We cook capellini directly in the tomato-based sauce, thickening it and imbuing the pasta with flavor while eliminating the need to boil water.** This is a delicious weeknight dinner as is, but also pairs wonderfully with grilled shrimp or pan-roasted white fish.

¼ cup extra-virgin olive oil, plus more to serve

3 medium garlic cloves, thinly sliced

1 tablespoon smoked paprika

½ cup dry sherry OR dry white wine

28-ounce can diced tomatoes

Kosher salt and ground black pepper

1 pound capellini

1 cup pitted green OR black olives
OR a combination, chopped

In a large pot over medium-high, heat the oil until shimmering. Add the garlic and paprika; cook, stirring, until fragrant, about 30 seconds. Stir in the sherry and cook until reduced by half, about 2 minutes.

Stir in the tomatoes with juices and 1 teaspoon salt; bring to a simmer, stirring occasionally. Add 4 cups water and the pasta; stir to combine. Bring to a boil, then reduce to medium and cook, uncovered and stirring occasionally, until the pasta is al dente. Off heat, stir in the olives. Taste and season with salt and pepper. Serve drizzled with additional oil.

Optional garnish: Roughly chopped fresh oregano OR finely grated manchego cheese OR both

Tomato Masala Pasta with Chicken

Start to finish: 40 minutes
Servings: 4 to 6

Both chicken tikka masala and butter chicken are relatively modern inventions, rising to popularity in the second half of the 20th century. Inspired by their warmly spiced, creamy-rich flavors, **this low-effort dish cooks pasta directly in a buttery, tomato-based sauce, thickening the mixture and infusing the noodles with bold flavor.**

1 tablespoon neutral oil

1 pound boneless, skinless chicken thighs, trimmed and cut into 1-inch pieces

Kosher salt and ground black pepper

2 tablespoons finely grated fresh ginger
OR 2 medium garlic cloves, minced OR both

1 tablespoon garam masala

4 tablespoons salted butter, cut into 1-tablespoon pieces, divided

28-ounce can diced fire-roasted tomatoes

1 pound farfalle

In a large pot over medium-high, heat the oil until shimmering. Add the chicken in an even layer and sprinkle with 1 teaspoon salt. Cook, without stirring, until well browned, 5 to 7 minutes. Add the ginger, garam masala and 2 tablespoons butter; cook, stirring, until fragrant, about 1 minute.

Stir in the tomatoes with their juices and 1 teaspoon salt, scraping up any browned bits. Bring to a simmer, stirring. Stir in 4 cups water and the pasta. Bring to a boil, then reduce to medium and cook, uncovered and stirring occasionally, until the pasta is al dente. Stir in the remaining 2 tablespoons butter, then taste and season with salt and pepper.

Optional garnish: Chopped fresh cilantro OR whole-milk Greek yogurt OR lime wedges OR red pepper flakes OR a combination

Orecchiette with Cherry Tomatoes and Mozzarella

Start to finish: 30 minutes
Servings: 4 to 6

This creamy, sweet-tart orecchiette dish takes inspiration from pasta alla Sorrentina, a southern Italian classic featuring fresh, quick-cooked tomatoes, mozzarella and aromatic basil. To make it, **we quickly infuse oil with garlic, then stir in whole cherry or grape tomatoes—no slicing or chopping necessary—and red pepper flakes. Orecchiette and a few cups of water are added to the mix, creating a silky-smooth sauce as they cook together.** Fresh mozzarella can become stringy and rubbery if over-mixed, so take care to stir just until it starts to melt.

¼ cup extra-virgin olive oil, plus
more to serve

2 medium garlic cloves, thinly sliced

2 pints cherry OR grape tomatoes

½ to 1 teaspoon red pepper flakes

Kosher salt and ground black pepper

1 pound orecchiette

8 ounces fresh mozzarella cheese
OR mozzarella di bufala OR burrata cheese,
cut into rough ½-inch cubes or torn into
small pieces

1 cup lightly packed fresh basil, torn

In a large pot over medium, heat the oil until shimmering. Add the garlic and cook, stirring, until fragrant, about 30 seconds. Add the tomatoes, pepper flakes and 1 teaspoon salt; stir to combine. Add 4 cups water and the pasta; stir to combine. Bring to a boil over medium-high, then reduce to medium and cook, uncovered and stirring occasionally, until the pasta is al dente. If needed, stir in additional water a few tablespoons at a time if the mixture looks dry.

Off heat, taste and season with salt and black pepper. Add half of the mozzarella, stirring just until beginning to melt. Serve topped with the remaining mozzarella and the basil and drizzled with additional oil.

Optional garnish: Finely grated Parmesan cheese OR flaky sea salt OR both

Carrot-Lime Soup with Cilantro

Start to finish: 30 minutes
Servings: 4

This creamy yet cream-free carrot soup is a riff on a recipe by Alice Waters. **We double down on some ingredients, using them at different times to add layers of flavor.** We start the soup with cilantro stems and lime zest, then finish it with a simple, relish-like garnish accented with cilantro leaves and lime juice along with fragrant coriander and spicy chilies. A drizzle of olive oil to serve adds fruity richness.

3 tablespoons extra-virgin olive oil, plus more to serve

1½ pounds carrots, peeled, halved lengthwise and cut into 1-inch pieces

2 tablespoons minced fresh cilantro stems, plus 1 cup lightly packed cilantro leaves, chopped, reserved separately

1 teaspoon grated lime zest, plus 2 teaspoons lime juice

1 or 2 Fresno OR jalapeño chilies, stemmed, seeded and minced

1 large shallot, minced

1 teaspoon ground coriander

Kosher salt and ground black pepper

In a large saucepan over medium-high, heat the oil until shimmering. Add the carrots, cilantro stems, lime zest, half of the chilies, half of the shallot, the coriander and 1 teaspoon salt. Cook, stirring, until the shallot is translucent, 2 to 4 minutes. Add 5 cups water and bring to a boil, then cook, uncovered and stirring occasionally, until the carrots are tender, 15 to 20 minutes. Meanwhile, in a small bowl, stir together the remaining chili, the remaining shallot, cilantro leaves and lime juice; season with salt and pepper, then set aside until ready to serve.

Using a blender, puree the soup in batches until smooth, then return to the pan. Thin to the desired consistency with water, then season with salt and pepper. Ladle into bowls, top with the cilantro mixture and drizzle with additional oil.

Optional garnish: Sour cream OR Mexican crema

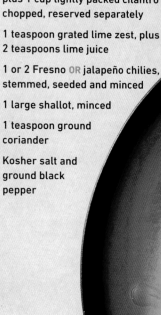

Chickpea, Chorizo and Spinach Soup

Start to finish: 45 minutes
Servings: 6

This hearty, simple meal in a bowl was inspired by Portuguese sopa de grão de bico, or chickpea soup. **We use a high-impact ingredient as a one-stroke flavor solution, leaning on Spanish dry-cured chorizo.** It infuses the broth with smoky, garlicky, paprika-forward intensity; don't use fresh Mexican chorizo in its place.

3 tablespoons extra-virgin olive oil

1 large yellow onion, halved and thinly sliced

4 ounces Spanish chorizo, thinly sliced

8 ounces Yukon Gold OR russet potatoes, unpeeled, cut into ½-inch cubes

Two 15½-ounce cans chickpeas, rinsed and drained

Kosher salt and ground black pepper

6 cups low-sodium chicken broth

5-ounce container baby spinach

In a large pot over medium, heat the oil until shimmering. Add the onion and cook, stirring occasionally, until golden brown, 8 to 10 minutes. Stir in the chorizo, potatoes, chickpeas and 1 teaspoon pepper, then add the broth. Bring to simmer over medium-high, then reduce to medium and cook, uncovered and stirring occasionally, until the potatoes are tender, 20 to 25 minutes.

Stir in the spinach and cook, stirring, until the leaves are fully wilted, about 1 minute. Off heat, taste and season with salt and pepper.

Pork Chops with Kimchi, Scallions and Browned Butter

Start to finish: 40 minutes
Servings: 4

Tart, spicy kimchi complements and contrasts sweet, juicy pork in this single-skillet meal. **We begin by searing the pork chops until caramelized, then use the remaining fat to build a bright, kimchi-based pan sauce,** balanced by rice vinegar and mirin (sake is a good, and slightly more savory, substitute). **Browned butter contributes rich, nutty notes, bringing everything together.** The chops finish cooking in the sauce, so don't worry if they're underdone after their initial sear. Serve with steamed rice, greens or both.

Four 1-inch-thick bone-in, center-cut pork loin chops (about 8 ounces each), patted dry

Kosher salt and ground black pepper

2 tablespoons neutral oil

2 cups chopped cabbage kimchi, plus 3 tablespoons kimchi juice

3 tablespoons salted butter, cut into 3 pieces

¼ cup mirin OR sake

1 tablespoon unseasoned rice vinegar

1 bunch scallions, thinly sliced on the diagonal

Season the pork chops on both sides with salt and pepper. In a 12-inch skillet over medium-high, heat the oil until barely smoking. Add the chops, reduce to medium and cook until browned on the bottoms, about 6 minutes. Flip and cook until lightly browned on the second sides (they will not be fully cooked), about 2 minutes. Transfer to a plate, then pour off and discard all but 1 tablespoon fat from the skillet.

Set the skillet over medium and heat the fat until shimmering. Add the kimchi and cook, stirring once or twice, until lightly browned in spots, about 4 minutes. Push the kimchi to the edges of the pan and add the butter to the center. Cook, without stirring, until the butter is browned and smells nutty, about 3 minutes. Stir the kimchi into the butter, then add the mirin and scrape up any browned bits. Add ½ cup water and bring to a simmer over medium-high. Nestle the chops, keeping the more deeply browned sides up, in the kimchi mixture, then add the accumulated juices. Cook, uncovered, until the thickest parts not touching bone reach 135°F, about 6 minutes.

Remove the pan from the heat. Transfer the chops to a platter or individual plates. Into the kimchi mixture, stir the kimchi juice, vinegar and about three-fourths of the scallions, then taste and season with salt and pepper. Spoon the mixture over the chops and sprinkle with the remaining scallions.

Optional garnish: Toasted sesame seeds OR toasted sesame oil

Curried Potato and Green Pea Frittata

Start to finish: 30 minutes
Servings: 4 to 6

This simple frittata, studded with warmly-spiced peas and potatoes, takes inspiration from Indian samosas. **We bloom curry powder and whole cumin seeds in oil, creating a flavor-rich base for cooking the vegetables. We start the cooking on the stovetop and finish in the oven to make sure the frittata is thick, flat and perfectly baked.** You will need a 10-inch oven-safe nonstick skillet. Serve with toasted bread, a leafy salad or both.

8 large eggs

¼ cup half-and-half

Kosher salt and ground black pepper

1 tablespoon extra-virgin olive oil

2 teaspoons curry powder

2 teaspoons cumin seeds

12 ounces Yukon Gold potatoes, peeled and cut into ½-inch cubes

1 cup frozen peas, thawed

Heat the oven to 400°F with a rack in the middle position. In a medium bowl, whisk together the eggs, half-and-half and ½ teaspoon salt; set aside.

In an oven-safe 10-inch nonstick skillet over medium, heat the oil, curry powder and cumin seeds, swirling, until sizzling and fragrant, about 1 minute. Stir in the potatoes, then distribute in an even layer. Cook, stirring occasionally, until the potatoes begin to brown, about 3 minutes. Add 1½ cups water and ½ teaspoon each salt and pepper; bring to a simmer and cook, uncovered and stirring occasionally, until the potatoes are tender and the water has evaporated, about 12 minutes.

Add the peas and cook, stirring, until heated through, about 1 minute. Add the egg mixture and cook, stirring constantly, just until large curds begin to form, about 1 minute. Transfer the skillet to the oven and bake until the center is set, 5 to 7 minutes. Remove from the oven (the handle will be hot), then run a silicone spatula around the edge and under the frittata to loosen. Slide it onto a platter and cut into wedges.

Optional garnish: Finely chopped fresh chives OR chopped fresh cilantro OR green chutney OR chili oil OR hot sauce OR a combination

Broccoli Rabe and Sausage

Start to finish: 30 minutes
Servings: 4 to 6

Simple and satisfying, the classic dish of broccoli e salsiccia—well-browned Italian sausage and tender broccoli rabe—was one of our favorite meals during a recent trip to Naples. The earthy, pleasantly bitter brassica pairs perfectly with spice-rich sausage. **The rendered fat from the sausage works well to sauté and season the sturdy greens.** Garlic and red pepper flakes, plus nutty Parmesan and a splash of tangy-bright lemon juice, round out the easy dish. Sweet or hot Italian sausage is great; use whichever you prefer. Serve with thick slices of warm, crusty bread.

1 tablespoon extra-virgin olive oil

1 pound sweet or hot Italian sausage, cut into 2½- to 3-inch sections

3 medium garlic cloves, chopped

½ to 1 teaspoon red pepper flakes

2 large bunches (2 pounds) broccoli rabe, trimmed and cut into 1-inch pieces

1 ounce Parmesan cheese, finely grated (½ cup), plus more to serve

2 tablespoons lemon juice, plus lemon wedges to serve

Kosher salt and ground black pepper

In a 12-inch nonstick skillet over medium, heat the oil until barely smoking. Add the sausage, cover and cook, turning occasionally, until well browned and the centers reach 160°F, 6 to 8 minutes. Transfer to a large plate; set aside.

To the skillet, add the garlic and pepper flakes, stirring. Add half the broccoli rabe and ½ cup water; using tongs, toss to combine. Cover and cook, tossing occasionally, until the rabe is wilted, 3 to 4 minutes. Scatter the remaining rabe on top, then cover and cook, tossing occasionally, until the stem pieces are tender, another 3 to 5 minutes.

Add the sausage, half of the Parmesan and the lemon juice; toss. Cook, uncovered and stirring, until the sausage is heated through, about 2 minutes. Taste and season with salt and black pepper. Serve sprinkled with additional Parmesan and lemon wedges on the side.

THE TARKA TECHNIQUE

Drizzling oil over a dish as a final flourish is an easy way to add richness and flavor. In India, cooks take it a step further, first infusing the oil with spices and aromatics, then pouring the mixture—seeds and all—onto cooked greens, raw vegetables and starchy legumes, adding taste and texture.

These seasoned oils, called tarka, often are made with ghee (clarified butter). At Milk Street, we've also developed variations using the more common refined coconut oil and neutral oils.

We use a small saucepan with high sides to keep the seeds from splattering the stove, and swirling, rather than stirring, is a better way to incorporate the seasonings.

We start with whole spices and once they sizzle and begin to darken at the edges, it's time to add any ground spices. They take just a few seconds to brown, then we add any fresh ingredients, such as ginger, chilies and fresh herbs. That's it. Remove from heat, swirling the pan to cool. Pour as desired.

RECIPES FROM TOP

| Coconut, Fennel Seed and Ginger Tarka | Spicy Garlic-Sesame Tarka | Caraway and Sage Tarka |

Caraway and Sage Tarka

Start to finish: 5 minutes
Makes about ¼ cup

Tarka is an Indian technique for building flavor into a dish by heating seasonings in fat. This one features ingredients that are more European than South Asian. It's the perfect counterpoint to mashed or roasted starchy vegetables, such as potatoes, sweet potatoes and winter squash. It also is delicious stirred into a bowl of beans or spooned over lentils. Use a mortar and pestle or the back of a small skillet to crush the caraway seeds.

3 tablespoons ghee OR salted butter,
cut into 3 pieces

1½ teaspoons caraway seeds,
lightly crushed

12 fresh sage leaves, roughly chopped

½ teaspoon red pepper flakes

Kosher salt

In a small saucepan or 8-inch skillet over medium-high, melt the ghee. Add the caraway seeds and cook, stirring, until beginning to sizzle, 45 to 90 seconds. Add the sage and stir until the leaves darken slightly and crisp, 20 to 30 seconds. Stir in the pepper flakes and ⅛ teaspoon salt, then remove from the heat. Use right away or transfer to a small bowl, cover and store at room temperature for a few hours; if the fat solidifies, rewarm before use.

Spicy Garlic-Sesame Tarka

Start to finish: 10 minutes
Makes about ⅓ cup

This tarka gets texture from sesame seeds, pungency from garlic and fresh chilies, and a rich red hue from Aleppo pepper (or sweet paprika plus red pepper flakes). It's delicious drizzled onto steamed vegetables, or roasted or grilled meats or seafood. It also is fantastic on avocado toast. **As soon as the garlic, chili, salt and pepper are stirred in, remove the pan from the burner. The residual heat will soften and mellow textures and flavors just enough, without dulling their vibrancy.**

3 tablespoons neutral oil

1 tablespoon sesame seeds

2 teaspoons Aleppo pepper
OR 1 teaspoon sweet paprika plus
½ teaspoon red pepper flakes

3 medium garlic cloves, minced

1 Fresno OR serrano chili, stemmed,
seeded and finely chopped

Kosher salt and ground black pepper

In a small saucepan or an 8-inch skillet, combine the oil and sesame seeds. Cook over medium, swirling the pan, heat until the seeds begin to sizzle and turn golden at the edges, 45 to 90 seconds. Add the Aleppo pepper and stir until the pepper just begins to darken, 20 to 30 seconds. Stir in the garlic, chili and ⅛ teaspoon salt and ¼ teaspoon black pepper, then remove from the heat. Use right away or transfer to a small bowl, cover and store at room temperature for a few hours.

Coconut, Fennel Seed and Ginger Tarka

Start to finish: 15 minutes
Makes about ¼ cup

This texture-rich tarka features the tropical flavor of flaked coconut plus the licorice notes of fennel seeds, with accents of fresh ginger and garlic. Curry powder goes in last to bloom for a few seconds, lending a golden hue and aromatic spiciness. **We cut the ginger into matchsticks so it has presence in the tarka, treating it almost like a vegetable as much as a seasoning.** To do so, thinly slice the peeled ginger, stack the slices, then cut them into slender matchsticks. Spooned onto dal, or Indian-style lentils, this tarka adds contrasting taste and texture. Or try it on creamy cauliflower, broccoli or winter squash soups.

3 tablespoons neutral oil

2 tablespoons unsweetened shredded coconut

1 teaspoon fennel seeds

2 tablespoons fresh ginger matchsticks (see headnote)

2 medium garlic cloves, minced

½ teaspoon curry powder

Kosher salt and ground black pepper

In a small saucepan or an 8-inch skillet over medium, heat the oil until shimmering. Add the coconut and fennel seeds; cook, stirring, until just beginning to sizzle, 30 to 45 seconds. Add the ginger and garlic; cook, stirring, until fragrant, about 30 seconds. Add the curry powder and ⅛ teaspoon salt and ¼ teaspoon black pepper; cook, stirring, until fragrant, about 30 seconds. Use right away or transfer to a small bowl, cover and store at room temperature for a few hours.

Paprika–Pinto Bean Soup with Collard Greens

Start to finish: 50 minutes
Servings: 6 to 8

This recipe was loosely inspired by Portuguese feijoada, a rustic stew of beans, cabbage, sausage and multiple cuts of pork. **Tomato paste is browned early in the cooking process to bring depth and umami to this hearty dish.** For the meat, we opted for chorizo, a flavor-packed sausage that boasts a robust, smoky taste. Be sure to use Spanish chorizo, a dry-cured sausage with a firm, sliceable texture, not fresh Mexican chorizo. Canned beans streamline prep and collards bring on the greens; after simmering low and slow for about half an hour, they become meltingly tender.

2 tablespoons extra-virgin olive oil, plus more to serve

2 medium yellow onions, finely chopped

Kosher salt and ground black pepper

4 ounces Spanish chorizo, quartered lengthwise and cut into ½-inch pieces

¼ cup tomato paste

2 tablespoons sweet paprika

Two 15½-ounce cans pinto beans OR pink beans, rinsed and drained

1 bunch collard greens OR lacinato kale, stemmed, leaves chopped

In a large Dutch oven over medium, heat 2 tablespoons oil until shimmering. Add the onions and ½ teaspoon salt; cook, stirring occasionally, until lightly browned, about 10 minutes. Add the chorizo and tomato paste, then cook, stirring often, until the paste browns and slightly sticks to the pan, about 2 minutes.

Add the paprika, beans, collard greens and 8 cups water. Bring to a boil over medium-high, then cover, reduce to low and simmer, stirring occasionally, until the greens are very tender, about 30 minutes. Off heat, taste and season with salt and pepper. Serve drizzled with additional oil.

Braised Cod with Tomatoes and Fennel Seed

Start to finish: 35 minutes
Servings: 4

Pesce all'acqua pazza, or "fish in crazy water," involves poaching mild-flavored white fish in a seasoned tomato broth, often enhanced by garlic and spices or herbs. For our weeknight-easy version, **fennel seeds and red pepper flakes are bloomed in olive oil to enhance flavors and aromas, then we add a hearty portion of dry white wine to reduce, flavoring the broth.** Serve with toasted or grilled crusty bread to soak up the spicy, sweet-tart sauce.

Four 6-ounce skinless cod fillets (about 1 inch thick)

Kosher salt and ground black pepper

2 tablespoons extra-virgin olive oil

3 medium garlic cloves, thinly sliced

½ to ¾ teaspoon red pepper flakes

1 teaspoon fennel seeds

½ cup dry white wine

1 pint cherry OR grape tomatoes, halved

Season the cod all over with ½ teaspoon each salt and black pepper; set aside. In a 12-inch skillet over medium, heat the oil until shimmering. Add the garlic and cook, stirring, until lightly browned, 1 to 2 minutes. Add the pepper flakes and fennel seeds; cook, stirring, until fragrant, about 30 seconds. Add the wine, bring to a simmer over medium-high and cook, uncovered, until the liquid has almost evaporated, 2 to 3 minutes. Stir in the tomatoes, 1 cup water and ½ teaspoon each salt and black pepper; cook, uncovered and stirring occasionally, until the tomatoes begin to break down, 8 to 10 minutes.

Reduce to medium-low, nestle the fish into the sauce and spoon some sauce onto the fillets. Cover and cook, spooning sauce onto the fish a couple more times, until the flesh flakes easily, 5 to 8 minutes. Using a slotted spatula, transfer the fillets to individual bowls or plates. Cook the sauce, stirring, until slightly thickened, about 1 minute. Off heat, taste and season with salt and black pepper. Spoon the sauce over the fish, then sprinkle with additional black pepper.

Optional garnish: Fresh basil, torn

Eggs in Purgatory

Start to finish: 25 minutes
Servings: 4

Eggs in purgatory—ova 'mpriatorio in the local dialect—is a Neapolitan classic. The whites of the eggs surrounded by the red of the tomato sauce are said to resemble religious depictions of souls in the fires of purgatory. An alternate explanation for the name of the dish is, simply, the spiciness of the sauce. **We use a covered 12-inch skillet to poach the eggs in a spicy tomato sauce, ensuring they cook gently and evenly, but quickly.** Our version has a medium, warming heat. For more bite, add ¼ to ½ teaspoon red pepper flakes along with the tomatoes. Or, if you prefer, tame the heat by seeding the chili before slicing it. Serve with crusty bread.

1 tablespoon extra-virgin olive oil, plus more to serve

2 medium garlic cloves, thinly sliced

1 Fresno OR jalapeño chili, stemmed and sliced into thin rings

28-ounce can whole peeled tomatoes, crushed by hand

1 sprig rosemary

Kosher salt and ground black pepper

6 large eggs

½ ounce Parmesan cheese, finely grated (¼ cup)

In a 12-inch skillet over medium-high, heat the oil until shimmering. Add the garlic and chili, then cook, stirring, until the garlic is lightly browned, 1 to 2 minutes. Add the tomatoes with juices, the rosemary, ½ teaspoon salt and ½ teaspoon pepper. Bring to a simmer and cook, stirring occasionally, until a spatula drawn through the sauce leaves a trail, 7 to 9 minutes. Remove and discard the rosemary, then taste and season with salt and pepper.

With the pan over medium-low, use the back of a spoon to form 6 evenly spaced wells in the sauce, each about 2 inches wide and deep enough that the bottom of the pan is visible. Crack 1 egg into each, then sprinkle with salt and pepper. Cover and cook until the egg whites are set but the yolks are still runny, 5 to 8 minutes, rotating the skillet about halfway through for even cooking. Off heat, sprinkle with Parmesan, then drizzle with additional oil.

Optional garnish: Roughly chopped fresh basil

Ginger-Curry Pork with Green Beans

Start to finish: 35 minutes
Servings: 4

Boneless pork shoulder has a rich, full flavor, but can be chewy if cooked quickly. **We slice tougher cuts thin for a more tender texture, which helps us get dinner on the table in about half an hour.** The dish starts as a stir-fry and ends as a braise, with green beans added for the second step, absorbing the spiced broth and providing a fresh, vegetal contrast. Curry powder provides a flavor base, but we add whole spices to amp up the intensity.

2 tablespoons neutral oil

1 pound boneless pork shoulder, trimmed, cut into 2-inch strips and sliced ¼ to ⅛ inch thick

2 teaspoons curry powder

Kosher salt and ground black pepper

1 medium yellow onion, finely chopped OR 8 medium garlic cloves, chopped OR both

1 tablespoon minced fresh ginger

3 cardamom pods, crushed OR 1 cinnamon stick OR 8 curry leaves OR a combination

8 ounces green beans, trimmed and halved on the diagonal

In a 12-inch skillet over medium-high, heat the oil until barely smoking. Add the pork, curry powder, 1½ teaspoons salt and ½ teaspoon pepper. Cook, stirring once or twice, until the pork is well browned, about 4 minutes. Add the onion, ginger and cardamom; cook, stirring, until the onion is browned, about 2 minutes. Add the beans and 1½ cups water; bring to a simmer, scraping up any browned bits.

Cover partially and cook, stirring occasionally, until the beans are tender and the sauce clings to the meat, about 15 minutes. Remove and discard the cardamom, then taste and season with salt and pepper.

Optional garnish: Chopped fresh cilantro OR toasted sesame seeds OR chopped chilies OR a combination

West African Peanut Chicken

Start to finish: 40 minutes
Servings: 4

This bright, bold dish inspired by Senegalese mafe (also spelled maafe or mafé) seasons boneless, skinless chicken thighs with the bold flavors of West African peanut stew. A single chili adds just enough spice and fruitiness. We use canned tomatoes and peanut butter for convenience and add fish sauce for instant, savory complexity. **The thighs stay put until they've browned long enough to release easily from the pan; the browning contributes flavor.** This is delicious with warm naan or pita bread.

2 pounds boneless, skinless chicken thighs, halved and patted dry

Kosher salt and ground black pepper

1 tablespoon neutral oil

14½-ounce can diced tomatoes

2 tablespoons fish sauce

1 habanero or Scotch bonnet chili
OR serrano chili, halved and seeded

¼ cup creamy peanut butter

Zest and juice of 1 lemon OR 1 lime

Season the chicken on all sides with salt and pepper. In a 12-inch skillet over medium-high, heat the oil until shimmering. Add the chicken and cook, undisturbed, until browned, 5 to 7 minutes. Add the tomatoes with juices, fish sauce and chili; scrape up any browned bits. Cover and cook until the chicken is tender.

Stir in the peanut butter and simmer until thickened. Taste and season with salt and pepper. Sprinkle with lemon zest and juice.

Optional garnish: Chopped fresh flat-leaf parsley

Harissa-Spiced Butternut Squash Soup with Toasted Pumpkin Seeds

Start to finish: 1 hour (40 minutes active)
Servings: 4 to 6

Harissa, a bright, tangy-hot chili paste from northern Africa, is the star of this creamy, comforting squash soup. Harissa varies in heat level, so use more or less depending on the brand and your spice tolerance. Paprika adds smoky sweetness, while cumin contributes warm, earthy notes. **We bloom the seasonings in oil to enhance their flavors and aromas.** Leeks' many layers can trap sand and dirt, so wash them thoroughly and drain them well before use. Toasted pumpkin seeds bring body, flavor and richness and provide texture as a crunchy garnish. Serve dolloped with plain yogurt for a touch of cool creaminess.

½ cup pumpkin seeds

2 tablespoons extra-virgin olive oil

1 tablespoon harissa paste

1 tablespoon sweet paprika

2 teaspoons cumin seeds OR ground cumin

2 medium leeks, white and light green parts thinly sliced, rinsed and drained

Kosher salt and ground black pepper

2-pound butternut squash, peeled, seeded and cut into ½-inch chunks

In a large pot over medium, toast the pumpkin seeds, stirring occasionally, until beginning to brown, 2 to 4 minutes. Transfer to a small bowl; set aside.

In the same pot over medium, heat the oil until shimmering. Add the harissa, paprika and cumin; cook, stirring, until fragrant, about 1 minute. Add the leeks and ¼ teaspoon salt; cook, stirring, until the leeks are softened, 3 to 4 minutes. Add the squash and another ½ teaspoon salt; cook, stirring occasionally, until the vegetables begin to brown, about 4 minutes.

Add half of the pumpkin seeds and 5 cups water; bring to a boil over medium-high, scraping up any browned bits. Cover and simmer, stirring occasionally, until a skewer inserted into the squash meets no resistance, 10 to 15 minutes. Remove from the heat and cool, uncovered, for 15 minutes.

Using a blender and working in 2 or 3 batches to avoid overfilling the jar, puree the squash mixture until smooth, 15 to 30 seconds. Return the soup to the pot. (Alternatively, puree the mixture directly in the pot with an immersion blender.) Heat over low, stirring, until warmed through. Taste and season with salt and pepper. Serve sprinkled with the remaining pumpkin seeds.

Optional garnish: Plain whole-milk yogurt OR lime wedges OR thinly sliced fresh mint OR a combination

Shiitake-Scallion
Chicken and Rice

Start to finish: 1 hour (20 minutes active)
Servings: 6 to 8

This one-pot dinner takes inspiration from a classic Cantonese comfort dish. **We use dried shiitake mushrooms, oyster sauce and soy sauce for a triple hit of umami savoriness** that pairs perfectly with chicken and fragrant jasmine rice. **Rehydrating the shiitakes creates a rich, earthy broth in which to cook the rice.** During steeping, some dirt or grit may settle in the bottom of the bowl; slowly pouring the liquid into the rice should help prevent it from escaping.

1 ounce (12 to 14 medium) dried
shiitake mushroom

2 cups boiling water

2 tablespoons neutral oil

1 bunch scallions, thinly sliced on the
diagonal, white and green parts
reserved separately

1 pound boneless, skinless chicken thighs,
trimmed and cut into ¾-inch pieces

Ground black pepper

¼ cup oyster sauce

2 tablespoons soy sauce

1½ cups jasmine rice, rinsed and drained

In a small heat-safe bowl, combine the shiitakes and boiling water. Soak until softened, 20 to 30 minutes. Remove the shiitakes, reserving the liquid. Remove and discard the stems; thinly slice the caps. Set aside.

In a large Dutch oven over medium-high, heat the oil until shimmering. Add the mushrooms and scallion whites; cook, stirring occasionally, until fragrant, about 1 minute. Add the chicken and ½ teaspoon pepper; cook, stirring occasionally, until the chicken begins to brown, 4 to 5 minutes.

Add the oyster and soy sauces; stir to coat, scraping up any browned bits. Stir in the rice. Slowly stir in the reserved mushroom liquid, leaving any grit in the bowl, and bring to a boil. Stir once or twice, then cover and reduce to low; cook until the water is absorbed and the rice is tender, about 15 minutes.

Remove the pan from the heat and let stand, covered, for 10 minutes. Uncover and fluff the rice with a fork. Serve sprinkled with the scallion greens.

Optional garnish: Chopped fresh cilantro OR chili oil OR both

Chicken Curry with Tomatoes and Yogurt

Start to finish: 40 minutes, plus marinating
Servings: 4 to 6

A yogurt-based marinade turns chunks of chicken perfectly succulent and tender while also bringing rich creaminess to the sauce. The marinade is enhanced by fresh ginger—or garlic, or, better yet, both—and curry powder. Cherry (or grape) tomatoes, cut in half so they readily break down into the sauce, add bright-tart notes and lend the sauce a vibrant red hue. Serve with basmati rice or naan to soak up the sauce.

½ cup plain whole-milk yogurt,
plus more to serve

2 tablespoons curry powder, divided

1 tablespoon finely grated fresh ginger
OR 3 medium cloves garlic, finely grated
OR both

Kosher salt and ground black pepper

2 pounds boneless, skinless chicken thighs,
trimmed and cut into 1-inch pieces

3 tablespoons neutral oil

1 medium yellow onion, chopped

1 pint cherry OR grape tomatoes, halved

In a large bowl, whisk together the yogurt, 1 tablespoon curry powder, the ginger, ¼ teaspoon salt and ½ teaspoon pepper. Add the chicken and toss. Let stand at room temperature for about 30 minutes.

In a 12-inch skillet over medium, heat the oil until shimmering. Add the onion and ¼ teaspoon salt; cook, stirring occasionally, until beginning to brown, 6 to 8 minutes. Add the remaining 1 tablespoon curry powder and cook, stirring, until fragrant, about 30 seconds. Stir in the chicken and any marinade in the bowl, then distribute in an even layer. Cook, uncovered and stirring occasionally, until the chicken is no longer pink and has released some juices, about 10 minutes.

Stir in the tomatoes and cook, uncovered and stirring occasionally, until the tomatoes break down and the sauce has reduced slightly and coats the chicken, 10 to 12 minutes; reduce the heat as needed as the mixture thickens. Off heat, taste and season with salt and pepper. Serve dolloped with additional yogurt.

Optional garnish: Chopped fresh cilantro OR lemon wedges OR both

Gingery Braised Greens with Berbere

Start to finish: 50 minutes
Servings: 4 to 6

These braised greens take inspiration from gomen wat, an Ethiopian stew of collard greens with alliums, ginger, fresh chilies and spices. **We put ginger on repeat, using a good measure in the braise and adding more at the end for a fresh infusion of bright, peppery-sweet flavor.** We start by browning a generous amount of onions, then along with the ginger, add berbere, an Ethiopian seasoning blend that combines chili heat with aromatics and warm spices. (If berbere is not available, equal parts ground coriander and smoked paprika work nicely.) Serve with rice.

3 tablespoons neutral oil

2 medium red onions, chopped

Kosher salt and ground black pepper

2 tablespoons minced fresh ginger, divided

2 tablespoons berbere OR 1 tablespoon ground coriander plus 1 tablespoon smoked paprika

2 bunches lacinato kale OR curly kale OR collard greens, stemmed, leaves torn into rough 2-inch pieces

1 quart low-sodium chicken broth OR vegetable broth

1 or 2 Fresno OR serrano chilies, stemmed, seeded and thinly sliced

In a large pot over medium, heat the oil until shimmering. Add the onions and ½ teaspoon salt; cook, stirring occasionally, until lightly browned, about 10 minutes.

Add 1½ tablespoons of the ginger and cook, stirring, until fragrant, about 1 minute. Add the berbere and ¼ cup water; cook, stirring, until the water has evaporated, about 1 minute. Add the kale a large handful at a time, stirring to slightly wilt after each addition. Stir in the broth, ¼ teaspoon salt and ½ teaspoon pepper.

Cover and cook over medium-low, stirring occasionally, until the mixture is saucy and the greens are fully tender, 20 to 30 minutes. Off heat, stir in the chili(es) and the remaining ½ tablespoon ginger. Taste and season with salt and pepper.

Optional garnish: Sliced scallions

Gochujang and Soy-Simmered Tofu

Start to finish: 45 minutes
Servings: 4

This vibrant spicy-sweet braise takes inspiration from the Korean soy-simmered tofu dish dubu jorim. Instead of using gochugaru (Korean hot pepper flakes), as is traditional, we call on gochujang, which adds ample umami as well as complexity and depth. **Pressing tofu removes excess moisture, making its texture in the finished dish firmer and meatier.** Serve over steamed white rice with a spoonful of the braising liquid and a crisp vegetable, such as stir-fried bok choy.

14-ounce container firm OR extra-firm tofu, drained and cut crosswise into ½-inch slices

3 tablespoons soy sauce

2 tablespoons gochujang

2 teaspoons white sugar

1 tablespoon neutral oil

2 teaspoons finely grated fresh ginger OR 2 medium garlic cloves, minced OR both

1 bunch scallions, whites thinly sliced, greens cut into 1-inch pieces, reserved separately

Cut the tofu in half lengthwise, then cut each half crosswise into ½-inch-thick slices. Stack 2 or 3 pieces, then cut into quarters diagonally, creating triangles. Line a rimmed baking sheet with a double layer of paper towels. Arrange the tofu in a single layer and cover with paper towels. Top with another baking sheet, then place cans or jars on top to weigh it down. Let stand 15 minutes. Meanwhile, in a small bowl, whisk together the soy sauce, gochujang, sugar and ½ cup water; set aside.

In a 12-inch nonstick skillet over medium-high, heat the oil until barely smoking. Remove the tofu from the baking sheet and add the slices to the skillet in a single layer; cook, without moving, until browned, 2 to 3 minutes. Using a spatula, carefully flip the tofu and cook until well browned on the second sides, about 2 minutes.

Gently push the tofu to one side of the skillet. Add the ginger and scallion whites to the clearing and cook, stirring, until fragrant, about 30 seconds. Pour the soy sauce mixture over the tofu, then stir everything together and evenly distribute the tofu. Bring to a simmer over medium-high and cook, occasionally shaking the pan, until the sauce thickens and clings to the tofu, about 3 minutes. Off heat, stir in the scallion greens.

Optional garnish: Toasted sesame seeds OR toasted sesame oil

Pasta

Charred Red Sauce Spaghetti

Start to finish: 30 minutes
Servings: 4 to 6

This is our method for making spaghetti all'assassina—or killer's spaghetti—a unique dish from Bari, Italy, in which the pasta is cooked from start to finish in a skillet. **A warm tomato broth is added to the noodles a little at a time, much like the classic technique for risotto. We cook pasta, undisturbed, in an even layer so it chars and crisps, adding texture and flavor.** The finished dish is dryish, but pleasantly so, and deliciously intense in flavor, with tasty, crunchy-chewy bits akin to edges of a baked lasagna. A few things of note: Basic brands of spaghetti, such as Barilla, work best for this, not high-end pastas with a rough, floury appearance, as they tend to release a large amount of starch during cooking. Second, for controlled charring, make sure to use a heavyweight nonstick 12-inch skillet. Lastly, the spaghetti strands must all be parallel when they go into the pan and they remain that way, more or less, throughout cooking.

14½-oz can tomato puree (1½ cups)

3 cups boiling water

1 tablespoon tomato paste

1 teaspoon white sugar

Kosher salt and ground black pepper

¼ cup extra-virgin olive oil

3 medium garlic cloves, finely chopped

¾ teaspoon red pepper flakes

12 ounces spaghetti (see headnote)

In a medium bowl or 1-quart liquid measuring cup, combine the tomato puree, the boiling water, tomato paste, sugar, 1 teaspoon salt and ½ teaspoon black pepper. Whisk until the tomato paste dissolves.

In a heavy-bottomed 12-inch nonstick skillet, combine the oil, garlic and pepper flakes. Set over medium-high and cook, stirring, until the garlic no longer smells raw, 1 to 2 minutes. Stir in ¾ cup of the tomato mixture. Place the spaghetti in the center of the pan with the noodles parallel to each other, distributing them in an even layer. Using a spatula, press down on the noodles. Cook without stirring and occasionally pressing down until the tomato mixture at the edges is reduced and deeply browned and the pasta is sizzling, about 5 minutes.

Slide a spatula under half of the spaghetti and flip the noodles, then do the same with the second half; the bottom of the noodles should be spottily charred. Once again, distribute the pasta as best you can in an even layer. Ladle on 1 cup of the tomato mixture, pouring it over and around the pasta. Cook without stirring but pressing down, until the liquid is reduced and once again browned at the edges of the pan and the pasta is sizzling, 3 to 4 minutes.

Flip the pasta in the same way and ladle on another 1 cup tomato mixture. Cook in this way until the pasta is al dente but crusty and spottily charred; this will require another 2 or 3 additions of tomato broth; you may not use all the broth. Finish with a flip of the pasta (not with an addition of broth). Off heat, taste and season with salt and black pepper.

Optional garnish: Finely grated pecorino Romano OR Parmesan cheese

Browned Butter and Lemon Pasta with Chicken

Start to finish: 35 minutes
Servings: 4 to 6

We cook butter until the milk solids caramelize to add nutty fragrance and flavor to this pasta dish. The richness of the browned butter is balanced with a generous measure of aromatic lemon zest and tart, tangy lemon juice. Either boneless chicken breasts or thighs work, and for allium savoriness, scallions, garlic or shallot all do well, so use whatever you prefer.

1 pound spaghetti OR capellini OR rigatoni OR penne

Kosher salt and ground black pepper

2 tablespoons extra-virgin olive oil

1½ pounds boneless, skinless chicken thighs OR breasts, trimmed and cut into ¾- to 1-inch chunks

4 tablespoons salted butter, cut into 4 pieces

1 bunch scallions, thinly sliced, whites and greens separated OR 2 medium garlic cloves, thinly sliced OR 1 medium shallot, halved and thinly sliced

1 tablespoon grated lemon zest, plus 3 tablespoons lemon juice

½ cup lightly packed fresh flat-leaf parsley

In a large pot, bring 4 quarts water to a boil. Add the pasta and 1 tablespoon salt, then cook, stirring occasionally, until just shy of al dente. Reserve 1 cup of the pasta cooking water, then drain and return to the pot; set aside.

In a 12-inch skillet over medium-high, heat the oil until shimmering. Add the chicken, ½ teaspoon salt and ¼ teaspoon pepper; cook, stirring occasionally, until the chicken is golden brown all over, 7 to 9 minutes. Reduce to medium and add the butter and scallion whites. Cook, stirring only once or twice, until the butter smells nutty and the chicken is well browned, about 4 minutes. Add the lemon zest and reserved pasta water, scraping up any browned bits.

Scrape the chicken mixture onto the pasta in the pot. Cook over medium, stirring and tossing, until the pasta is al dente, 2 to 3 minutes. Off heat, stir in the lemon juice and parsley. Taste and season with salt. Serve sprinkled with pepper.

Optional garnish: Red pepper flakes OR finely grated pecorino Romano cheese OR both

Farfalle with Spinach and Lemon Pesto

Start to finish: 25 minutes
Servings: 4 to 6

This speedy pasta was inspired by the spaghetti al pesto di limone that Giovanna Aceto made for us on her family's farm in Amalfi, Italy. Instead of lemon juice, which is sharp and acidic, we use lemon zest, where the essential oils reside. **We use lemon zest in two ways, half in the cooking water and half in the pesto. The result is well-rounded lemony flavor without a hint of harshness.** For textural contrast, we sprinkle on toasted almonds before serving.

4 lemons

1 cup slivered almonds

1 pound farfalle OR penne OR spaghetti OR linguine

Kosher salt and ground black pepper

1 ounce Parmesan cheese, finely grated (½ cup), plus more to serve

⅓ cup extra-virgin olive oil, plus more to serve

5-ounce container baby spinach

Chopped fresh chives OR basil, to serve

Using a vegetable peeler (preferably a Y-style peeler), remove the zest from the lemons in long strips; try to remove only the colored portion of the peel, not the white pith just underneath. You should have about ⅔ cup zest strips.

In a large pot over medium-low, toast the almonds, stirring, until golden brown, about 5 minutes. Transfer to a small plate. In the same pot, bring 3 quarts water to a boil. Stir in the pasta and 2 teaspoons salt, then cook, stirring occasionally, until just shy of al dente. Stir in half of the zest strips and cook until the pasta is al dente. Remove the pot from heat. Using tongs, transfer the zest strips to a food processor. Reserve 1 cup of the cooking water, then drain the pasta and return it to the pot.

To the food processor, add the remaining zest strips, ¾ cup of the almonds, the Parmesan and ¼ teaspoon each salt and pepper. Process until the mixture resembles coarse sand, 10 to 20 seconds. Add the oil and process until incorporated (the mixture will not be smooth), about 10 seconds. Add the pesto to the pasta, along with the spinach and reserved pasta water; toss to combine. Taste and season with salt and pepper. Serve drizzled with additional oil and sprinkled with chives and the remaining almonds; serve additional Parmesan on the side.

Fettuccine with Miso and Kale Pesto

Start to finish: 30 minutes
Servings: 4 to 6

Bold, salty-sweet white miso forms the backbone of this vegan earthy kale and basil-based pesto. For richness and body, we add walnuts, echoing miso's umami punch (pine nuts are a good stand-in for those who aren't fans of walnuts). **A few splashes of starchy pasta water both thicken and smooth the vibrant pesto, which we pair with long, al dente noodles, providing plenty of surface area for the sauce to cling to.**

1 pound fettuccine OR spaghetti

Kosher salt and ground black pepper

5-ounce container baby kale
OR 1 small bunch lacinato kale, stemmed
and roughly chopped

½ cup lightly packed fresh basil

½ cup walnuts OR pine nuts, plus
¼ cup chopped walnuts OR pine nuts

¼ cup white miso

2 medium garlic cloves, smashed
and peeled

½ cup neutral oil

In a large pot, bring 4 quarts water to a boil. Add the pasta and 1 tablespoon salt, then cook, stirring occasionally, until al dente. Reserve ½ cup of the cooking water, then drain and return the pasta to the pot.

In a food processor, combine the kale, basil, ½ cup walnuts, miso, garlic and ½ teaspoon pepper. Process until the mixture resembles coarse sand, 10 to 20 seconds. With the machine running, stream in the oil, followed by the reserved cooking water; process, scraping the bowl as needed, until almost completely smooth, about another 20 seconds.

Add the pesto to the pasta in the pot and stir. Taste and season with salt and pepper. Serve sprinkled with the chopped walnuts.

Optional garnish: Lemon wedges

Lemon-Garlic Shrimp with Spaghetti

Start to finish: 40 minutes
Servings: 4 to 6

Spaghetti aglio e olio is a three-ingredient Italian classic starring extra-virgin olive oil (olio), garlic (aglio) and, of course, spaghetti. This version adds shrimp, incorporating pops of briny-sweet flavor. **Toasting thinly sliced garlic in olive oil infuses the oil, later used for cooking the shrimp, and creates a crispy garnish. We boil the spaghetti until just shy of al dente in minimal water, yielding an extra-starchy liquid ideal for making a silky sauce; the pasta finishes cooking directly in the mix so the noodles absorb the seasonings.** To finish, lemon zest, juice and parsley are tossed in, imbuing each bite with fresh, bright notes.

Kosher salt and ground black pepper

1 pound spaghetti OR linguine

4 tablespoons extra-virgin olive oil, divided

5 medium garlic cloves, thinly sliced

1 pound extra-large shrimp (21/25 per pound), peeled (tails removed), deveined and patted dry

½ teaspoon red pepper flakes

2 teaspoons grated lemon zest, plus 2 tablespoons lemon juice

½ cup lightly packed fresh flat-leaf parsley OR basil OR chives, chopped

In a large pot, bring 3 quarts water to a boil. Add 2 teaspoons salt and the pasta; cook, stirring occasionally, until just shy of al dente. Reserve 1 cup of the cooking water, then drain and return the pasta to the pot; set aside.

Meanwhile, in a 12-inch skillet over medium, combine 2 tablespoons oil and the garlic; cook, stirring occasionally, until lightly browned, 1 to 2 minutes. Remove from the heat and, using a slotted spoon, transfer the garlic to a small bowl. Return the skillet to medium and heat the oil until shimmering. Add the shrimp in an even layer and cook without stirring until browned on the bottom, 2 to 3 minutes.

Scrape the shrimp and oil onto the pasta in the pot and add the remaining 2 tablespoons oil, half the garlic, the pepper flakes, 1 teaspoon black pepper and ½ cup of the reserved cooking water. Cook over medium, tossing with tongs, until the pasta is al dente and the shrimp are cooked through, 3 to 4 minutes; add more reserved water as needed if the mixture looks dry.

Off heat, toss in the lemon zest and juice and the parsley. Taste and season with salt and black pepper. Serve sprinkled with the remaining garlic.

BROWN YOUR TOMATO PASTE

Out of season, transforming tomatoes into a bright, flavorful pasta sauce can be a gamble. Too often, supermarket tomatoes look red and ripe, but taste dull and anemic. For surefire flavor, we bet on a sure thing, tomato paste.

Tomato paste already is brimming with naturally sweet, umami-rich flavor, but we take things up a notch by deeply browning the paste, caramelizing its sugars to make it richer and more savory. This becomes the base of our sauce.

We often start by toasting sliced garlic in olive oil, maybe with some herbs or spices, then add the paste and, finally, add some slightly undercooked pasta along with some of the cooking water to create a loose-but-clingy sauce that coats the noodles evenly as they finish cooking.

RECIPES FROM TOP

| Tomato Sauce with Vermouth and Fennel Seeds | Tomato Sauce with Browned Butter and Cumin | Tomato Sauce with Saffron, Garlic and Orange |

Tomato Sauce with Vermouth and Fennel Seeds

Start to finish: 20 minutes
Makes 1¼ cups

For this multi-purpose sauce, **we pair a 6-ounce can of tomato paste with fennel seeds, ground coriander and red pepper flakes, all bloomed in olive oil.** Browning the tomato paste and adding umami-packed anchovies enriches the sauce even further, while vermouth brings crisp, subtly bitter notes. This recipe yields enough sauce to dress 1 pound of pasta, but also is delicious on gnocchi or spooned over chicken cutlets or grilled, seared or sautéed fish fillets. Chopped fresh flat-leaf parsley or basil is a nice herbal flourish to dishes dressed with this sauce.

3 tablespoons extra-virgin olive oil

2 teaspoons fennel seeds

1 teaspoon ground coriander

½ teaspoon red pepper flakes

6-ounce can tomato paste (⅔ cup)

Kosher salt and ground black pepper

2 oil-packed anchovy fillets

¼ cup dry vermouth OR dry white wine

In a 12-inch skillet over medium-high, combine the oil, fennel seeds, coriander and pepper flakes. Cook, stirring constantly, until the seeds are sizzling and the mixture is fragrant, 1 to 2 minutes.

Add the tomato paste, 1 teaspoon salt and ½ teaspoon black pepper; cook, stirring often, until the paste browns and slightly sticks to the pan, 1 to 3 minutes. Add the anchovies and cook, breaking them into small bits, until fragrant, about 30 seconds. Add the vermouth and cook, stirring, until mostly dry, about 1 minute; add 1 cup water and scrape up any browned bits. Bring to a simmer, then reduce to medium-low and cook, stirring occasionally, until slightly thickened, about 2 minutes. Off heat, taste and season with salt and black pepper.

Tomato Sauce with Browned Butter and Cumin

Start to finish: 20 minutes
Makes 1¼ cups

Deeply savory and packed with umami, browned tomato paste makes an excellent base for this Turkish-inspired sauce, enhanced by butter and spices. Dried mint has a distinct menthol-like tang that balances the mixture's richness, but dried oregano works well, too. This recipe yields enough to coat 1 pound of pasta— also toss in a dollop of plain whole-milk yogurt for a play on Turkish dumplings called manti. The sauce also complements hearty grains, such as bulgur or freekeh, and is delicious over lamb chops or salmon. We recommend finishing dishes featuring this sauce with a sprinkle of chopped fresh flat-leaf parsley or mint.

4 tablespoons salted butter, cut into 4 pieces

1 teaspoon cumin seeds

6-ounce can tomato paste (⅔ cup)

Kosher salt and ground black pepper

1 teaspoon Aleppo pepper OR ½ teaspoon sweet paprika plus ¼ teaspoon red pepper flakes

2 medium garlic cloves, finely grated

1 teaspoon dried mint OR dried oregano

In a 12-inch skillet over medium, melt the butter. Add the cumin seeds and cook, stirring often, until the seeds are sizzling and the butter is golden brown with a nutty aroma, 1 to 2 minutes.

Add the tomato paste, 1 teaspoon salt and ½ teaspoon black pepper; cook, stirring often, until the paste browns and slightly sticks to the pan, 1 to 3 minutes. Add the Aleppo pepper, garlic and mint; cook, stirring, until fragrant, about 30 seconds. Add 1 cup water and bring to a simmer over medium-high, scraping up any browned bits. Reduce to medium-low and cook, stirring, until slightly thickened, about 2 minutes. Off heat, taste and season with salt and black pepper.

Tomato Sauce with Saffron, Garlic and Orange

Start to finish: 20 minutes
Makes 1¼ cups

To make this Provençal-inspired sauce, **we bloom saffron threads in water to draw out their flavor and aroma. The golden liquid then is stirred into a base of sautéed garlic and tomato paste that has been browned to develop depth of flavor.** Saffron adds inimitable notes of earth, flowers and minerals, but is quite pricey. The sauce still will be delicious made without, as it derives ample flavor from orange zest, pepper flakes and fresh thyme. If omitting the saffron, simply add ¾ cup water to the browned tomato paste along with the orange juice. This recipe yields enough sauce to dress 1 pound of pasta, however, it's also delicious over seafood; chopped fresh flat-leaf parsley or basil are ideal herbal garnishes.

½ teaspoon saffron threads, crushed (optional; see headnote)

1 cup boiling water

2 tablespoons extra-virgin olive oil

2 medium garlic cloves, minced

6-ounce can tomato paste (⅔ cup)

½ teaspoon red pepper flakes

Kosher salt and ground black pepper

2 teaspoons grated orange zest, plus ¼ cup orange juice

2 teaspoons fresh thyme OR oregano OR tarragon, chopped

Stir the saffron into the boiling water; set aside. In a 12-inch skillet over medium, combine the oil and garlic; cook, stirring, until the garlic begins to brown, about 1 minute. Add the tomato paste, pepper flakes, 1 teaspoon salt and ½ teaspoon black pepper. Cook, stirring, until the paste browns and slightly sticks to the pan, 1 to 3 minutes.

Add the orange juice and saffron water; stir to combine, scraping up any browned bits. If desired, thin the sauce with water, adding 1 tablespoon at a time. Off heat, stir in the orange zest and thyme. Taste and season with salt and black pepper.

Pasta with Tomatoes,
Sweet Corn and Avocados

Start to finish: 40 minutes
Servings: 4 to 6

This colorful pasta salad is best made with in-season tomatoes and sweet, fresh corn. In non-summer months, however, frozen corn works well. **The kernels are dropped into the pasta during the final minutes of boiling and cooked only briefly so they retain some snappy texture.** We frequently salt then drain fresh tomatoes to remove excess moisture. But here **we salt tomatoes and retain their juices, using the liquid to coat and season the pasta.**

1 pint cherry or grape tomatoes, halved

1 tablespoon extra-virgin olive oil,
plus more to serve

Kosher salt and ground black pepper

8 ounces orecchiette OR campanelle
OR fusilli

3 cups fresh corn kernels (from about 4 ears corn)
OR frozen corn kernels

2 Fresno OR habanero chillies, stemmed,
seeded and minced

1 medium garlic clove, finely grated

2 ripe avocados, halved, pitted, peeled
and cut into ½-inch cubes

In a large bowl, toss together the tomatoes, oil and 1 teaspoon salt; let stand while you cook the pasta.

In large pot, bring 3 quarts water to a boil. Add the pasta and 2 teaspoons salt, then cook, stirring often, until just shy of al dente. Add the corn and cook until the pasta is al dente and the corn is tender-crisp, about 2 minutes. Drain in a colander and rinse under cold water, tossing, until cool to the touch. Drain again, shaking to remove as much water as possible.

Into the tomatoes, stir the chilies, garlic and ½ teaspoon pepper. Add the avocados and pasta-corn mixture; toss, then let stand for about 15 minutes, tossing once or twice. Taste and season with salt and pepper. Serve drizzled with additional oil.

Optional garnish: Crumbled feta cheese OR fresh basil OR lime wedges OR a combination

Rigatoni with Turkey Sausage and Tomato-Cream Sauce

Start to finish: 35 minutes
Servings: 4 to 6

This comforting pasta dish is our re-creation of a favorite from Bar Pitti in New York City. Italian sausage made with turkey or chicken is best, as its leaner, milder flavor is a better match than pork-based sausage for the creamy tomato sauce and sweet peas. There's no need to thaw the peas before use; they have plenty of time to defrost in the pot. **We drain the pasta when it's slightly underdone—just shy of al dente—and finish cooking it directly in the sauce so the noodles soak up the flavors.**

1 pound rigatoni OR ziti

Kosher salt and ground black pepper

2 tablespoons extra-virgin olive oil

8 ounces hot OR sweet fresh Italian turkey OR chicken sausage, casing removed

14½-ounce can tomato puree (1½ cups)

½ to 1 teaspoon red pepper flakes

1 cup frozen peas

¾ cup heavy cream

In a large pot, bring 4 quarts water to a boil. Add the pasta, 1 tablespoon salt and cook until just shy of al dente. Reserve about 1 cup of the cooking water, then drain and return the pasta to the pot.

Meanwhile, in a 12-inch skillet over medium-high, heat the oil until shimmering. Add the sausage and ½ teaspoon each salt and pepper. Cook, stirring occasionally and breaking up the meat into very small bits, until the sausage is lightly browned, 4 to 5 minutes. Stir in the tomato puree and pepper flakes; bring to a simmer and cook, stirring occasionally, until the sauce is slightly reduced, about 5 minutes. Stir in the peas and cream, then cook, stirring, until the mixture is heated through, about 1 minute.

Add the sauce and ½ cup reserved pasta water to the pasta in the pot. Cook over low, stirring, until the pasta is al dente, 1 to 2 minutes; add more reserved water as needed so the noodles are lightly sauced. Off heat, taste and season with salt and black pepper.

Optional garnish: Finely grated Parmesan cheese

Pasta with Creamy Cauliflower and Cheese Sauce

Start to finish: 40 minutes
Servings: 4 to 6

In this one-pot-plus-blender recipe, mild cauliflower pairs with pasta and rich Italian cheese. The cauliflower, cut into florets and simmered in the water that's later used to cook the pasta, plays a dual role. Some is tossed with the noodles, bringing a contrasting texture to the mix. **We also blend cauliflower with some of its cooking water and oil to create a velvety sauce base without adding dairy or starch.** The result is a delicious, easy—and light—take on macaroni and cheese. A short, twisty pasta that the sauce easily grips is best; we like campanelle, cavatappi and fusilli.

4 medium garlic cloves, smashed and peeled

4 thyme sprigs OR 2 rosemary springs AND 2 teaspoons minced fresh thyme

2-pound cauliflower head, trimmed, cored and cut into ½- to 1-inch florets

Kosher salt and ground black pepper

1 pound campanelle OR cavatappi OR fusilli

2 tablespoons extra-virgin olive oil

4 ounces provolone OR fontina cheese, shredded (1 cup) OR 4 ounces taleggio cheese, trimmed of rind and cut into rough ½-inch pieces

Chopped fresh chives, to serve

In a large pot over medium-high, combine 3 quarts water, the garlic and thyme sprigs. Cover and bring to a boil. Stir in the cauliflower and 1 tablespoon salt. Re-cover, reduce to medium and simmer, stirring occasionally, until the cauliflower is fully tender, 10 to 12 minutes. Off heat, use a slotted spoon to transfer 3 cups of the cauliflower to a bowl; set aside. Transfer the remaining cauliflower, the garlic and ½ cup of the cooking liquid to a blender. Remove and discard the thyme sprigs.

Bring the water remaining in the pot to a boil over medium-high. Add the pasta and cook, stirring occasionally, until al dente. Reserve 1 cup of the cooking water, then drain and return the pasta to the pot; set aside.

To the blender, add the oil and ½ teaspoon salt. Blend on high until smooth, about 1 minute. Transfer the puree to the pasta and add the cheese, the reserved cauliflower florets, the minced thyme and ½ teaspoon pepper. Cook over low, stirring often and adding reserved cooking water as needed, until the sauce coats the pasta, 2 to 3 minutes. Off heat, taste and season with salt and pepper. Serve sprinkled with chives.

Pasta Salad with Charred Corn and Cilantro

Start to finish: 30 minutes
Servings: 4 to 6

Creamy-rich yet bright and fresh, this pasta salad takes inspiration from Mexican esquites, corn that typically is grilled or roasted and finished with a mixture of herbs, lime, chili and cheese. **We simmer corn cobs in the water that's later used for cooking the pasta to add sweet, grassy flavor.** The kernels, meanwhile, are charred and tossed with brine from pickled jalapeños, cilantro, Mexican crema and salty cotija. And if fresh corn is out of season, frozen kernels that have been thawed and patted dry work nicely; you'll need 2 pounds. If using frozen kernels, you won't have cobs to simmer, so simply boil the pasta in the water.

5 cups fresh corn kernels from about
5 ears of corn, cobs reserved (see headnote)

8 ounces ditalini OR penne
OR elbow macaroni

Kosher salt and ground black pepper

2 tablespoons neutral oil

½ cup Mexican crema OR ½ cup sour cream
whisked with 2 tablespoons water

2 ounces cotija cheese, finely grated (½ cup)

1 cup lightly packed fresh cilantro,
roughly chopped

⅓ cup pickled jalapeños, chopped,
plus 3 tablespoons brine

In a large pot, combine 4 quarts water and the corn cobs. Bring to a boil and cook for 10 minutes, then remove and discard the cobs. Stir in the pasta and 1 tablespoon salt, then cook, stirring occasionally, until fully tender. Drain in a colander and rinse under cold water, tossing, until cool to the touch. Drain again, shaking the colander to remove as much water as possible; set aside.

In a 12-inch skillet over high, heat the oil until barely smoking. Add the corn in an even layer and cook without stirring for about 3 minutes, allowing the kernels to char. Stir once, then cook without stirring until most of the kernels are fully charred, about 2 minutes. Set aside off heat.

In a large bowl, whisk together the crema, half of the cotija, the cilantro, pickled jalapeños and their brine and ½ teaspoon each salt and pepper. Stir in the corn and pasta, then taste and season with salt and pepper. Transfer to a serving bowl and sprinkle with the remaining cotija.

Optional garnish: Chili powder OR lime wedges OR sliced scallions OR a combination

Ziti with Sweet Peppers, Bacon and Paprika

Start to finish: 30 minutes
Servings: 4 to 6

Loosely inspired by Hungary's ubiquitous pepper stew, lescó, this dish combines smoky bacon with bell peppers and onion, creating a luscious vegetable-packed sauce. **We use extra-starchy pasta water as a thickener, made by boiling the noodles in a bare amount of liquid.** Sweet paprika lends bold color and fruity, earthy notes, while lightly browned tomato paste provides umami-rich depth. We love this topped with spoonfuls of ricotta cheese; its creaminess brings everything together beautifully.

1 pound ziti OR penne

Kosher salt and ground black pepper

2 teaspoons extra-virgin olive oil

4 ounces bacon OR pancetta, roughly chopped

3 medium red OR yellow bell peppers OR a combination, stemmed, seeded and cut into ½-inch pieces

1 medium yellow onion, chopped

2 tablespoons tomato paste

1 tablespoon sweet paprika

In a large pot, bring 3 quarts water to a boil. Add the pasta and 2 teaspoons salt, then cook, stirring often, until al dente. Reserve about 2 cups of the cooking water, then drain. Return the pasta to the pot; set aside.

In a 12-inch skillet over medium, combine the oil and bacon; cook, stirring occasionally, until the bacon is crisp, about 5 minutes. Using a slotted spoon, transfer the bacon to a small bowl; set aside. Increase to high and heat until the fat is barely smoking. Add the bell peppers, onion and 1 teaspoon salt. Cook, stirring once or twice, until the vegetables are charred and tender, 8 to 10 minutes.

Add the tomato paste and paprika; cook, stirring often, until the paste slightly sticks to the pan, 2 to 4 minutes. Add 1½ cups of the reserved cooking water and ½ teaspoon pepper, stirring and scraping up any browned bits. Transfer the sauce to the pot with the pasta, add the bacon and cook over medium-high, stirring, until heated through, 2 to 3 minutes; if needed, add reserved cooking water 1 tablespoon at a time if the mixture looks dry. Taste and season with salt and pepper.

Optional garnish: Ricotta cheese OR chopped fresh flat-leaf parsley OR sliced scallions OR a combination

SUPER-STARCH PASTA

Creamy pastas are great, but they don't need to rely on cheese or cream to deliver, particularly because they tend to leave the finished dish feeling heavy and dense. Our choice more often is something most people pour down the drain—the water used to cook the pasta.

We prefer to follow the example of Italian cooks and hang on to some of the cooking liquid left over when we drain our pasta. The starch from the noodles leaches into the water as they cook, creating a good base for sauces, especially when you cook the pasta in slightly less than the typical amount of water. Normally, we cook 1 pound of pasta in 4 quarts water. To create super-starched water, we reduce that to 3 quarts and scoop out a cupful or so just before draining.

When combined with other sauce ingredients, this starchy liquid creates naturally creamy, thick sauces that cling to the pasta without weighing it down.

RECIPES FROM TOP

| Caramelized Onion and Pecorino Pasta | Penne Carbonara with Zucchini | Gemelli and Peas with Lemon, Herbs and Ricotta |

Gemelli and Peas with Lemon, Herbs and Ricotta

Start to finish: 30 minutes
Servings: 4 to 6

Citrusy and herbaceous, this easy, spring-inspired meal features garlic, peas and plenty of lemon, both zest and juice. We heat the thawed frozen peas by putting them in a colander and draining the cooked pasta over them. **To create an extra-starchy liquid, ideal for thickening the sauce and giving it an especially silky texture, we cook the pasta in just 3 quarts of water.** A few handfuls of fresh, fragrant herbs complete the vibrant dish, which is topped with soft, sweet whole-milk ricotta.

1½ cups frozen peas, thawed

1 pound gemelli OR casarecce OR penne

Kosher salt and ground black pepper

3 tablespoons extra-virgin olive oil, plus more to serve

3 medium garlic cloves, minced

2 cups lightly packed fresh dill OR flat-leaf parsley OR mint OR a combination, chopped

1 tablespoon grated lemon zest, plus 3 tablespoons lemon juice, plus lemon wedges to serve

1 cup whole-milk ricotta cheese

Put the peas in a colander and set the colander in the sink. In a large pot, bring 3 quarts water to a boil. Add the pasta and 2 teaspoons salt, then cook, stirring occasionally, until al dente. Reserve about 1½ cups of the cooking water, then drain the pasta over the peas; set aside.

In the same pot over medium, combine the oil and garlic; cook, stirring, until the garlic is lightly browned, 1 to 2 minutes. Add the pasta-pea mixture and 1 cup of the reserved cooking water. Cook, stirring, until the pasta is lightly sauced, about 2 minutes; add more reserved water as needed if the mixture looks thick

and dry. Add the dill and lemon zest and juice; toss. Off heat, taste and season with salt and pepper. Serve dolloped with the ricotta, drizzled with additional oil and with lemon wedges on the side.

Caramelized Onion and Pecorino Pasta

Start to finish: 30 minutes
Servings: 4 to 6

The mild, wheaty taste of pasta is a great backdrop for super-sized flavors. This recipe is a delicious combination of contrasts. The sweetness of deeply caramelized onions is balanced by salty, umami-packed anchovies (fish sauce is a good substitute) and funky pecorino Romano cheese (Parmesan is great, too). A splash of vinegar brings brightness and chives (or scallions) offer color and herbal freshness. **We cook the pasta in a scant amount of water—only 3 quarts—then use some of the extra-starchy liquid to build sauciness in the dish.**

1 pound linguine OR spaghetti OR fettuccine

Kosher salt and ground black pepper

3 tablespoons extra-virgin olive oil

2 large yellow onions, halved and thinly sliced

2 oil-packed anchovy fillets OR 1 tablespoon fish sauce

1 tablespoon white wine vinegar

⅓ cup fresh chives cut into ½-inch lengths OR 4 scallions, thinly sliced

1 ounce pecorino Romano OR Parmesan cheese, finely grated (½ cup)

In a large pot, bring 3 quarts water to a boil. Add the pasta and 2 teaspoons salt, then cook, stirring occasionally, until just shy of al dente. Reserve about 1½ cups of the pasta cooking water, then drain.

Meanwhile, in a 12-inch skillet over medium-high, heat the oil until shimmering. Add the onions and ½ teaspoon salt; cook, stirring only occasionally at the start then more often as the onions brown, until crisped and deeply caramelized, about 15 minutes; reduce the heat as needed to prevent scorching. Stir in the anchovies, vinegar and ¾ teaspoon pepper, then add the pasta and 1 cup reserved pasta water. Cook over medium, stirring and tossing, until the pasta is al dente, about 3 minutes.

Off heat, stir in the chives. Taste and season with salt and pepper. Serve sprinkled with the cheese.

Penne Carbonara with Zucchini

Start to finish: 30 minutes
Servings: 4 to 6

Traditionally made with eggs, cured pork, hard cheese and plenty of pepper, carbonara is classic Italian comfort fare. For a lighter, equally delicious version, we've replaced the pancetta or guanciale typically used with zucchini (or yellow summer squash). Sautéed in olive oil and seasoned with garlic and pepper flakes, the zucchini takes on a richness that stands in for the pork. **To build the dish's creamy, silky-smooth sauce, a paste of eggs and Parmesan is combined with pasta cooking liquid, made especially starchy by boiling the noodles in a bare amount of water.**

1 pound medium zucchini OR yellow summer squash

1 pound penne OR ziti

Kosher salt and ground black pepper

¼ cup extra-virgin olive oil

2 medium garlic cloves, thinly sliced

½ to 1 teaspoon red pepper flakes, plus more to serve

2 large eggs, plus 4 large egg yolks

3 ounces Parmesan cheese, finely grated (1½ cups), plus more to serve

Thinly slice the zucchini on the diagonal. Stack several slices and cut lengthwise into matchsticks. Repeat with the remaining slices; set the zucchini aside.

In a large pot, bring 3 quarts water to a boil. Add the pasta and 2 teaspoons salt, then cook, stirring occasionally, until al dente. Reserve about 1 cup of the cooking water, then drain and return the pasta to the pot; set aside.

Meanwhile, in a 12-inch skillet over medium, heat the oil until simmering. Add the zucchini and ½ teaspoon salt. Cook, stirring occasionally, until the zucchini is softened and beginning to brown, about 4 minutes. Add the garlic and pepper flakes; cook, stirring, until fragrant, 1 to 2 minutes. Set aside off the heat.

In a medium bowl, whisk together the whole eggs plus yolks, ½ teaspoon salt and ¼ teaspoon black pepper. Whisk in the cheese about ¼ cup at a time; the mixture will be thick and paste-like.

Return the pot to low and stir in ½ cup of the reserved cooking water, the zucchini and the egg-cheese mixture. Cook, stirring constantly, until the sauce is silky, thickened and coating the pasta, 2 to 3 minutes. If needed, toss in reserved cooking water 1 tablespoon at a time to adjust the consistency. Off heat, taste and season with salt and black pepper. Serve sprinkled with additional pepper flakes and Parmesan.

Optional garnish: Chopped fresh mint OR fresh basil

One-Pot Tortellini with Cherry Tomatoes and Salami

Start to finish: 40 minutes
Servings: 4 to 6

There's no need to boil a large pot of water for this recipe because **we cook the pasta in the sauce for better flavor absorption. But we first brown the filled pasta in olive oil, a step that builds flavor in the dish.** Then cherry (or grape) tomatoes go into the pot along with a little water, some garlic and chopped salami. As the tortellini simmer and soften in the mix, they absorb the seasonings. Fresh tortellini, the type sold in the refrigerator case of the supermarket, is what you'll want to use here, not the shelf-stable variety sold alongside dried pasta.

3 tablespoons extra-virgin olive oil, plus more to serve

16- to 20-ounce package store-bought fresh tortellini

4 ounces salami OR pepperoni, chopped

2 medium garlic cloves, smashed and peeled

2 pints cherry OR grape tomatoes, halved

Kosher salt and ground black pepper

1 ounce pecorino Romano OR Parmesan cheese, finely grated (1 cup), plus more to serve

½ cup lightly packed fresh basil, torn

In a large Dutch oven over medium-high, heat the oil until shimmering. Add the tortellini, distributing them in an even layer, and cook, uncovered and without stirring, until well browned on the bottom, 3 to 4 minutes. Stir in the salami, garlic, tomatoes, ½ teaspoon pepper and 1 cup water. Bring to a simmer, then reduce to medium, cover and cook, stirring occasionally, until the tomatoes have softened and the tortellini are tender, 4 to 5 minutes.

Remove the pot from the heat. If desired, remove and discard the garlic. Stir in the cheese and basil, then taste and season with salt and pepper. Serve drizzled with additional oil and sprinkled with additional cheese.

Tomato-Harissa Toasted Pearl Couscous with Mint

Start to finish: 40 minutes (20 minutes active)
Servings: 4

This bright, zesty dish stars harissa, North Africa's smoky-spicy chili condiment, as well as fresh mint, tangy lemon, sweet-tart tomatoes and briny olives. **Toasting the couscous before cooking it brings out its nuttier notes; dressing it while warm ensures maximum flavor absorption.** The couscous, after tossing with the tomatoes and olives, can be covered and refrigerated for up to eight hours; bring to room temperature before serving, then stir in the mint. Delicious as both an easy side dish and simple dinner, we love topping the mix with high-quality oil-packed tuna and fresh greens.

1½ cups pearl couscous

¼ cup extra-virgin olive oil

1½ tablespoons grated lemon zest, plus 3 tablespoons lemon juice

3 teaspoons harissa paste, divided, plus more if desired

Kosher salt and ground black pepper

1 pint cherry OR grape tomatoes, halved

½ cup pitted green OR black olives OR a combination, chopped

1 cup lightly packed fresh mint OR flat-leaf parsley OR a combination, torn

In a medium saucepan over medium, combine the couscous and oil. Cook, stirring, until golden brown, about 4 minutes. Add 3 cups water, the lemon zest, 2 teaspoons harissa, 1½ teaspoons salt and ¼ teaspoon pepper. Bring to a simmer and cook, stirring occasionally, until the couscous has absorbed the liquid and is tender, 10 to 13 minutes.

Meanwhile, in a large bowl, toss the tomatoes with ¼ teaspoon salt and the remaining 1 teaspoon harissa.

When the couscous is tender, add it to the tomatoes along with the olives and lemon juice; toss. Taste and add additional harissa if desired. Let stand 15 minutes, stirring once or twice, then stir in the mint. Taste and season with salt and pepper.

Optional garnish: Chopped hard-cooked egg OR chopped pistachios OR both

Fettuccine Alfredo

Start to finish: 30 minutes
Servings: 4 to 6

Made the Italian way, fettuccine Alfredo bears little resemblance to the cream-based pasta dish that's popular in the U.S. True fettuccine Alfredo consists of only fresh pasta, Parmigiano Reggiano cheese, butter and salt. **To keep the sauce light and aerated, we skip the cream and line a serving bowl with butter, adding the hot, cooked pasta and tossing to incorporate, followed by the cheese.** Purchase a hefty chunk of true Parmigiano Reggiano—not the pre-shredded stuff—trim off the rind, cut 6 ounces into rough ½-inch pieces and whir them in a food processor until very finely ground. At the grocery store, some types of high-fat butter are labeled "European-style"; Plugrá and Kerrygold are widely available.

8 tablespoons salted European-style butter (see headnote), sliced about ½ inch thick

6 ounces Parmigiano Reggiano cheese (without rind), cut into rough ½-inch chunks

16 to 18 ounces fresh fettuccine

Kosher salt

Line a large bowl with the butter slices, placing them in a single layer along the bottom and up the sides of the bowl; let stand at room temperature until the butter is softened.

Meanwhile, in a food processor, process the cheese until very finely ground, about 40 seconds; transfer to a medium bowl (you should have about 1½ cups).

In a large pot, bring 2 quarts water to a boil. Add the pasta and 1½ teaspoons salt, then cook, stirring often, until al dente. Remove the pot from the heat. Using tongs, transfer the pasta from the pot, with ample water clinging to it, to the butter-lined bowl; reserve the water in the pot. Using the tongs, quickly stir and toss the pasta, incorporating the butter, until the butter is fully melted. Add ½ cup of the reserved pasta water and toss until the water has been absorbed.

Add 1 cup of the cheese ⅓ cup at a time, tossing and adding the next addition only after the previous one has been incorporated. Next, toss in ½ to 1 cup more pasta water, about ¼ cup at a time, until the sauce clings to the pasta and only a small amount pools at the bottom of the bowl.

Let stand for 2 minutes to allow the sauce to thicken slightly. If needed, toss in additional pasta water a little at a time until the sauce once again clings to the pasta and only a small amount pools at the bottom of the bowl. Taste and season with salt. Divide among warmed serving bowls and serve immediately with the remaining cheese on the side.

Pasta with Parsley, Garlic and Parmesan Breadcrumbs

Start to finish: 30 minutes
Servings: 4

Crisp, flavored breadcrumbs add flavor and texture to a weeknight-easy pasta recipe. We deepen their flavor by toasting them in olive oil and stirring in some savory Parmesan cheese. We were inspired by gremolata, a toss of chopped parsley, lemon and garlic used in Italian cooking as a finishing touch to bring herbal notes, citrusy freshness and allium savoriness—plus vivid color—to any dish. First we toast panko (light, fluffy Japanese breadcrumbs), then stir in some Parmesan (or pecorino) and the gremolata elements. We then dress al dente pasta with a little more cheese, plus some starchy cooking water so the noodles are lightly sauced.

4 tablespoons extra-virgin olive oil, divided, plus more to serve

¾ cup panko breadcrumbs

3 ounces Parmesan OR pecorino Romano cheese, finely grated (1½ cups)

Kosher salt and ground black pepper

1 pound gemelli OR casarecce OR penne

Leaves from 1 large bunch fresh flat-leaf parsley, finely chopped (about ¾ cup)

2 medium garlic cloves, finely chopped

1 teaspoon grated lemon zest, plus lemon wedges to serve

In a large pot over medium, heat 3 tablespoons oil until shimmering. Add the panko and cook, stirring occasionally, until golden brown, about 5 minutes. Transfer to a medium bowl. Stir in half of the cheese and ½ teaspoon salt; set aside.

In the same pot, bring 4 quarts water to a boil. Stir in the pasta and 1 tablespoon salt. Cook, stirring occasionally, until al dente. Reserve about 1¼ cups of the cooking water, then drain and return the pasta to the pot.

To the panko mixture, add the parsley, garlic, lemon zest and the remaining 1 tablespoon oil; toss to combine.

Set the pot over medium, add the remaining Parmesan and toss until the cheese is evenly dispersed. While tossing, gradually add the reserved pasta water; after about 2 minutes, the pasta will be lightly sauced. Off heat, taste and season with salt and pepper. Transfer to a serving dish, drizzle with additional oil and top with the breadcrumb mixture. Serve with lemon wedges.

Optional garnish: Red pepper flakes

Pasta with Pecorino-Zucchini Sauce and Basil

Start to finish: 40 minutes
Servings: 4 to 6

From Italy's Amalfi Coast, pasta alla nerano features long, thin pasta tossed with a velvety sauce made with pureed zucchini. It's an elegant yet easy dish that's luxurious but not heavy. **We use a minimal amount of water to cook the pasta, then blend some of the starchy liquid with tender, sautéed zucchini to create creamy consistency without cream.** If you own an immersion blender, it works well for making the zucchini-garlic puree; simply transfer the ingredients to be blended to a medium bowl. When smooth, return the mixture to the pot.

1½ pounds medium zucchini

1 pound spaghetti OR bucatini

Kosher salt and ground black pepper

3 tablespoons extra-virgin olive oil,
plus more to serve

3 medium garlic cloves, smashed and peeled

2 tablespoons salted butter, cut into 2 pieces

2 ounces pecorino Romano cheese,
finely grated (1 cup), plus more to serve

½ cup lightly packed fresh basil, chopped

Thinly slice the zucchini on the diagonal. Stack several slices and cut lengthwise into matchsticks. Repeat with the remaining slices; set the zucchini aside.

In a large pot, bring 3 quarts water to a boil. Add the spaghetti and 2 teaspoons salt, then cook, stirring occasionally, until al dente. Reserve about 1½ cups of the cooking water, then drain; set aside.

In the same pot, combine the oil and garlic. Cook over medium, stirring, until the garlic is golden brown, 1 to 2 minutes. Transfer the garlic to a small plate, then add the zucchini to the pot. Cook, stirring occasionally, until the zucchini is lightly browned and soft enough to mash with a fork, 10 to 12 minutes. Remove the pot from the heat. Add half of the zucchini to a blender along with the garlic and ½ cup reserved pasta water. Puree until the mixture is smooth, about 30 seconds.

To the zucchini in the pot add the puree, drained pasta, butter, pecorino, basil and another ½ cup reserved pasta water. Cook over medium, tossing, until heated through and the mixture is creamy and the pasta is lightly sauced, 2 to 3 minutes; add more reserved water as needed if the mixture looks thick and dry. Off heat, taste and season with salt and pepper. Serve drizzled with additional oil and sprinkled with additional cheese.

Stir-Fried

Stir-Fried Rice Noodles with Broccolini and Oyster Sauce

Start to finish: 45 minutes
Servings: 4

This rice noodle stir-fry is a simplified, six-ingredient version of pad see ew, a Thai favorite. Oyster sauce, fish sauce and sugar supply the umami-rich salty-sweet flavors. Instead of Chinese broccoli, we use Broccolini, which we cut into 1½-inch pieces. **We use our sear-then-steam technique to develop flavorful browning on the vegetable before tenderizing it with a little water and a lid.** Rice stick noodles are the type used to make pad Thai. They vary in width; for this, opt for ones that are at least ¼-inch wide.

10 ounces dried rice stick noodles
(see headnote)

⅓ cup oyster sauce

2 tablespoons packed light brown sugar

4 teaspoons fish sauce

Ground black OR white pepper

4 tablespoons neutral oil, divided

1 pound Broccolini, trimmed and
cut into 1½-inch pieces

2 medium garlic cloves, minced

Place the noodles in a large bowl and add hot water to cover. Let stand, stirring occasionally, for about 30 minutes; the noodles will become pliable but not fully tender. In a small bowl, whisk together the oyster sauce, sugar, fish sauce and ¼ teaspoon pepper; place near the stove.

Drain the noodles in a colander. Shake the colander to remove excess water and set near the stove.

In a 12-inch nonstick skillet over medium-high, heat 2 tablespoons oil until barely smoking. Add the Broccolini and cook, without stirring, until beginning to char. Stir in the garlic and cook, stirring occasionally, until the Broccolini begins to soften, about 2 minutes. Add 3 tablespoons water, then immediately cover and reduce to low. Cook, stirring only once or twice, until the Broccolini is tender-crisp and the pan is dry, about 3 minutes.

Add the remaining 2 tablespoons oil and the noodles; increase to medium-high and cook, tossing, until sizzling, about 1 minute. Pour in the sauce mixture around the perimeter of the pan. Cook, tossing, until the noodles have absorbed the sauce and are tender, 1 to 2 minutes; if the noodles are still too firm, drizzle in water 2 tablespoons at a time and cook, stirring, until tender. Off heat, taste and season with pepper and fish sauce.

Optional garnish: Red pepper flakes OR lime wedges OR both

Buttery Udon with Shiitake Mushrooms

Start to finish: 30 minutes
Servings: 4

They may seem an unlikely pairing, but sweet, creamy butter and bold, salty soy sauce are a fantastic flavor match. In this recipe, the duo adds richness and umami to Japanese udon, wheat noodles that cook up with a satisfying chewiness. Fresh shiitake mushrooms sautéed in butter bring a meatiness to the vegetarian dish and make it feel more complete. If you like, top each serving with a runny-yolked fried egg.

12 ounces dried udon noodles

4 tablespoons salted butter,
cut into 1-tablespoon pieces, divided

8 ounces shiitake mushrooms,
stemmed, caps sliced about ¼ inch thick

2 medium garlic cloves, finely grated
OR 2 teaspoons finely grated fresh ginger OR both

¼ cup soy sauce, plus more if needed

Toasted sesame seeds, to serve

In a large pot, bring 3 quarts water to a boil. Add the noodles and cook, stirring occasionally, until just shy of al dente. Reserve ¼ cup of the cooking water, then drain the noodles in a colander. Rinse under cold water until cool to the touch, then drain again; set aside.

In the same pot over medium-high, melt 2 tablespoons butter. Add the mushrooms and cook, stirring occasionally, until beginning to brown, about 3 minutes. Reduce to medium and add the garlic; cook, stirring, until fragrant, about 30 seconds. Add the noodles, followed by the soy sauce; cook over medium-high, stirring and tossing, until heated, about 1 minute.

Add the reserved cooking water and the remaining 2 tablespoons butter; cook, tossing, until the noodles are slick, glossy and tender, about 2 minutes. Off heat, taste and season with additional soy sauce. Serve sprinkled with sesame seeds.

Optional garnish: Thinly sliced scallions OR shichimi togarashi OR both

Sizzled-Oil Oyster Sauce Noodles

Start to finish: 20 minutes
Servings: 4

These noodles are simple to make and require only a few ingredients—ones we keep on hand because they instantly add big, bold flavor. Oyster sauce is the major player here, lending salty-sweetness, plus loads of umami. This is a deconstructed stir-fry. **We borrow a Chinese technique and use hot oil to tame the pungency of garlic and scallions and bloom their aromas.** Then we add the aromatics to the noodles and toss to incorporate. To make the noodles heartier, serve them topped with runny-yolked fried eggs.

12 ounces dried lo mein OR dried udon noodles OR dried non-instant ramen OR linguine

2 tablespoons toasted sesame oil

1 tablespoon neutral oil

3 scallions, whites thinly sliced, greens thinly sliced on the diagonal, reserved separately

2 medium garlic cloves, finely grated OR 2 teaspoons finely grated fresh ginger OR both

½ teaspoon red pepper flakes

⅓ cup oyster sauce

In a large pot, bring 4 quarts water to a boil. Add the noodles and cook, stirring occasionally, until tender. Drain in a colander and rinse under cold water, tossing, until cool to the touch. Drain again, shaking the colander to remove as much water as possible, then return the noodles to the pot.

In an 8-inch skillet over medium-high, heat both oils until barely smoking. Remove the pan from the heat and quickly stir in the scallion whites, garlic and pepper flakes. Whisk in the oyster sauce and ¼ cup water. Pour the mixture over the noodles in the pot, then cook over medium-low, tossing, until heated through, about 2 minutes. Serve sprinkled with scallion greens.

Optional garnish: Chopped roasted peanuts or toasted sesame seeds OR chili oil OR chili crisp OR a combination

Stir-Fried Beef and Tomatoes

Start to finish: 35 minutes
Servings: 4

This stir-fry of beef with tomatoes, known as "beef tomato," is a popular dish in Hawaii. It actually has Cantonese origins and was brought to the islands by immigrants. In our six-ingredient version, **we coat the meat with a cornstarch slurry to promote tenderness and to thicken the sauce to a gravy-like richness. Salting tomatoes before adding them to the hot skillet helps remove excess moisture,** then we cook them briefly along with aromatic ginger. Oyster sauce or hoisin sauce contributes the characteristic salty-sweet flavor to the dish. Serve over steamed rice.

4 tablespoons oyster sauce
OR hoisin sauce, divided

1½ tablespoons cornstarch

Kosher salt and ground white
OR black pepper

1 pound flank steak, cut with the grain
into 2- to 3-inch pieces, then thinly sliced
against the grain

1 pound plum tomatoes, cored and
cut into ½-inch wedges

3 tablespoons neutral oil, divided

2 teaspoons minced fresh ginger
OR 3 medium garlic cloves, minced OR both

1 bunch scallions, cut on the diagonal
into 1-inch lengths

In a medium bowl, whisk 1 tablespoon oyster sauce, the cornstarch, ½ teaspoon pepper and 1 tablespoon water. Add the beef, stirring; let stand at room temperature for 15 minutes or cover and refrigerate for 1 hour. Meanwhile, place the tomatoes on a paper towel-lined plate and sprinkle with ¼ teaspoon salt; set aside.

In a 12-inch skillet over high, heat 2 tablespoons oil until barely smoking. Add the beef in an even layer and cook without stirring until well browned and the pieces release easily from the skillet, 2 to 3 minutes. Stir, then transfer to a large plate.

In the same skillet over medium-high, heat the remaining 1 tablespoon oil until shimmering. Add the tomatoes and ginger; cook, scraping up any browned bits, until the tomatoes soften and the ginger is aromatic, 30 to 60 seconds. Add the beef and any juices, then stir in the remaining 3 tablespoons oyster sauce and 2 tablespoons water. Cook, stirring, until the meat is tender and the sauce has thickened, 1 to 2 minutes. Stir in the scallions to wilt slightly, about 30 seconds. Off heat, taste and season with salt and pepper.

Optional garnish: Toasted sesame oil

Stir-Fried Gochujang Chicken

Start to finish: 30 minutes
Servings: 4

Flavor-packed, spicy-sweet gochujang elevates a couldn't-be-simpler chicken stir-fry. The complexly flavored Korean refrigerator staple is balanced by the pepperiness and pungency of ginger and garlic, plus a splash of salty soy sauce and a spoonful of sugar rounding everything out. **We get deeply flavorful browning on the chicken by cooking it on each side without stirring.** Serve with steamed rice and a chilled beer.

¼ cup gochujang

3 tablespoons soy sauce

1 tablespoon white sugar

3 tablespoons neutral oil

1½ pounds boneless, skinless chicken thighs, trimmed and cut crosswise into thirds

3 medium garlic cloves, finely chopped

3 tablespoons finely chopped fresh ginger

In a small bowl, whisk together the gochujang, soy sauce and sugar; set aside.

In a 12-inch skillet over medium-high, heat the oil until shimmering. Add the chicken in an even layer and cook without stirring until browned on the bottom, about 5 minutes. Reduce to medium, then flip the chicken and cook without stirring until browned on the second sides, 3 to 4 minutes.

Add the garlic and ginger; cook, stirring, until fragrant, about 30 seconds. Add the gochujang mixture and cook, scraping up any browned bits and occasionally turning the chicken, until the sauce has thickened lightly and coats the chicken, 2 to 3 minutes.

Optional garnish: Toasted sesame seeds OR sliced scallions OR both

Thai Stir-Fried Chicken and Asparagus

Start to finish: 30 minutes
Servings: 4

This weeknight-easy chicken and asparagus stir-fry takes inspiration from pad prik khing, a Thai classic in which long beans and protein are cooked with red curry paste. We tested a variety of Thai red, green and yellow curry pastes—all work deliciously, though we recommend tasting a small amount before deciding exactly how much to use, as they vary in spiciness. To round out the paste's bold, zingy notes, we combine it with fish sauce and sugar. **We toss the chicken with a seasoning paste before and after browning to develop flavor-building caramelization while creating delicious layers of complexity and intensity.** Serve with steamed jasmine rice.

2 to 3 tablespoons Thai green OR red OR yellow curry paste (see headnote)

2 tablespoons fish sauce

1 tablespoon packed brown sugar

1 pound boneless, skinless chicken breasts, sliced crosswise about ¼ inch thick

3 tablespoons neutral oil, divided

8 ounces asparagus OR green beans, trimmed and cut on the diagonal into 1-inch pieces

1 medium red onion, halved and cut into ½-inch wedges, layers separated

Kosher salt and ground black pepper

In a medium bowl, stir together the curry paste, fish sauce and sugar. In another medium bowl, combine 1 tablespoon of the curry paste mixture with the chicken, then toss until coated; let stand for about 10 minutes.

In a 12-inch nonstick skillet over high, heat 2 tablespoons oil until barely smoking. Add the chicken in an even layer and cook, without stirring, until well browned on the bottom, about 2 minutes; the chicken will not be fully cooked. Transfer to the bowl with the remaining curry paste mixture; set aside.

In the same skillet over high, heat the remaining 1 tablespoon oil until shimmering. Add the asparagus and onion; cook, without stirring, until browned on the bottom, about 2 minutes. Add the chicken-curry paste mixture; cook, stirring, until the sauce has thickened slightly and the vegetables are tender-crisp, about 1 minute. Off heat, taste and season with salt and pepper.

Optional garnish: Chopped fresh cilantro OR basil OR lime wedges OR a combination

BLOOM SPICES FOR BIGGER FLAVOR

Blooming—or heating spices in hot fat, such as butter, ghee or oil—works two ways. It extracts flavors and aromas and creates new and more complex compounds through heat and oxidation.

There are a few rules for getting spices bloomed just right. Size matters, so larger spices, such as whole seeds (mustard, coriander) and sticks (cinnamon) require more time for the heat to draw the volatile oil-soluble compounds to the surface of the spice. Ground spices, on the other hand, require less time. We usually start with cool or warm oil and heat slowly. This prevents the spices from burning and turning bitter before they have time to reach full bloom.

For spices that will be pulverized in a grinder, we use the same approach minus the fat and dry-toast the spices in a hot skillet. Once again, timing is dependent on size; it takes no more than a few minutes to wake up the flavors. Once the spices have cooled, they're ready to grind.

RECIPES FROM TOP

| Potatoes and Peas with Sizzled Cumin and Mustard Seeds | Stir-Fried Sichuan Pepper Chicken | Coconut Curry Beef |

Potatoes and Peas with Sizzled Cumin and Mustard Seeds

Start to finish: 30 minutes
Servings: 4

Heating whole spices in hot fat not only enhances their flavors and aromas, it also crisps their texture. And the fat itself becomes an infusion that carries the seasoning throughout the dish. In this recipe inspired by Indian sabzi—a category of boldly spiced cooked vegetable dishes—earthy cumin and pungent mustard seeds give character to a basic backdrop of potatoes (or cauliflower, or both) that are skillet-cooked with onion and garlic. Green peas added at the end bring sweetness and pops of color. This is hearty enough to be a vegetarian main but also works as a side to meats and fatty fish.

¼ cup neutral oil

1 tablespoon cumin seeds

1 tablespoon brown OR yellow mustard seeds

Kosher salt and coarsely ground black pepper

1 medium red onion, halved and thinly sliced

2 medium garlic cloves, minced

2 pounds Yukon Gold potatoes, peeled and cut into 1-inch cubes OR 2-pound cauliflower head, trimmed, cored and cut into 1-inch florets OR a combination

1½ cups thawed frozen peas

In a 12-inch skillet over medium, heat the oil, cumin seeds, mustard seeds and ½ teaspoon coarsely ground pepper. Bloom the spices, stirring, until fragrant and the seeds begin to pop, about 1 minute. Add the onion, garlic and ½ teaspoon salt; cook, stirring occasionally, until the onion begins to soften, about 1 minute.

Stir in the potatoes, 1 teaspoon salt and 1 cup water. Cover and cook, stirring occasionally, until the potatoes are tender and only a little liquid remains, 13 to 15 minutes. Add the peas and cook, uncovered and stirring occasionally, until the peas are heated through, 3 to 5 minutes. Taste and season with salt and pepper.

Stir-Fried Sichuan Pepper Chicken

Start to finish: 30 minutes
Servings: 4

Sichuan peppercorns—which come from the prickly ash tree and are unrelated to black peppercorns—bring a pleasantly tingly, mouth-numbing effect to dishes. **In this recipe, we combine them with fennel seeds and black pepper—first toasting the spices in a dry pan to enhance their flavor and fragrance before coarsely grinding them—**and use them in a simple chicken stir-fry. A little honey balances the spices and soy. Serve with steamed or stir-fried vegetables and jasmine rice.

2 tablespoons soy sauce

4 teaspoons honey

1 tablespoon finely grated fresh ginger OR 3 medium cloves garlic, finely grated OR both

2 teaspoons Sichuan peppercorns

2 teaspoons fennel seeds

Kosher salt and whole black peppercorns

2 tablespoons neutral oil

1½ pounds boneless, skinless chicken thighs, trimmed and sliced crosswise about ¼ inch thick

In a small bowl, whisk together the soy sauce, honey and ginger; set aside. In a 12-inch nonstick skillet over medium, toast the Sichuan peppercorns, fennel seeds and 2 teaspoons black peppercorns, stirring often, until fragrant, 1 to 2 minutes. Transfer to a spice grinder or mortar and let cool; reserve the pan. Add ¼ teaspoon salt to the spices, then grind or crush with the pestle until coarsely ground; set aside.

In the same skillet over medium-high, heat the oil until barely smoking. Add the chicken, and cook, stirring often, until well browned and no longer pink when cut into, 7 to 9 minutes. Add the soy sauce mixture and spices; cook, scraping up any browned bits, until the sauce thickens and coats the chicken, 2 to 3 minutes.

Coconut Curry Beef

Start to finish: 30 minutes
Servings: 4

For an easy, dry-style curry inspired by those of southern India, we bloom whole spices in oil, then toss in a ready-made spice blend. Fresh ginger adds warm, punchy heat, while scallions contribute bright allium notes. To finish, thinly sliced beef is cooked quickly in the fragrant, flavor-packed oil and combined with toasty wide-flaked coconut. Serve over a bowl of steamed basmati rice and garnish as you like; we love this topped with a handful of fresh herbs and yogurt.

1 cup dried unsweetened wide-flaked coconut OR ¾ cup unsweetened shredded coconut

3 tablespoons neutral oil

1 tablespoon coriander seeds OR cumin seeds OR mustard seeds OR a combination

2 tablespoons minced fresh ginger

1 bunch scallions, thinly sliced, whites and greens reserved separately

2 teaspoons garam masala OR curry powder

1 pound beef sirloin tips OR tri-tip, cut with the grain into 2- to 3-inch pieces, then thinly sliced against the grain

Kosher salt and ground black pepper

In a 12-inch skillet over medium, toast the coconut, stirring occasionally, until lightly browned and fragrant, 3 to 5 minutes. Transfer to a small bowl and set aside.

Return the skillet to medium-high and add the oil and coriander. Cook, occasionally stirring and swirling, until sizzling and fragrant, 30 to 60 seconds. Add the ginger and scallion whites; cook, stirring, until browned and fragrant, 1 to 2 minutes. Add the garam masala and cook, stirring, until fragrant, about 20 seconds. Add the beef; cook, stirring, until mostly browned but some pink still remains, 1½ to 2 minutes.

Add half of the coconut, 1 teaspoon salt, ½ teaspoon pepper and ⅓ cup water, stirring to scrape up any browned bits. Cook until the liquid has evaporated and the beef is fully browned and tender, 2 to 4 minutes. Off heat, stir in the scallion greens, then taste and season with salt and pepper. Serve sprinkled with the remaining coconut.

Optional garnish: Minced fresh chilies OR chopped cilantro OR plain whole-milk yogurt OR lime wedges OR a combination

Stir-Fried Peppers and Eggplant with Black Bean Sauce

Start to finish: 30 minutes
Servings: 4 to 6

This salty-sweet stir-fry calls on one of our favorite powerhouse ingredients: black bean–garlic sauce. Made with salted fermented black beans, jarred Chinese black-bean garlic sauce is deeply savory and packed with umami. Look for it in the international aisle. We pair it with hoisin and Shaoxing wine (or dry sherry) to yield a flavor-rich blend, perfect for coating silky eggplant and tender-crisp bell peppers. **We cook the eggplant and peppers in batches to avoid crowding the pan, which would cause the vegetables to steam rather than sear, and develop flavorful browning.** Serve this as a side to any grilled, roasted or seared meat, poultry or fish, or over rice as a light vegetarian main.

¼ cup Shaoxing wine OR dry sherry

3 tablespoons hoisin sauce

2 tablespoons black bean–garlic sauce (see headnote)

4 tablespoons neutral oil, divided

1½ pounds Japanese OR Chinese eggplant, trimmed, halved lengthwise and cut crosswise into 3-inch pieces

1 yellow OR orange OR red bell pepper, stemmed, seeded and sliced into ½-inch strips

3 tablespoons finely grated fresh ginger

In a medium bowl, stir the Shaoxing wine, hoisin and bean sauce; set aside. In a 12-inch nonstick skillet over medium, heat 2 tablespoons oil until shimmering. Add half of the eggplant and cook, turning occasionally, until lightly browned and tender, 4 to 6 minutes; transfer to a large plate. Using the remaining 2 tablespoons oil, cook the remaining eggplant in the same way; transfer to the plate with the first batch and set aside.

To the skillet still over medium, add the bell pepper and cook, stirring occasionally, until softened and blistered in spots, about 3 minutes; transfer to the plate with the eggplant. Add the ginger and sauce mixture; cook, stirring, until fragrant and bubbling, about 30 seconds. Return the eggplant and pepper to the skillet, then cook, stirring occasionally, until heated through and lightly sauced, 2 to 3 minutes.

Optional garnish: Red pepper flakes OR thinly sliced fresh chilies OR sliced scallions OR chopped fresh cilantro OR a combination

Stir-Fried Hoisin Pork and Broccoli

Start to finish: 50 minutes (30 minutes active)
Servings: 4

In this savory-sweet stir-fry, lightly charred broccoli contrasts tender, succulent meat. The pork tenderloin is thinly sliced before cooking, creating pieces with lots of surface area. **We freeze the tenderloin, uncovered, until firm. This makes it easier to cut into thin slices.** After slicing, the pork is coated with a cornstarch slurry so that when cooked, it browns well and develops flavor while the sauce thickens. Serve with steamed rice.

1¼-pound pork tenderloin, trimmed of silver skin

3½ tablespoons soy sauce, divided

1 tablespoon cornstarch

Kosher salt and ground white OR black pepper

¼ cup hoisin sauce

4 tablespoons neutral oil, divided

1 pound broccoli, stems peeled and thinly sliced, florets cut into 1- to 1½-inch pieces

1 tablespoon minced fresh ginger OR 3 medium garlic cloves, minced OR both

Set the pork on a large plate and freeze until the meat is firm and partially frozen, 20 to 30 minutes. Meanwhile, in a medium bowl, whisk together 2 tablespoons soy sauce, the cornstarch and ½ teaspoon pepper.

Using a chef's knife, cut the partially frozen pork crosswise into slices about ⅛ inch thick. Add the pork to the soy-cornstarch mixture and stir to coat; let stand at room temperature for 15 minutes. Meanwhile, in a small bowl, whisk together the hoisin, the remaining 1½ tablespoons soy sauce, ½ teaspoon pepper and ⅓ cup water; set aside.

In a 12-inch skillet over medium-high, heat 2 tablespoons oil until barely smoking. Add the broccoli and cook, stirring occasionally, until charred in spots and tender-crisp, 4 to 6 minutes. Transfer to a large plate; set aside.

In the same skillet over high, heat the remaining 2 tablespoons oil until barely smoking. Add the pork in an even layer and cook without stirring until golden brown on the bottom and the pieces release easily from the skillet, about 2 minutes. Add the ginger and, using a metal spoon or spatula, stir and scrape up the pork and cook until the ginger is aromatic, about 30 seconds. Add the broccoli and hoisin mixture. Cook, stirring, until the sauce is syrupy and the pork is tender, about 3 minutes. Off heat, taste and season with salt and pepper.

Optional garnish: Toasted sesame seeds OR sesame oil OR sliced scallions OR a combination

Chicken Yakisoba

Start to finish: 30 minutes
Servings: 4

Yakisoba, a stir-fry of ramen noodles, vegetables and salty-sweet seasonings, is a Japanese mainstay. It's such a popular dish that grocery stores sell yakisoba kits that include fresh noodles and seasoning packets, as well as instant versions requiring only boiling water and a couple minutes to prepare. This is an easy homemade version that uses dried non-instant ramen and adds chicken and cabbage to make a complete meal. **A trio of pantry staples—soy sauce, ketchup and Worcestershire sauce—provide big, bold flavor that the noodles absorb during stir-frying.**

8 ounces dried non-instant ramen noodles

¼ cup soy sauce

3 tablespoons ketchup

2 tablespooons Worcestershire sauce

2 tablespoons neutral oil, divided

1 pound boneless, skinless chicken thighs, cut into ¾-inch chunks

Kosher salt and ground black pepper

8 ounces green cabbage, cored and thinly sliced (about 3 cups)

In a large pot, bring 3 quarts water to a boil. Add the ramen and cook, stirring occasionally, until tender. Drain in a colander and rinse under cold water, tossing, until cool, then drain again. In a medium bowl, whisk together the soy sauce, ketchup and Worcestershire sauce; set aside.

In a 12-inch nonstick skillet over medium-high, heat 1 tablespoon oil until shimmering. Add the chicken and sprinkle with ½ teaspoon salt. Cook, stirring occasionally, until well browned, about 8 minutes; transfer to a plate.

To the now-empty skillet over medium-high, add the remaining 1 tablespoon oil and heat until shimmering. Add the cabbage and ¼ teaspoon each salt and pepper. Cook, stirring occasionally, until lightly browned, about 5 minutes. Add the noodles, soy mixture and chicken with accumulated juices. Cook, tossing, until the noodles absorb the seasonings and the pan is dry, about 2 minutes. Off heat, taste and season with salt and pepper.

Optional garnish: Pickled ginger OR crumbled nori snacks OR furikake OR a combination

Stir-Fried Sriracha Eggplant with Basil

Start to finish: 30 minutes
Servings: 4 to 6

In this Thai-inspired stir-fry, **we first brown eggplants and onion in hot oil to caramelize the exteriors, then the pan is covered, trapping moisture inside to steam the eggplants until perfectly tender.** Two powerhouse ingredients—Sriracha and fish sauce—bring on the umami, balanced by a touch of brown sugar. Fresh basil adds pops of color and bright herbal flavor. Serve over steamed rice if you like. Be sure to use Japanese or Chinese eggplants, as the globe variety won't work well in this recipe.

2 tablespoons Sriracha

2 tablespoons fish sauce

2 teaspoons packed light OR dark brown sugar

¼ cup neutral oil

1½ pounds medium Japanese OR Chinese eggplants, trimmed, halved lengthwise and cut crosswise into 2-inch pieces

1 medium yellow onion, halved and cut into 1-inch wedges, layers separated

2 cups lightly packed fresh Thai OR Italian basil, torn if large

In a small bowl, whisk together the Sriracha, fish sauce and sugar; set aside. In a 12-inch nonstick skillet over medium-high, heat the oil until shimmering. Add the eggplants and cook, stirring once halfway through, until browned on both sides, about 2 minutes. Stir in the onion, then cook without stirring until it begins to soften, about 2 minutes. Cover the pan, reduce to medium and cook until the eggplants are tender, about 3 minutes.

Uncover and cook, stirring once, until some of the moisture released by the eggplants has evaporated, about 2 minutes. Add the Sriracha mixture, then stir until the vegetables are coated, about 30 seconds. Off heat, stir in the basil.

Optional garnish: Lime wedges OR chopped roasted peanuts OR both

Sweet-and-Sour Cauliflower

Start to finish: 30 minutes
Servings: 4

This flavor-packed stir-fry utilizes our go-to sear and steam technique, yielding perfectly tender-crisp and caramelized cauliflower florets. They're coated in a salty-sweet mixture of tangy rice vinegar, umami-rich hoisin sauce and fresh ginger, garlic and chili, contributing bright, zesty notes throughout. Serve as a side dish or as a vegetarian main with steamed rice.

¼ cup neutral oil

2½-pound head cauliflower, trimmed, cored and cut into 1-inch florets

Kosher salt

2 medium garlic cloves, minced

1 tablespoon minced fresh ginger

1 Fresno OR jalapeño chili, stemmed, seeded and thinly sliced

¼ cup unseasoned rice vinegar

¼ cup hoisin sauce

In a 12-inch skillet over medium-high, heat the oil until barely smoking. Add the cauliflower and stir, then distribute evenly. Cook without stirring until beginning to brown on the bottom, 3 to 5 minutes. Stir, add ¼ cup water and ¼ teaspoon salt, then immediately cover. Cook until just tender and the liquid has evaporated, about 3 minutes, stirring once about halfway through. Add the garlic, ginger and chili; cook, uncovered and stirring occasionally, until fragrant, about 2 minutes.

Increase to medium-high, then add the vinegar, hoisin and ¼ teaspoon salt. Cook, stirring occasionally, until the sauce thickens and clings to the cauliflower, 1 to 2 minutes.

Optional garnish: Thinly sliced scallions OR chopped roasted peanuts OR toasted sesame seeds OR a combination

Stir-Fried Kimchi with Bacon

Start to finish: 25 minutes
Servings: 4

This spicy-sweet stir-fry takes inspiration from a Korean side called kimchi bokkeum. Though typically made with kimchi and pork belly, we found the fatty, smoky qualities of bacon to be an ideal match for brightly acidic pickled cabbage. **Gochujang, the Korean fermented chili paste, is a one-stroke flavor solution, adding spicy, sweet and umami-rich notes.** A pinch of sugar and splash of sesame oil round out the dish. Serve over steamed rice.

6 ounces bacon, preferably thick-cut, cut crosswise into ¼-inch pieces

3 cups well-drained napa cabbage kimchi, roughly chopped

2 tablespoons gochujang

1 bunch scallions, white parts thinly sliced, green parts cut into 1-inch pieces

1 teaspoon white sugar

1 tablespoon toasted sesame oil, plus more to serve (if desired)

In a 12-inch nonstick skillet over medium, cook the bacon, stirring, until well browned, 10 to 12 minutes. Using a slotted spoon, transfer to a paper towel-lined plate; set aside. Pour off and discard all but 2 tablespoons of fat from the skillet.

Set the skillet over medium-high and heat the fat until shimmering. Add the kimchi, gochujang, scallion whites and sugar; stir. Cook, undisturbed, until the kimchi is charred in spots and barely tender, 4 to 5 minutes. Stir in the bacon and half the scallion greens. Off heat, stir in the sesame oil. Serve sprinkled with remaining scallion greens and, if desired, drizzled with additional sesame oil.

Optional garnish: Toasted sesame seeds

Five-Spice Carrot and Ginger Stir-Fry

Start to finish: 30 minutes
Servings: 4

Fresh ginger usually is a supporting player, bringing spicy-sweetness to a dish. But here **we give ginger a starring role. We treat it almost like a vegetable, upping the quantity and cooking it with carrots to mellow its bite.** Chinese five-spice powder lends warmth and complexity to this easy stir-fry. The recipe uses a two-step cooking process: First the carrots and ginger are seared in the skillet, then they are gently steamed in honey-infused water, which reduces to a light glaze. Be sure to slice the carrots on the diagonal to maximize the surface area for browning.

2-inch piece fresh ginger, peeled

2 tablespoons neutral oil

1½ pounds medium carrots, peeled and thinly sliced on the diagonal

Kosher salt and ground black pepper

1 teaspoon Chinese five-spice powder

2 tablespoons honey

4 scallions, thinly sliced OR ½ cup lightly packed fresh cilantro, roughly chopped

Thinly slice the ginger on the diagonal. Stack several slices and cut lengthwise into matchsticks. Repeat with the remaining slices.

In a 12-inch nonstick skillet over high, heat the oil until barely smoking. Add the carrots, ginger and ½ teaspoon salt; cook, stirring only once or twice, until the carrots are beginning to char at the edges, 3 to 5 minutes. Reduce to medium-high, then add the five-spice powder and 1 teaspoon each salt and pepper. Cook, stirring, until fragrant, about 1 minute.

Add the honey and ½ cup water; cook, stirring and scraping up any browned bits, until the carrots are tender-crisp and glazed, 4 to 5 minutes. Off heat, taste and season with salt and pepper. Transfer to a serving dish and sprinkle with the scallions.

FLAVOR IN A SLURRY

Stir-frying is an undeniably quick way to get supper on the table. But the result often is disappointingly flavorless meat in a gloopy, slapped-on sauce. We've found a quick and easy technique to up the flavor and build a perfectly thickened sauce: a seasoned slurry.

We coat sliced pork or chicken or chunks of fish fillets in corn-starch mixed with a little water plus a high-flavor ingredient, such as soy sauce, chili-garlic sauce or miso. The coating browns when it hits the hot oil, developing depth of flavor that stays on the meat. Next, vegetables go in for a brief stir-fry, and finally meat and vegetables are reunited and finished with a simple sauce that echoes or comple-ments the seasonings in the slurry.

The sauce thickens slightly thanks to the cornstarch, forming a savory-sweet glaze which clings well to the coating. Made with a multi-tasking seasoned slurry, a stir-fry tastes much more than the sum of its parts.

RECIPES FROM TOP

| Sweet and Spicy Stir-Fried Fish with Snow Peas | Stir-Fried Orange-Miso Chicken | Honey and Soy-Glazed Stir-Fried Pork |

Stir-Fried Orange-Miso Chicken

Start to finish: 30 minutes
Servings: 4

This recipe adds rich umami flavor to thinly sliced chicken thanks to a cornstarch slurry spiked with white miso. To finish the stir-fry, we add more miso plus fresh ginger, orange zest and juice; this mixture thickens lightly thanks to the starch and forms a savory-sweet glaze for the chicken and red onion. Steamed rice is the perfect accompaniment. Be sure to use white miso for this recipe, as it has a milder, more delicate taste than yellow or red miso.

3 tablespoons white miso, divided

1 tablespoon cornstarch

Kosher salt and ground black pepper

1½ pounds boneless, skinless chicken breasts, halved lengthwise and sliced crosswise about ¼ inch thick

1 tablespoon grated orange zest, plus ⅓ cup orange juice

1 tablespoon finely grated fresh ginger

3 tablespoons neutral oil, divided

1 large red onion, halved and sliced ½ inch thick

In a medium bowl, whisk together 1 tablespoon miso, the cornstarch, ¼ teaspoon salt, 1 teaspoon pepper and 2 tablespoons water until smooth. Add the chicken and toss to coat; set aside.

In a small bowl, whisk together the remaining 2 tablespoons miso, the orange zest and juice, ginger and ½ teaspoon pepper; set aside.

In a 12-inch nonstick skillet over medium-high, heat 1 tablespoon oil until barely smoking, swirling to coat. Add half of the chicken mixture; cook, stirring often and scraping up any browned bits, until the chicken is well browned, 2 to 3 minutes. Transfer to another medium bowl. Repeat with 1 tablespoon of the remaining oil and the remaining chicken mixture, adding any marinade in the bowl; transfer to the bowl with the first batch.

In the same skillet over medium-high, add the remaining 1 tablespoon oil and the onion. Cook, stirring and scraping up any browned bits, until the onion is just beginning to brown, 1 to 2 minutes. Stir in the chicken and any accumulated juices, then add the miso-orange mixture. Cook, stirring and scraping, until the sauce thickens slightly and coats the chicken and onion, 2 to 3 minutes. Off heat, taste and season with salt and pepper.

Optional garnish: Chopped fresh basil OR cilantro

Honey and Soy-Glazed Stir-Fried Pork

Start to finish: 30 minutes
Servings: 4

Tossed with a cornstarch slurry that also includes soy sauce, thin slices of pork tenderloin absorb tons of salty-savory flavor. For contrasting texture, we pair the juicy meat with tender-crisp bell pepper strips. The dish is finished with a sauce made from more soy sauce and honey plus a splash of rice vinegar, creating a perfect balance of salty, sweet and tangy. If you like, garnish with sesame seeds, and accompany with steamed rice.

3 tablespoons soy sauce, divided

1 tablespoon cornstarch

Kosher salt and ground black pepper

1¼- to 1½-pound pork tenderloin, trimmed of silver skin and sliced crosswise about ¼ inch thick

1½ tablespoons honey

3 tablespoons neutral oil, divided

1 medium red bell pepper, stemmed, seeded and sliced into ¼-inch strips

1 tablespoon unseasoned rice vinegar

In a medium bowl, whisk together 1 tablespoon soy sauce, the cornstarch, ¼ teaspoon salt, 1 teaspoon pepper and 2 tablespoons water until smooth. Add the pork and toss to coat; set aside. In a small bowl,

whisk together the remaining 2 tablespoons soy sauce, the honey and ½ teaspoon pepper; set aside.

In a 12-inch nonstick skillet over medium-high, heat 1 tablespoon oil until barely smoking, swirling to coat. Add half of the pork mixture; cook, stirring often and scraping up any browned bits, until well browned, 2 to 3 minutes. Transfer to another medium bowl. Repeat with 1 tablespoon of the remaining oil and the remaining pork mixture, adding any marinade in the bowl; transfer to the bowl with the first batch.

In the same skillet over medium-high, add the remaining 1 tablespoon oil and bell pepper. Cook, stirring and scraping up any browned bits, until tender-crisp, 1 to 2 minutes. Stir in the pork and any accumulated juices, then add the soy-honey mixture. Cook, stirring and scraping, until the sauce thickens slightly and coats the pork and bell pepper, 2 to 3 minutes.

Off heat, stir in the vinegar, then taste and season with salt and pepper.

Optional garnish: Toasted sesame seeds OR sliced scallions OR both

Sweet and Spicy Stir-Fried Fish with Snow Peas

Start to finish: 30 minutes
Servings: 4

This dish pops with vibrant color and spicy, garlicky notes thanks to a powerhouse pantry ingredient. **We whisk chili-garlic sauce into a cornstarch slurry and briefly marinate the fish so it soaks up all the big flavors. Near the end of cooking, we stir in more chili-garlic sauce plus a touch of honey to balance the heat; the cornstarch adds body to the sauce and allows it to cling to the fish.** Choose a thick white fish that will hold up well when cooked with crisp snow peas. Fresh or frozen mahi mahi, cod or snapper are all good options. Serve on a bed of sliced cabbage, watercress or steamed rice.

4½ tablespoons chili-garlic sauce OR Sriracha, divided

1½ tablespoons cornstarch

Kosher salt and ground black pepper

1½ pounds skinless mahi mahi OR cod OR snapper fillets (1 to 1½ inches thick), patted dry and cut into 2-inch chunks

1½ tablespoons honey

2 tablespoons neutral oil, divided

1 bunch scallions, thinly sliced, white and green parts reserved separately

8 ounces snow peas, trimmed

In a medium bowl, whisk together 1½ tablespoons chili-garlic sauce, the cornstarch, ¼ teaspoon salt, ½ teaspoon pepper and 1 tablespoon water until smooth. Add the fish and toss to coat; set aside. In a small bowl, whisk together the remaining 3 tablespoons chili-garlic sauce, the honey and ½ teaspoon pepper; set aside.

In a 12-inch nonstick skillet over medium-high, heat 1 tablespoon oil until barely smoking, swirling to coat. Add the fish mixture in a single layer along with any marinade in the bowl; cook until the fish is well browned on the bottoms, 2 to 3 minutes. Using a wide spatula, flip the fish and cook until browned on the second sides and almost cooked through at the center, another 2 to 3 minutes; transfer to a plate.

To the skillet over medium-high, add the remaining 1 tablespoon oil and scallion whites. Cook, stirring and scraping up any browned bits, until the scallions begin to soften, 1 to 2 minutes. Stir in the snow peas. Add the fish and any accumulated juices, then pour in the chili garlic-honey mixture. Cook, flipping the fish occasionally, until the sauce thickens slightly, the fish flakes easily and the peas are tender-crisp, 2 to 3 minutes. Off heat, taste and season with salt and pepper. Serve sprinkled with the scallion greens.

Optional garnish: Pickled jalapeños OR lime wedges

Chili-Garlic Glazed Tofu

Start to finish: 30 minutes
Servings: 4 to 6

This meat-free but flavor-packed skillet dish calls on a few Asian pantry staples. **We coat cubes of extra-firm or firm tofu with cornstarch, then brown them in a skillet. The cornstarch creates a crust that crisps in hot oil, then a salty-sweet, umami-rich mix of soy sauce, chili-garlic sauce and sugar goes into the pan and cooks down to a glaze that clings deliciously to the tofu.** This is great made with ginger or garlic—and is even better with both. Serve with steamed rice.

¼ cup soy sauce

1 to 2 tablespoons chili-garlic sauce

3½ teaspoons white sugar

¼ cup cornstarch

Kosher salt and ground black pepper

Two 14-ounce containers extra-firm OR firm tofu, drained, cut into ¾-inch cubes and patted dry

4 tablespoons neutral oil, divided

1 tablespoon finely grated fresh ginger OR 4 medium garlic cloves, finely grated OR both

In a small bowl, stir together the soy sauce, chili-garlic sauce and sugar; set aside. Add the cornstarch to a large bowl, then add the tofu and toss to coat, gently pressing to adhere.

In a 12-inch nonstick skillet over medium-high, heat 3 tablespoons oil until shimmering. Add the tofu, distributing it in an even layer, and cook without stirring until golden brown on the bottom, 4 to 6 minutes. Stir, redistribute the tofu in an even layer and cook without stirring until the second sides are golden brown, 4 to 6 minutes.

Push the tofu to one side. To the clearing, add the remaining 1 tablespoon oil and the ginger; cook, stirring, until fragrant, about 30 seconds. Add the soy mixture and cook, gently stirring the sauce into the tofu, until most of the sauce is absorbed, about 1 minute. Off heat, taste and season with salt and pepper.

Optional garnish: Sliced scallions OR chopped fresh cilantro OR lime wedges OR a combination

Dry-Fried Green Beans with Pork and Scallions

Start to finish: 35 minutes
Servings: 4

This is our spin on a favorite Sichuan dish that uses a technique called dry-frying. **We precook green beans in a small amount of oil to lightly char them and evaporate any moisture, which concentrates their flavor.** Then the beans are stir-fried with ground pork and garlic plus a splash of Shaoxing wine and soy sauce for sweet-salty flavor. Be sure to pat the beans thoroughly dry before cooking. To add a touch of heat, garnish with sliced fresh chili or a drizzle of chili oil.

2 tablespoons Shaoxing wine OR dry sherry

1½ tablespoons soy sauce

3 tablespoons neutral oil

12 ounces green beans, trimmed, halved on the diagonal and thoroughly dried

Kosher salt and ground black pepper

8 ounces ground pork

1 bunch scallions, white parts finely chopped, green parts cut into 1-inch pieces, reserved separately

3 medium garlic cloves, minced

In a small bowl, stir together the Shaoxing wine and soy sauce; set aside. In a 12-inch skillet over medium, heat the oil until shimmering. Add the green beans and a pinch of salt. Toss, then distribute in an even layer and cook, stirring once every few minutes, until spottily browned and beginning to shrivel, 10 to 12 minutes. Transfer to a paper towel-lined plate.

In the same skillet over medium-high, add the pork, scallion whites, garlic and ¼ teaspoon each salt and pepper. Cook, breaking up the meat, until the pork is no longer pink, about 3 minutes. Stir in the Shaoxing mixture, then cook until the liquid has reduced, about 1 minute.

Return the beans to the skillet and add the scallion greens. Cook, stirring occasionally, until heated through and coated with the sauce, 1 to 2 minutes.

Optional garnish: Sliced fresh chilies OR chili oil OR sesame seeds OR toasted sesame oil OR a combination

Lemon-Miso Stir-Fried Zucchini

Start to finish: 45 minutes (15 minutes active)
Servings: 4

From zucchini to pattypan, summer squash has a reputation for being bland and uninteresting. To combat this, **we brown summer squash quickly over high-heat, facilitating caramelization, then toss it with a light and zingy sauce.** Miso contributes salty-sweet, umami-rich notes. Paired with bright, tangy lemon, it makes for a dynamic, well-rounded mixture, transforming zucchini into a flavor-packed affair. This is a wonderful side to roasted fish or chicken, but also is delicious simply over brown rice.

2-inch piece fresh ginger, peeled

2 tablespoons lemon juice

2 tablespoons white miso

1 tablespoon mirin OR honey

1 tablespoon toasted sesame oil
OR toasted sesame seeds OR both

Kosher salt and ground black pepper

2 tablespoons neutral oil

3 medium zucchini OR summer squash
(about 1½ pounds), halved lengthwise and
sliced ½ inch thick on the diagonal

Thinly slice the ginger on the diagonal. Stack several slices and cut lengthwise into matchsticks. Repeat with the remaining slices; set aside. Whisk together the lemon juice, miso, mirin, sesame oil, ¼ cup water and ½ teaspoon pepper; set aside.

In a 12-inch skillet over medium-high, heat the oil until shimmering. Add the zucchini and cook, stirring occasionally, until well browned in spots, about 4 minutes. Add the ginger and cook, stirring, until lightly browned all over, 1 to 2 minutes. Add the lemon-miso mixture and cook, stirring occasionally, until the zucchini has absorbed the sauce and is tender-crisp, 2 to 3 minutes. Off heat, taste and season with salt and pepper.

Optional garnish: Chili oil OR chopped fresh mint OR chopped fresh basil OR a combination

Stir-Fried Tofu and Mushrooms with Lemon Grass

Start to finish: 35
Servings: 4

In this Southeast Asian-inspired stir-fry, we toss mild tofu with two powerhouse ingredients, fish sauce and Sriracha, then brown the cubes in hot oil. When the tofu comes out of the pan, we stir-fry meaty mushrooms and add citrusy lemon grass and savory scallions, building layers of contrasting flavors, and finish by tossing everything together. **Be sure to pat the tofu dry after cubing it. Wicking away excess moisture means the tofu will better absorb seasonings and brown better.** Serve the stir-fry with steamed jasmine rice.

3 tablespoons fish sauce

3 teaspoons Sriracha OR
chili-garlic sauce, divided

Kosher salt and ground white pepper
OR black pepper

14-ounce container extra-firm
OR firm tofu, drained, cut into ¾-inch cubes
and patted dry

4 tablespoons neutral oil, divided

12 ounces cremini mushrooms, thinly sliced
OR shiitake mushrooms (stemmed), thinly sliced
OR a combination

2 stalks fresh lemon grass, trimmed to
the bottom 6 inches, dry outer layers
discarded, minced

1 bunch scallions, thinly sliced, whites
and greens reserved separately

In a medium bowl, stir together the fish sauce, 1 teaspoon Sriracha and ½ teaspoon pepper. Add the tofu and toss to coat. In a 12-inch nonstick skillet over medium-high, heat 2 tablespoons oil until barely smoking. Add the tofu, distributing it in an even layer. Cook, stirring, until golden brown on most sides, 3 to 4 minutes. Transfer to a paper towel-lined plate; set aside.

In the same skillet over medium-high, heat the remaining 2 tablespoons oil until barely smoking. Add the mushrooms and cook, stirring occasionally, until tender and lightly browned, about 3 minutes. Add the lemon grass, scallion whites and the remaining 2 teaspoons Sriracha; cook, stirring, until fragrant, about 1 minute. Add the tofu and cook, stirring occasionally, until heated through, about 2 minutes.

Off heat, stir in half of the reserved scallion greens. Taste and season with salt and pepper. Serve sprinkled with the remaining scallion greens.

Optional garnish: Lime wedges OR chopped roasted peanuts OR chopped fresh cilantro OR a combination

Stir-Fried Black Pepper Beef

Start to finish: 20 minutes
Servings: 4

This stir-fry is an homage to pepper steak, the Chinese-American takeout staple. A combination of high-impact ingredients like savory-sweet oyster sauce, spicy black peppercorns and umami-rich soy sauce yields a punchy yet well-rounded dish. Though beef is typical, thinly sliced chicken thighs also work. For maximum heat, use the full 2 tablespoons peppercorns and crush them fresh. A mortar and pestle are best, but if you don't have one, you also can crush them under a heavy skillet, rocking the pan back and forth over the peppercorns so they crack rather than scatter. **Cooking the crushed peppercorns for a couple minutes with the onion and bell pepper blooms their fragrance and flavors.**

3 tablespoons neutral oil, divided

1 medium red OR yellow onion, halved and sliced ½ inch thick

1 medium red bell pepper, stemmed, seeded and cut into ½-inch strips OR 3 medium celery stalks, thinly sliced on the diagonal

1½ to 2 tablespoons black peppercorns, coarsely cracked (see headnote)

1 pound flank steak, cut with the grain into 2- to 3-inch pieces, then thinly sliced against the grain OR 1 pound boneless, skinless chicken thighs, trimmed and cut into thin strips

2 tablespoons oyster sauce

2 tablespoons soy sauce

In a 12-inch skillet over high, heat 2 tablespoons oil until barely smoking. Add the onion and bell pepper; cook, stirring often, until the onion begins to wilt, about 2 minutes. Add the peppercorns and cook, stirring, until the mixture is fragrant and the onion begins to brown at the edges, 1 to 2 minutes. Transfer to a plate and set aside.

In the same skillet over high, heat the remaining 1 tablespoon oil until barely smoking. Add the beef in an even layer and cook, without stirring, until well browned on the bottom and the pieces release easily from the skillet, 2 to 3 minutes. Stir in the vegetable-peppercorn mixture. Add the oyster and soy sauces; cook, stirring, until the beef is tender and the sauce clings to the meat, 1½ to 3 minutes.

Optional garnish: Chopped cilantro OR lime wedges OR a combination

High Heat

Broiled Ginger and Yogurt Shrimp

Start to finish: 50 minutes
Servings: 4

A marinade of thick, creamy Greek yogurt seasoned with fresh ginger, paprika, lemon zest and honey helps flavorings adhere to shrimp and aids in caramelization. The prep for this dish is minimal, and cooking happens in a matter of minutes, so the shrimp can be on the table in under an hour. Mango chutney or green chutney (also called cilantro chutney) are excellent condiments to offer on the side. Serve with basmati rice or warm naan, or add the shrimp to a grain-based or leafy salad.

½ cup plain, whole-milk Greek yogurt

1 tablespoon neutral oil

1 tablespoon finely grated fresh ginger

1 teaspoon hot paprika OR ¾ teaspoon sweet paprika plus ¼ teaspoon cayenne pepper

1 teaspoon grated lemon zest, plus lemon wedges to serve

1 teaspoon honey

Kosher salt and ground black pepper

1½ pounds extra-large (21/25 per pound) shrimp, peeled and deveined

In a medium bowl, whisk together the yogurt, oil, ginger, paprika, lemon zest, honey and ½ teaspoon each salt and pepper. Add the shrimp, toss to coat; let stand at room temperature for about 30 minutes.

Heat the oven to broil with a rack about 4 inches from the element. Set a wire rack in a broiler-safe rimmed baking sheet. Distribute the shrimp in an even layer on the rack. Broil until the shrimp are just opaque and lightly charred, 4 to 5 minutes.

Optional garnish: Chopped fresh cilantro

Garlic-Ginger Beef Skewers

Start to finish: 30 minutes
Servings: 4

We add flavor at the start and end of cooking to give these curried beef skewers extra kick. If you like, trim the ends off 2 medium shallots, then peel and halve them lengthwise; before cooking, cap each beef skewer with a shallot. Broiling will char the shallots' outer layers and the interiors will be sweet and tender, a nice complement to the beef. Serve with fragrant basmati or jasmine rice.

¼ cup neutral oil

2 tablespoons fish sauce

1½ tablespoons finely grated fresh ginger

8 medium garlic cloves, finely grated

1½ teaspoons curry powder

Grated zest of 1 lime, plus lime wedges to serve

Ground black pepper

1½ pounds beef flat iron steak OR boneless short ribs, trimmed and sliced against the grain into ½-inch-thick strips

Heat the broiler with a rack about 4 inches from the element. Stir together the oil, fish sauce, ginger, garlic, curry powder, lime zest and a pinch of pepper. In a medium bowl, toss the steak with half the seasoning paste. Scrunch the meat onto metal skewers, then arrange on a rimmed baking sheet. Broil until charred on both sides, 6 to 10 minutes, flipping once. Brush the skewers with the remaining seasoning paste, then let stand for 10 minutes. Serve with lime wedges.

Optional garnish: Fried shallots OR hot sauce OR chopped roasted peanuts OR Fresno or jalapeño chilies, stemmed and chopped

Baharat Mushrooms with Tahini-Lemon Sauce

Start to finish: 50 minutes (25 minutes active)
Servings: 4

Jerusalem mixed grill is a popular Israeli street food. It includes an assortment of meats griddled with onions and spices. It inspired this recipe that roasts mushrooms until meaty and well browned—and that bears a surprising resemblance to the real deal. Baharat is a Middle Eastern blend of earthy, warm spices. If not available, replace with 1¼ teaspoons each ground coriander and ground cumin. **Don't use a bowl to toss the mushrooms, oil and seasonings. Instead, toss the ingredients directly on the baking sheet; this leaves the pan slicked with oil for better caramelization.** Serve as a side to chicken or beef, or make it into a vegetarian main with rice pilaf alongside.

¼ cup plus 2 tablespoons olive oil

2½ teaspoons baharat (see headnote), divided

Kosher salt and ground black pepper

1½ pounds cremini OR button mushrooms OR a combination, trimmed, quartered if large, halved if medium or small

1 medium red onion, halved and sliced about ¼ inch thick

¼ cup tahini

3 tablespoons lemon juice, plus lemon wedges, to serve

1 tablespoon finely chopped fresh chives OR fresh flat-leaf parsley

Heat the oven to 450°F with a rack in the middle position. On a rimmed baking sheet, stir together the oil, 2 teaspoons baharat, ½ teaspoon salt and ¼ teaspoon pepper. Add the mushrooms and onion; toss to coat, then distribute in an even layer. Roast until the mushrooms are tender and well browned, about 30 minutes, stirring once about halfway through.

Meanwhile, in a small bowl, whisk together the tahini, lemon juice, 2 tablespoons hot water, ¼ teaspoon salt and the remaining ½ teaspoon baharat, adding additional hot water 1 teaspoon at a time as needed to thin to the desired consistency.

Transfer the mushrooms to a serving dish. Taste and season with salt and pepper. Spoon on the tahini sauce or serve on the side. Sprinkle the mushrooms with the chives and serve with lemon wedges.

Grilled Harissa-Spiced Chicken

Start to finish: 45 minutes (25 minutes active),
plus marinating
Servings: 4

Spicy, smoky and tangy, harissa is a fragrant chili
paste ubiquitous in North African cuisine. We temper
its zingy heat by combining it with cool yogurt and
mint, as well as bright lemon juice and zest, to make
both a marinade and serving sauce for grilled chicken.
**We make yogurt work two ways; it tenderizes chicken
and helps seasonings stick to the skin.** If your grill
pan is on the smaller side, simply cook the chicken in
batches. Serve with warmed flatbread or couscous,
or slice the chicken for adding to salads or tucking
into sandwiches.

8 tablespoons (½ cup) plain
whole-milk yogurt, divided

2 tablespoons harissa

2 tablespoons extra-virgin olive oil

2 tablespoons finely chopped fresh mint,
plus more to serve

1 medium garlic clove, finely grated

1 teaspoon grated lemon zest, plus 1 teaspoon
lemon juice, plus wedges to serve

Kosher salt and ground black pepper

1½ pounds boneless, skinless chicken breasts,
trimmed and pounded to ½-inch thickness OR
boneless, skinless chicken thighs, trimmed

In a large bowl, whisk together 2 tablespoons yogurt,
the harissa, oil, mint, garlic, lemon zest and juice,
1½ teaspoons salt and ½ teaspoon pepper. Measure
1 tablespoon of the mixture into a small bowl, then
stir in the remaining 6 tablespoons yogurt; cover and
refrigerate until ready to serve. Add the chicken to the
large bowl with the remaining yogurt mixture and
turn to coat. Let stand at room temperature for about
30 minutes.

Heat a 12-inch grill pan over medium-high until barely
smoking. Meanwhile, scrape the marinade off the
chicken and pat dry with paper towels. Add the chicken
to the pan and cook until well browned on the bottom,
4 to 6 minutes. Flip and cook until the second sides are
well browned and the thickest part reaches 160°F for
breasts or 175°F for thighs, another 4 to 6 minutes.
Transfer the chicken to a platter. Sprinkle with
additional mint and serve with the yogurt sauce.

Chipotle and Cumin Marinated Flank Steak

Start to finish: 25 minutes, plus marinating
Servings: 4

This recipe takes inspiration from Peruvian anticuchos, a favorite street food of skewered grilled meat. Our version combines flank steak (beef sirloin tips work well, too) and chipotle chilies in adobo for smoky heat. To streamline prep, we skip the skewers, cook the beef under the broiler and slice it for serving. Vinegar, dried oregano and cumin add tang and herbal notes. **A no-knife-needed seasoning mix does double duty: a portion is used to marinate the meat and the rest is served as a sauce.**

½ cup red wine vinegar

2 chipotle chilies in adobo sauce, plus 1 tablespoon adobo sauce

2 tablespoons soy sauce

2 tablespoons neutral oil

2 tablespoons dried oregano

2 teaspoons ground cumin

Kosher salt and ground black pepper

1½ pounds flank steak OR beef sirloin tips

In a blender, combine the vinegar, chipotles and adobo sauce, soy sauce, oil, oregano, cumin and ½ teaspoon each salt and pepper. Blend on high until smooth, about 1 minute. Place the steak in a wide, shallow container; add ¼ cup of the vinegar-soy mixture, turning to coat; reserve the remaining mixture. Let the beef stand at room temperature for 30 minutes, turning once or twice.

Heat the broiler with a rack about 4 inches from the element. Set a wire rack in a broiler-safe rimmed baking sheet and mist it with cooking spray. Remove the steak from the marinade, scraping off the excess, and place on the rack. Broil until lightly charred on both sides and the center reaches 125°F for medium rare, 8 to 10 minutes, flipping once halfway through.

Transfer the steak to a cutting board, tent with foil and let rest for about 5 minutes. Thinly slice against the grain, transfer to a platter and drizzle with the accumulated juices. Serve with the reserved vinegar-soy mixture.

Optional garnish: Chopped fresh cilantro OR thinly sliced red onion OR lime wedges OR a combination

NO-COOK SAUCES

The right sauce paired with a quick-cooked protein—think sizzled steak or seared salmon fillet—is a winning combination. Trouble is, we don't always have the time or the energy for the standing, seasoning and stirring classic sauces can require.

Enter the no-cook sauce. We blitz a handful of ingredients in the blender, or simply stir them in a bowl, and in just a few minutes we're done. The secret is using high-impact ingredients that let us take a few shortcuts without shorting ourselves on flavor.

We blend savory miso and spicy gochujang for a sauce inspired by Korean ssamjang that's great with grilled meats. Walnuts add creaminess and flavor to a parsley sauce that's terrific on steak, fish or even roasted vegetables. And smoked paprika and sherry vinegar team up for our easy take on Catalan romesco, which is good spooned over grilled meats and vegetables or tucked into a grilled cheese sandwich.

RECIPES FROM TOP

| Smoky Roasted Pepper Sauce with Almonds and Sherry Vinegar | Walnut, Parsley and Caper Sauce | Miso-Gochujang Umami Sauce |

Walnut, Parsley and Caper Sauce

Start to finish: 15 minutes
Makes 1 cup

Walnuts give this easy, no-cook sauce an amazing richness and depth of flavor, along with a creamy consistency. Herbs add color and freshness, while capers and lemon zest and juice balance with tangy brightness. **Though the ingredients are blitzed in a food processor, roughly chopping them first ensures they readily break down.** Spoon this pesto-like sauce onto seared or grilled steak or fish or even on roasted vegetables. It also makes a great spread for crostini or sandwiches.

½ cup lightly packed fresh flat-leaf parsley, roughly chopped

½ cup walnuts, roughly chopped

2 tablespoons fresh oregano, roughly chopped

2 tablespoons drained capers, roughly chopped

1 medium garlic clove, smashed and peeled

¼ cup extra-virgin olive oil

1 teaspoon grated lemon zest, plus 2 tablespoons lemon juice

Kosher salt and ground black pepper

In a food processor, combine the parsley, walnuts, oregano, capers and garlic. Process until finely ground, about 10 seconds. Add the oil, lemon zest and juice, 3 tablespoons water and ¼ teaspoon each salt and pepper; pulse until well combined, 8 to 10 pulses, scraping the bowl as needed. Taste and season with salt and pepper. Use immediately or refrigerate in an airtight container for up to 3 days.

Miso-Gochujang Umami Sauce

Start to finish: 10 minutes
Makes ¾ cup

Korean ssamjang, a salty, spicy condiment used with foods that often are wrapped in lettuce for eating, inspired this umami-packed no-cook sauce. **It gets its rich, spicy-sweet flavor from a combination of white miso and gochujang—two high-impact ingredients we always keep on hand**—plus toasted sesame oil. Scallions and garlic add allium pungency. Serve with grilled or roasted meat, poultry or seafood, or even on runny-yolked fried eggs on top of a bowl of rice.

¼ cup white miso

2 tablespoons gochujang

1½ tablespoons toasted sesame oil

4 scallions, thinly sliced

1 medium garlic clove, finely grated

2 teaspoons white sugar

In a small bowl, whisk together all ingredients and ¼ cup water. Use immediately or refrigerate in an airtight container for up to 2 weeks.

Optional add-ins: Chopped toasted walnuts OR toasted sesame seeds OR both

Smoky Roasted Pepper Sauce with Almonds and Sherry Vinegar

Start to finish: 15 minutes
Makes 1 cup

This sauce is a simple rendition of Catalan romesco, a blend that traditionally includes roasted tomatoes, nuts, garlic, ñora chilies, olive oil and bread for thickening. In our six-ingredient version, **we add smoked paprika and woodsy sherry vinegar—two ingredients that give the sauce a decidedly Spanish flavor and aroma.** It's a delicious accompaniment to grilled vegetables and grilled or seared steaks, lamb or chops. Or smear it onto sandwiches or include it in a grilled cheese.

½ cup roasted red peppers, patted dry

½ cup roasted almonds, roughly chopped

½ cup extra-virgin olive oil

2 tablespoons sherry vinegar

2 tablespoons tomato paste

1 teaspoon smoked paprika

1 medium garlic clove, smashed and peeled

Kosher salt and ground black pepper

In a food processor, combine the roasted peppers, almonds, oil, vinegar, tomato paste, paprika, garlic and ½ teaspoon each salt and pepper. Pulse to combine, then process until smooth, 1 to 2 minutes, scraping the bowl as needed. If desired, thin the sauce by processing in up to 1 tablespoon water. Taste and season with salt and pepper. Use immediately or refrigerate in an airtight container for up to 3 days.

Broiled Salmon with Yogurt, Citrus and Warm Spices

Start to finish: 25 minutes
Servings: 4

A stir-together sauce of Greek yogurt, spices and citrus zest does double duty with this rich, meaty salmon. We slather some of the mixture onto salmon fillets before broiling, then turn the rest into a sauce for drizzling over just before serving. Baharat is a Middle Eastern spice blend; it's sold in spice shops and many well-stocked supermarkets. If you can't find it, simply use an equal amount of ground cumin or coriander, or ½ teaspoon of each. Complete the meal with a leafy salad and rice pilaf.

Four 6-ounce salmon fillets, each about 1 inch thick

Kosher salt and ground black pepper

½ cup plain whole-milk Greek yogurt

3 teaspoons extra-virgin olive oil, divided, plus more for the baking sheet

1 teaspoon baharat OR ground cumin OR ground coriander

½ teaspoon ground turmeric OR ½ teaspoon ground ginger

⅛ teaspoon ground cloves OR ground cinnamon

1 tablespoon grated lime zest OR lemon zest, plus 1½ tablespoons lime OR lemon juice, plus wedges, to serve

Heat the broiler with a rack about 6 inches from the element. Lightly coat a broiler-safe rimmed baking sheet with oil. Season the salmon with salt and pepper. In a small bowl, stir together the yogurt, 2 teaspoons of the oil, the baharat, turmeric, cloves, lime zest and a pinch of salt. Measure 2 tablespoons of the mixture into another small bowl, then smear the remainder onto all sides of the salmon.

Place the fillets skin side down on the prepared baking sheet and broil until spotty brown and the flesh flakes easily, 4 to 6 minutes; transfer to individual plates. Stir the lime juice and the remaining 1 teaspoon oil into the reserved yogurt mixture and drizzle onto the salmon. Serve with lime wedges.

Optional garnish: Chopped fresh cilantro OR dill OR mint OR a combination

Sweet-and-Savory Broiled Eggplant with Peanuts

Start to finish: 20 minutes
Servings: 4 to 6

This recipe was inspired by Vietnamese cooking, where grilled eggplant is commonly paired with nước chấm, a savory-sweet blend of fish sauce, sugar, lime juice, chilies and garlic. Our version swaps the grill for a broiler and builds the dressing on a base of garlicky chili sauce. **We also pair mellow, broiled eggplant with savory fish sauce and chopped peanuts for crunchy contrast.** Serve with steamed jasmine rice for a main or offer it as a side to simply grilled meats, poultry or seafood.

1½ pounds Japanese OR Chinese eggplant, stemmed and halved lengthwise

3 tablespoons neutral oil

Kosher salt and ground black pepper

3 tablespoons fish sauce

3 tablespoons lime juice, plus lime wedges to serve

2 tablespoons white sugar

1 tablespoon chili-garlic sauce OR Sriracha

½ cup roasted, salted peanuts, chopped

Heat the broiler with a rack about 4 inches from the element. Set a wire rack in a broiler-safe rimmed baking sheet and mist it with cooking spray.

Brush the eggplant on all sides with the oil, then sprinkle with 1 teaspoon salt and ½ teaspoon pepper. Arrange cut side up on the prepared rack and broil until well charred and a skewer inserted through the thickest parts meets no resistance, 8 to 10 minutes, rotating the baking sheet about halfway through. Meanwhile, in a small bowl, stir together the fish sauce, lime juice, sugar, chili-garlic sauce and 3 tablespoons water; set aside.

Transfer the eggplant to a cutting board, cut into 1½- to 2-inch pieces and place on a platter. Spoon the sauce over the top, then sprinkle with peanuts.

Optional garnish: Fresh cilantro OR mint OR both

Cilantro, Garlic and Lime Marinated Pork Skewers

Start to finish: 1 hour 20 minutes (20 minutes active)
Servings: 4 to 6

Cilantro leaves are delicate and tender, but the sturdier stems are even more flavor-packed and are a great way to bring fresh, herbal notes to a dish. For this salty-sweet Southeast Asian-inspired marinade, we pair the stems' bright, grassy flavor with the leaves, tangy lime juice, brown sugar, garlic and umami-rich fish sauce. Thinly slicing the pork allows it to absorb seasonings, tenderize and cook quickly, but cutting raw meat into small pieces can be tricky. To remedy this, we place it in the freezer for 30 minutes beforehand, firming up the pork for easy knife-work.

2 pounds boneless pork shoulder, trimmed of surface fat and halved lengthwise

1 bunch cilantro, leaves and stems roughly chopped (about 2 cups)

⅓ cup lime juice, plus lime wedges to serve

3 tablespoons fish sauce

3 tablespoons packed light OR dark brown sugar

6 medium garlic cloves, smashed and peeled

1 tablespoon neutral oil

Kosher salt and ground black pepper

Set the pork on a large plate and freeze until the meat is firm and partially frozen, 30 to 60 minutes. Meanwhile, in a blender, combine the cilantro, lime juice, fish sauce, sugar, garlic, oil, ¼ teaspoon salt and 2 teaspoons pepper. Puree until smooth, about 1 minute, scraping the blender jar as needed.

Using a sharp chef's knife, slice the partially frozen pork crosswise into pieces about ⅛ inch thick. The slices will be irregularly shaped; cut them into strips 1 to 1¼ inches wide (it's fine if the strips are not uniform). In a large bowl, combine the pork and cilantro puree; and mix with your hands until evenly coated. Cover and refrigerate for about 30 minutes.

Heat the broiler with a rack about 6 inches from the element. Set a wire rack in a rimmed broiler-safe baking sheet and mist the rack with cooking spray. Thread the pork onto ten 10- to 12-inch metal skewers, scraping off excess marinade, scrunching it together and packing it quite tightly. If some pieces are too wide, too wispy or awkwardly shaped, fold the meat or tuck in the edges as you skewer. Place the skewers on the prepared rack.

Broil until lightly charred on top, 6 to 8 minutes. Remove from the oven, flip the skewers and broil until the second sides are charred, another 6 to 8 minutes. Serve with lime wedges.

Optional garnish: Thai sweet chili sauce OR thinly sliced fresh mint OR sliced Fresno or jalapeño chilies

Broiled Lemon-Garlic Salmon with Arugula

Start to finish: 30 minutes
Servings: 4

Salmoriglio is a simple southern Italian marinade and sauce that marries extra-virgin olive oil, garlic, herbs and lemon. The combination is perfect for rich, meaty salmon. The ingredients do double duty, seasoning the fish before cooking, then creating the sauce that finishes the dish. **We broil lemon halves alongside the salmon; this renders the fruit extra-juicy while tempering its acidity.** Baby arugula or spinach makes a colorful bed for the fillets and pairs beautifully with the sauce.

1 lemon

1 medium garlic clove, finely grated

1 teaspoon minced fresh oregano
OR ½ teaspoon dried oregano, crumbled

Kosher salt and ground black pepper

3 tablespoons extra-virgin olive oil, divided

1½ teaspoons honey

Four 6-ounce salmon fillets, each about 1 inch thick

5-ounce container baby arugula
OR baby spinach

Heat the broiler with a rack about 6 inches from the element. Set a broiler-safe wire rack in a broiler-safe rimmed baking sheet, then mist with cooking spray.

Grate 2 teaspoons zest from the lemon; set the lemon aside. In a small bowl, combine the zest, garlic, oregano and ½ teaspoon each salt and pepper. Measure ½ teaspoon of this mixture into a wide, shallow dish. Stir 2 tablespoons oil into the remaining zest mixture in the bowl; set aside.

To the zest mixture in the shallow dish, stir in the remaining 1 tablespoon oil, honey, ¼ teaspoon salt and ½ teaspoon pepper. Add the salmon and turn to coat, rubbing the seasonings in. Place the fillets skin side down on the prepared rack. Halve the reserved lemon crosswise and trim the ends so the halves sit stably; place cut sides up alongside the salmon. Broil until the edges of the fillets are firm to the touch and the flesh flakes easily, 4 to 6 minutes.

Squeeze the juice from the lemon halves into the reserved zest-oil mixture; whisk to combine, then taste and season with salt and pepper. Place the arugula on a serving platter, creating a bed for the fish. Nestle the fillets into the greens and drizzle with the sauce.

Grilled Zucchini with Lemony Ricotta

Start to finish: 30 minutes
Servings: 4 to 6

The contrast of silky grilled zucchini, creamy ricotta and crunchy nuts provides this dish with satisfying textural complexity. **We incorporate lemon two ways, stirring the zest into the ricotta and grilling the halved fruit to bring out a gentler acidity in the juice.** Be sure to use a high-quality full-fat ricotta cheese to ensure a creamy texture; low-fat versions can be watery and granular. Also, look for slightly larger zucchini and slice on a sharp diagonal—the larger slices are easier to manage on the grill. Serve with thick slices of grilled bread and a drizzle of syrupy aged balsamic.

1 lemon

1 cup whole-milk ricotta cheese

3 tablespoons extra-virgin olive oil, divided

¼ teaspoon red pepper flakes

Kosher salt and ground black pepper

3 medium zucchini OR yellow summer squash (about 1½ pounds total), sliced about ¼ inch thick on a sharp diagonal

¼ cup lightly packed fresh mint OR dill OR basil OR flat-leaf parsley OR a combination, chopped

3 tablespoons pistachios, roughly chopped OR pine nuts, toasted

Grate 1 tablespoon zest from the lemon, then halve the lemon crosswise and set aside. In a medium bowl, stir together the lemon zest, ricotta, 1 tablespoon oil, the red pepper flakes and ¼ teaspoon each salt and black pepper; set aside.

Heat a 12-inch grill pan over medium-high until barely smoking. Meanwhile, in a large bowl, toss the zucchini with the remaining 2 tablespoons oil and ½ teaspoon salt. Working in batches if needed, add the zucchini to the pan and cook, turning occasionally, until charred and tender-crisp, about 3 minutes per side. Transfer to a serving platter and cool slightly.

Grill the lemon halves cut side down until lightly charred, 2 to 3 minutes. Squeeze 1 tablespoon juice from a grilled lemon half, then stir it into the ricotta mixture. Taste and season with salt and pepper. Dollop the ricotta mixture onto the zucchini, then sprinkle with mint and pistachios. Serve with the remaining lemon half for squeezing.

Optional garnish: Balsamic vinegar

SPICE RUBS

Marinades and even brining have their place, but when we want to add flavor to roasted meat or vegetables fast, we prefer rubs. A few pulses in a spice grinder is all it takes to turn out punchy seasonings tailored to whatever we're roasting or steaming.

Getting spice rubs right means balancing flavors so the mix doesn't teeter too-hot or too-salty. Our takes include a blend inspired by Madeira's espetada, beef skewers heavy on the bay and garlic. We added heat and sharpness via red chili and black pepper and tossed in a bit of brown sugar to keep the savory notes from dominating.

For a smoked paprika spice paste, drawn from typical flavors of Spanish cooking, we use cumin and oregano along with the paprika and keep the mixture from feeling heavy by adding ground coriander and grated lemon zest. To add texture, we use whole cumin seeds and pulse just a few times so they still have some crunch.

Thyme and fennel go into a rub that evokes the South of France. Orange zest matches the herbs' earthy, licorice notes with tangy sweetness and, if you like, you can add a touch of color and nuanced, floral flavor with crushed saffron threads.

RECIPES FROM TOP

| Smoked Paprika Spice Paste with Cumin and Oregano | Thyme, Fennel and Orange Zest Spice Paste | Bay, Garlic and Black Pepper Spice Paste |

Thyme, Fennel and Orange Zest Spice Paste

Start to finish: 5 minutes
Makes about ¼ cup

With bright, floral notes plus woodsy herbs and licorice-like fennel, this spice rub is evocative of the flavors of Provence. **We rub orange zest into the spices to release its oils and evenly distribute citrus flavor.** The inimitable taste and vibrant hue of saffron is a welcome addition, but even without it, this seasoning mix offers a well-balanced mix of savory, sweet and citrusy. It's especially good on steamed or seared seafood, and is a delicious match for pork and lamb.

2 teaspoons dried thyme OR 1½ teaspoons dried rosemary OR 1 teaspoon each

1½ teaspoons fennel seeds

1 teaspoon coriander seeds

¼ teaspoon saffron threads, crushed (optional)

Kosher salt and ground black pepper

1 tablespoon grated orange zest

½ teaspoon granulated garlic

2 tablespoons extra-virgin olive oil

In a spice grinder, pulse the thyme, fennel seeds, coriander seeds, saffron (if using) and ½ teaspoon salt until finely ground, about 6 pulses. Transfer to a small bowl and add the orange zest, granulated garlic and ¼ teaspoon pepper. With your fingertips, rub the mixture until well combined and evenly moistened. Stir in the oil. Use immediately or refrigerate in an airtight container for up to 3 days (if refrigerated, bring to room temperature before use).

Bay, Garlic and Black Pepper Spice Paste

Start to finish: 5 minutes
Makes about ¼ cup

This spice rub takes inspiration from espetada, beef skewers from Madeira that are redolent of bay and garlic. **And the bay doesn't just put in its usual cameo appearance; it's ground into the mix to add earthy flavor.** We add subtle heat with dried red chili and some sharpness and pungency with black pepper, while brown sugar keeps the savoriness in check. This bold rub is a great match for beef or lamb, as well as a fat-rich cut of pork, such as shoulder. The recipe makes enough to season about 1½ pounds of meat.

8 bay leaves, crumbled

1 dried árbol chili OR ½ teaspoon red pepper flakes

2 teaspoons black peppercorns

2 teaspoons packed light brown sugar

1½ teaspoons granulated garlic

Kosher salt

2 tablespoons extra-virgin olive oil

In a spice grinder, combine the bay, chili and peppercorns. Process to a fine powder, 30 to 60 seconds, occasionally shaking the spice grinder. Transfer to a small bowl, then stir in the sugar, granulated garlic and 1 teaspoon salt, followed by the oil. Use immediately or refrigerate in an airtight container for up to 2 weeks (if refrigerated, bring to room temperature before use).

Smoked Paprika Spice Paste with Cumin and Oregano

Start to finish: 10 minutes
Makes about ¼ cup

A combination of rich, smoked paprika, earthy cumin and herbal fresh oregano (dried oregano works well, too), this richly hued spice rub is Spanish in its inspiration. To keep the flavor profile from feeling heavy, we also include ground coriander and grated lemon zest—both add light, citrusy notes. **We use cumin seeds and pulse them only a few times in a spice grinder, leaving some not fully ground so they add texture as much as flavor.** This mix is ideal for mild, lean meats such as chicken or pork. It's also great tossed with cauliflower before roasting.

2 teaspoons cumin seeds

2 teaspoons ground coriander

1½ teaspoons smoked paprika

2 teaspoons grated lemon zest

1 teaspoon minced fresh oregano
OR ½ teaspoon dried oregano

Kosher salt and ground black pepper

2 tablespoons extra-virgin olive oil

In a spice grinder, pulse the cumin seeds until a mixture of coarsely and finely ground, about 3 pulses. Transfer to a small bowl and stir in the coriander, paprika, lemon zest, oregano, ¾ teaspoon each salt and pepper, followed by the oil. Use right away or refrigerate in an airtight container for up to 3 days (if refrigerated, bring to room temperature before use).

Baked Feta with Tomatoes, Olives and Oregano

Start to finish: 50 minutes (15 minutes active)
Servings: 4 to 6

For our rendition of baked feta, feta sto fourno in Greek, we combine cherry or grape tomatoes—dependably good year-round—with sliced red onion, chopped olives, seasonings and, of course, a generous glug of extra-virgin olive oil. With feta layered on top and baked for 35 minutes, the tomatoes form a tangy-sweet sauce that's a delicious match for the briny, creamy-crumbly cheese. **We include oregano in two forms— dried adds woodsy, earthy notes and fresh sprinkled on top after baking brings bright hints of mint and citrus.** Seek out high-quality feta sold in blocks and slice it into moderately thick slabs (about ¾ inch thick). Serve warm as an appetizer with crusty bread, or make it into a light main with a salad.

⅓ cup extra-virgin olive oil

1¼ teaspoons Aleppo pepper, divided,
or ½ teaspoon red pepper flakes, divided

½ teaspoon dried oregano

Kosher salt and ground black pepper

1 pint cherry or grape tomatoes, halved

1 medium red onion, halved and sliced
¼ inch thick

⅓ cup pitted Kalamata olives, chopped

1 pound feta cheese, sliced ¾ inch thick
(see headnote)

3 tablespoons chopped fresh oregano

Heat the oven to 425°F with a rack in the middle position. In a 9-by-13-inch baking dish, stir together the oil, 1 teaspoon of the Aleppo pepper (or ¼ teaspoon of the pepper flakes), the dried oregano and ¼ teaspoon salt. Add the tomatoes, onion and olives; toss until well coated. Place the feta on top in an even layer and sprinkle with ¼ teaspoon black pepper.

Bake, uncovered, until the feta is browned at the edges, the tomatoes break down and the mixture is saucy and bubbling, about 35 minutes. Remove from the oven and sprinkle with the remaining ¼ teaspoon Aleppo pepper (or pepper flakes) and the fresh oregano. Let stand for about 10 minutes, then serve warm directly from the baking dish or transfer to a platter.

Oven-Baked Eggs in a Hole with Toasted Parmesan

Start to finish: 20 minutes
Servings: 4

The childhood favorite, egg in a hole, gets a boost in flavor from the garlic clove that's rubbed onto the bread before toasting and the Parmesan cheese that browns and crisps during cooking. **For ease, we use a baking sheet to make eggs in a hole, not a skillet, so four servings can be made simultaneously.** Be sure to choose sturdy bread that's sliced about ¾ inch thick. Thinner slices won't be deep enough to hold the cracked egg in the center cutouts. This recipe can easily be increased by half to make six servings.

4 slices hearty bread (see headnote)

1 medium garlic clove, halved lengthwise

2 tablespoons salted butter, melted

2 tablespoons extra-virgin olive oil

4 large eggs

Kosher salt and ground black pepper

1 ounce Parmesan cheese, finely grated (½ cup)

Heat the oven to 475°F with a rack in the middle position. Mist a rimmed baking sheet with cooking spray. Rub each slice of bread on both sides with the cut side of the garlic, then place the slices in a single layer on the prepared baking sheet; discard the garlic. In a small bowl, stir together the butter and oil. Brush both sides of each slice with the butter-oil mixture.

Using a 2½- to 3-inch round biscuit cutter, stamp out the center of each slice of bread and place the cutouts on the baking sheet. Crack 1 egg into the hole of each slice of bread. Sprinkle salt and pepper onto the eggs and the bread, including the cutouts, followed by the Parmesan. Bake until the bread is toasted and the eggs are just set, 3 to 4 minutes for runny yolks or 5 minutes for fully set eggs.

Using a wide metal spatula, transfer each egg in a hole and its cutout to an individual plate.

Optional garnish: Chopped fresh flat-leaf parsley OR thinly sliced scallions OR hot sauce OR a combination

Berbere-Spiced Chicken Skewers

Start to finish: 30 minutes
Servings: 4

These vibrant chicken skewers get deep flavor from berbere, Ethiopia's signature spice blend. Made with dried alliums, chilies and warm spices, berbere features complex flavor and a rich, earthy aroma. Look for it in spice shops or well-stocked grocery stores. If you can't find it, use a mixture of ground coriander and smoked paprika. **We combine berbere with softened butter, lime juice and honey, making a spicy-sweet seasoning mix ideal for clinging to the chicken before cooking.**

4 tablespoons salted butter, room temperature

2 tablespoons berbere OR 1 tablespoon ground coriander plus 1 tablespoon smoked paprika

2 tablespoons honey, plus more to serve

1 tablespoon grated lime zest, plus
2 tablespoons lime juice, plus lime wedges, to serve

Kosher salt and ground black pepper

1½ pounds boneless, skinless chicken thighs, trimmed and cut into 1½-inch pieces

2 medium red OR orange OR yellow bell peppers OR a combination, stemmed, seeded and cut into 1½-inch pieces

Set a wire rack in a broiler-safe rimmed baking sheet and mist with cooking spray. In a large bowl, mix the butter, berbere, honey, the lime zest and juice, 1 teaspoon salt and ½ teaspoon pepper. Measure 2 tablespoons of the mixture into a small bowl; set aside for brushing.

Add the chicken and peppers to the bowl with the remaining berbere mixture and mix with your hands to coat. Thread the chicken, alternating with the peppers, onto four 12-inch metal skewers. Place the skewers on the prepared rack, spacing them evenly. Let stand at room temperature while the broiler heats.

Heat the broiler with a rack about 6 inches from the element. Broil the skewers until lightly charred, 6 to 7 minutes. Remove from the oven, flip and broil until charred on the second sides, another 6 to 7 minutes. Transfer to a serving platter, brush with the reserved butter mixture and drizzle with additional honey. Serve with lime wedges.

Pan-Seared Steak with Mustard Seeds, Black Pepper and Rosemary

Start to finish: 30 minutes
Servings: 4 to 6

We give meat an acidic finish to lighten and brighten flavors by finishing pan-fried steaks with a quick pan sauce made with whole-grain mustard, plus a little shallot and butter. The flavor combination was inspired by the late Floyd Cardoz's "Flavorwalla." Be sure the pan is off the burner when the butter is whisked into the sauce at the end so the butter doesn't "break" and become watery.

1 tablespoon yellow mustard seeds

1½ teaspoons black peppercorns

1 tablespoon fresh rosemary

Kosher salt and ground black pepper

Two 1-pound beef strip steaks, trimmed

2 tablespoons neutral oil

3 tablespoons salted butter, cut into 1-tablespoon pieces, divided

1 medium shallot, finely chopped

2 tablespoons whole-grain Dijon mustard

In a spice grinder, pulse the mustard seeds, peppercorns, rosemary and 1 tablespoon salt until coarsely ground. Season the steaks on all sides with the mixture. In a 12-inch skillet, heat the oil over medium-high until barely smoking. Add the steaks and brown on both sides until the centers reach 120°F (for medium-rare). Transfer to a platter.

To the skillet, add 1 tablespoon of the butter and the shallot. Cook over medium, stirring, until the shallot is softened. Add ⅔ cup water and the Dijon mustard. Cook, stirring, until slightly thickened. Off heat, whisk in the remaining 2 tablespoons butter and the accumulated steak juices. Taste and season with salt and pepper. Slice the steaks, return to the platter and pour the sauce over them.

Pan-Seared Brussels Sprouts with Feta and Honey

Start to finish: 25 minutes
Servings: 4

For these skillet-charred Brussels sprouts, salty feta, sweet honey, spicy red pepper flakes and a dose of lemon juice create a delicious interplay of contrasting flavors. **Cooking the sprouts in a searing-hot skillet creates a deep caramelization of natural sugars that counters the vegetable's tendency to bitterness.** Chopped almonds contribute a rich, nutty crunch; pomegranate seeds, if in season, also work nicely, adding pops of color and fruity freshness. Be sure to reduce the heat to medium once you've added the sprouts; this ensures they char and become tender but don't burn. And choose Brussels sprouts that are similarly sized. Small to medium ones work best.

1 pound small to medium Brussels sprouts, trimmed and halved

1 tablespoon neutral oil

2 teaspoons plus 2 tablespoons honey, divided, plus more to serve

Kosher salt and ground black pepper

½ to ¾ teaspoon red pepper flakes

1 ounce feta cheese, crumbled (¼ cup)

¼ cup roasted almonds, roughly chopped OR pomegranate seeds OR a combination

1 tablespoon lemon juice

In a medium bowl, toss the sprouts with the oil, 2 teaspoons honey, ½ teaspoon salt and ¼ teaspoon black pepper. Heat a 12-inch cast-iron skillet over medium-high until water flicked onto the surface immediately sizzles and evaporates. Place the sprouts cut side down in the pan, then reduce to medium; reserve the bowl. Cook without stirring until deeply browned on the bottoms, 5 to 7 minutes.

Using tongs, flip the sprouts and cook, stirring occasionally, until a skewer inserted into the largest sprout meets just a little resistance, 4 to 6 minutes; lower the heat if the sprouts brown too quickly. Return the sprouts to the bowl, then immediately add the remaining 2 tablespoons honey and pepper flakes; toss. Add the feta, almonds and lemon juice; toss again. Taste and season with salt and black pepper. Transfer to a serving dish and, if desired, drizzle with additional honey.

Optional garnish: Chopped fresh flat-leaf parsley OR chopped fresh chives

Sesame-Crusted Salmon with Black Pepper–Lime Sauce

Start to finish: 25 minutes
Servings: 4

For this simple salmon dish, we coat fillets with sesame seeds, which form a crisp, nutty-tasting crust as the fish cooks. We balance the rich fattiness of the salmon with the peppery-lime brightness of the pleasantly pungent Cambodian black pepper and lime sauce called tuk meric. The sauce traditionally is paired with the beef stir-fry known as loc lac, but we find it brightens up a host of other foods, including seafood. Be sure to grind the peppercorns coarsely, not finely, for the sauce using a spice mill or a mortar and pestle.

2 teaspoons coarsely ground black pepper (see headnote)

¼ cup lime juice, plus lime wedges to serve

1½ tablespoons packed light brown sugar

2 tablespoons fish sauce, divided

1 jalapeño OR Fresno chili, stemmed and sliced into thin rings (optional)

½ cup white sesame seeds OR a mix of white and black sesame seeds

Four 6-ounce center-cut salmon fillets (each 1 to 1¼ inches thick), patted dry

1 tablespoon grapeseed or other neutral oil

In a 12-inch nonstick skillet over medium, toast the pepper, stirring often, until fragrant and lightly smoking, about 2 minutes. Transfer to a small bowl; reserve the skillet. Into the toasted pepper, stir the lime juice, the sugar, 1 tablespoon fish sauce, the chili (if using) and 2 tablespoons water; set aside for serving.

Put the sesame seeds in a pie plate or other wide, shallow dish. Brush the tops of the salmon with the remaining 1 tablespoon fish sauce. One at a time, press the flesh side of the salmon into the sesame seeds to form an even crust; coat only the tops of the fillets.

In a 12-inch nonstick skillet over medium-high, heat the oil until shimmering. Add the salmon, seed side down, then immediately reduce to medium. Cook, undisturbed, until the sesame seeds are golden, about 6 minutes. Using a wide, thin spatula, flip the fillets, then cover the skillet and remove from the heat. Let stand until the thickest parts of the fillets reach 120°F or are nearly opaque when cut into, about 4 minutes for 1-inch-thick fillets and up to 8 minutes for thicker fillets. Serve with the sauce and lime wedges on the side.

Optional garnish: 2 scallions, thinly sliced on the diagonal OR 2 tablespoons roughly chopped fresh cilantro

OVEN-FRIED VEGETABLES

Frying vegetables on the stovetop is messy, fussy and too often produces oil-sodden results. So we're always happy to step aside and let the oven do the work for us.

To make sure our vegetables turn out crisp and flavorful, we rub them with oil and seasonings and give them a dusting of cornstarch; it helps produce a flavorful crust that contrasts beautifully with the tender roasted vegetables.

We then slide them into a hot oven on low-rimmed baking sheets, which promote fast and even cooking. While they roast, we use the time to make stir-together sauces that offer cool, tangy contrast.

All kinds of vegetables lend themselves to this treatment; our takes include paprika-spiced potato wedges; earthy butternut squash paired with pickled jalapeños; and cauliflower florets served with a kung pao-inspired sauce of chili crisp, rice vinegar and soy sauce. If you have them, some chopped roasted peanuts tossed on top add a finishing bit of crunch.

RECIPES FROM TOP

| Butternut Squash with Pumpkin Seeds, Cilantro and Pickled Jalapeños | Cauliflower with Salty-Sweet Chili Crisp Sauce | Sliced Potato Wedges with Pickled Peppers |

Spiced Potato Wedges with Pickled Peppers

Start to finish: 45 minutes (15 minutes active)
Servings: 4

To make these oven-fried potato wedges, smoky and earthy spices are combined with cornstarch, creating a flavorful coating. The starchy mixture becomes golden-brown and crisp in the oven, while the potatoes' insides roast until perfectly tender. The final touch is a smattering of pickled peppers, which add tanginess and crunch. Top with sour cream and chopped chives, if desired.

¼ cup cornstarch

1 tablespoon smoked OR sweet paprika

2 teaspoons ground coriander
OR ground cumin OR fennel seeds,
lightly crushed OR a combination

1 teaspoon white sugar

Kosher salt and ground black pepper

2 pounds medium (2-inch) Yukon Gold potatoes, unpeeled, cut into 1-inch wedges

⅓ cup neutral oil

⅓ cup drained Peppadew peppers
OR sweet cherry peppers, patted dry and sliced into thin rings

Heat the oven to 475°F with a rack in the middle position. In a small bowl, whisk together the cornstarch, paprika, coriander, sugar and ¾ teaspoon each salt and pepper.

In a large bowl, toss the potatoes and oil until evenly coated. Sprinkle with the cornstarch mixture and toss again, pressing the starch mixture onto the potatoes. Transfer to a rimmed baking sheet and arrange in a single layer, turning the pieces cut side down as much as possible. Roast until golden brown on the bottom, about 20 minutes.

Using a wide metal spatula, flip the potatoes, then redistribute in a single layer. Roast until deep golden brown on the second side, 10 to 12 minutes. Transfer to a platter and top with the Peppadew peppers.

Optional garnish: Sour cream OR chopped chives OR both

Butternut Squash with Pumpkin Seeds, Cilantro and Pickled Jalapeños

Start to finish: 40 minutes (20 minutes active)
Servings: 4

Employing our oven-fried vegetable technique, we roast cubes of nutty-sweet squash tossed in a mixture of cornstarch and oil, plus a few seasonings. The starchy coating creates a crisp, well-browned crust while the interiors become silky and tender. While the squash cooks, we whip up a bright and herbaceous sauce starring fresh cilantro and pickled jalapeños. This is delicious paired with roast turkey, chicken or fish.

½ cup cornstarch

¼ cup pumpkin seeds, chopped

1 tablespoon chili powder

Kosher salt and ground black pepper

2-pound butternut squash, peeled, seeded and cut into 1-inch chunks

⅓ cup neutral oil

¾ cup lightly packed fresh cilantro, finely chopped

¼ cup finely chopped pickled jalapeños, plus 2 tablespoons brine

Heat the oven to 475°F with a rack in the middle position. In a small bowl, whisk together the cornstarch, half of the pumpkin seeds, the chili powder and 1 teaspoon each salt and pepper.

In a large bowl, toss the squash and oil until evenly coated. Sprinkle with the cornstarch mixture and toss again, pressing the starch mixture into the squash. Transfer to a rimmed baking sheet and arrange in a single layer. Roast until golden brown on the bottom, 10 to 12 minutes.

Meanwhile, in a small bowl, stir together the cilantro, pickled jalapeños and brine and 1 tablespoon water; set aside. In a small skillet over medium, toast the remaining pumpkin seeds, stirring occasionally, until beginning to brown, about 3 minutes; set aside off heat.

Using a wide metal spatula, flip the squash, then redistribute in a single layer. Roast until deep golden brown on the second side, 10 to 12 minutes. Taste and season with salt and pepper, then transfer to a platter. Spoon the cilantro mixture over the top and sprinkle with the toasted pumpkin seeds.

Cauliflower with Salty-Sweet Chili Crisp Sauce

Start to finish: 40 minutes (15 minutes active)
Servings: 4

Sweet, salty and tangy with a chili kick, this kung pao-inspired cauliflower makes a great starter, side dish or rice-bowl topper. **Utilizing our easy oven-frying method, we coat the cauliflower in a mixture of oil and cornstarch before roasting in a hot oven; this yields florets that are golden-crisp on the outside, yet tender within.** A sauce of spicy chili crisp, punchy rice vinegar and umami-rich soy sauce, all rounded out by brown sugar, contributes a vibrant reddish hue and bright, layered flavor.

½ cup cornstarch

Kosher salt and ground black pepper

2- to 2½-pound head cauliflower, trimmed and cut into 1½-inch florets

⅓ cup neutral oil

2 tablespoons chili crisp

2 tablespoons soy sauce

2 tablespoons unseasoned rice vinegar

2 tablespoons firmly packed light
OR dark brown sugar

Heat the oven to 475°F with a rack in the middle position. In a small bowl, whisk together the cornstarch and ¾ teaspoon each salt and pepper.

In a large bowl, toss the cauliflower with the oil, using your hands to rub the oil into the florets. Sprinkle with the cornstarch mixture and toss, pressing the cornstarch into the cauliflower. Transfer the florets to a rimmed baking sheet, shaking off excess cornstarch and turning the pieces cut side down as much as possible. Roast until golden brown on the bottom, about 15 minutes. Meanwhile, in a small bowl, stir together the chili crisp, soy sauce, vinegar and sugar; set aside.

Using a wide metal spatula, flip the cauliflower, then roast until deep golden brown, another 10 minutes. Transfer to a platter and drizzle with the chili crisp mixture.

Optional garnish: Chopped roasted peanuts OR chopped fresh cilantro OR thinly sliced scallions OR a combination

Sweet and Salty Galbi-Style Skirt Steak

Start to finish: 30 minutes, plus marinating
Servings: 4

Korean yangneom galbi—often shortened to "galbi"—are short ribs marinated in a salty-sweet, umami-rich mix of ingredients. It inspired this simple recipe for skirt or flank steak. In addition to soy sauce and sesame oil, Asian pear is a traditional galbi ingredient, but the fruits are seasonal and can be pricey; we've found that any pear variety works nicely. A blender makes quick work of the marinade. **The fruit adds a subtle flavor, gives a little body to the marinade, and contains enzymes that help tenderize the steak. We layer on the flavor by using most of the marinade to soak the steak, but save some to create a simple sauce that adds a final fresh jolt of seasoning.**

1½ pounds skirt steak OR flank steak, trimmed

1 ripe pear OR 1 Asian pear (see headnote), peeled, cored and cut into large chunks

6 medium garlic cloves, smashed and peeled

¼ cup plus 1 tablespoon soy sauce, divided

3 tablespoons white sugar

2 tablespoons toasted sesame oil, divided

Kosher salt and ground black pepper

Poke the steak all over with the tip of a paring knife, then cut with the grain into pieces about 5 inches wide. Place in a wide, shallow dish. In a blender, combine the pear, garlic, ¼ cup soy sauce, sugar, 1 tablespoon sesame oil, ½ teaspoon salt and 1 teaspoon pepper. Blend on high until smooth, about 1 minute, scraping the blender jar as needed.

Measure 2 tablespoons of the marinade into a small bowl; cover and refrigerate. Pour the remainder over the steak, turn to coat and arrange in an even layer. Cover and refrigerate at least 2 hours or up to 24 hours, turning the pieces once or twice.

Remove the reserved soy mixture from the refrigerator. Heat a 12-inch grill pan over medium-high until water flicked onto the surface immediately sizzles and evaporates. Remove the steak from the marinade, allowing excess to drip off. Working in batches if needed, place the steak in the pan and cook until nicely charred on the bottom, 2 to 3 minutes. Flip and cook until the second sides are nicely charred and the center reaches 125°F for medium-rare, 2 to 4 minutes. Transfer to a platter, tent with foil and let rest for 5 minutes.

Whisk the remaining 1 tablespoon sesame oil and 1 tablespoon soy sauce into the reserved soy mixture. Transfer the steak to a cutting board, then thinly slice it against the grain. Whisk the accumulated juices on the platter into the soy-sesame mixture. Return the steak to the platter and drizzle with the soy-sesame mixture.

Optional garnish: Thinly sliced scallions OR toasted sesame seeds OR both

Sweet and Sour–Glazed
Pork Chops with Hoisin

Start to finish: 20 minutes, plus marinating
Servings: 4

Inspired by a recipe from "Korean BBQ" by Bill Kim and Chandra Ram, **we use a five-ingredient, savory-sweet-sour hoisin mixture to first marinate, then later sauce bone-in pork chops** that are charred under the intense heat of the broiler. The first application of the sauce caramelizes under the heat while the second stays fresh and vibrant.

¼ cup hoisin sauce

2 tablespoons balsamic vinegar

1 tablespoon toasted sesame oil

1 tablespoon chopped fresh rosemary

2 medium garlic cloves, finely grated

Four 1-inch-thick bone-in, center-cut pork chops (12 to 14 ounces each)

In a small bowl, whisk together the hoisin, vinegar, sesame oil, rosemary and garlic. Transfer about three-fourths of the marinade to a wide, shallow dish; set the remainder aside. Place the chops in the dish and turn to coat. Marinate at room temperature for about 30 minutes or up to 1 hour.

Heat the broiler with a rack about 6 inches from the element. Set a wire rack in a broiler-safe rimmed baking sheet and mist it with cooking spray. Remove the chops from the marinade and pat dry with paper towels. Place the chops on the rack, spacing them evenly, and broil until charred at the edges and the thickest parts not touching bone reach 135°F, about 10 to 12 minutes, flipping them once about halfway through. Transfer to a platter and brush with the reserved hoisin mixture.

Souvlaki-Inspired Pork Skewers

Start to finish: 30 minutes
Servings: 4

In Greece, skewers of garlicky grilled meat called souvlaki are sold on street corners, in restaurants and at the beach. Inspired by the ubiquitous snack, our broiler-cooked iteration incorporates sweet-tart tomatoes, which blister and char in the oven. Zucchini cut into chunks works nicely, too—or even a combination. **A yogurt marinade isn't traditional for pork souvlaki, but we like the tenderizing effect it has on the meat.** It also makes a creamy, tangy sauce. Serve with rice, orzo pilaf or warmed pita bread.

¾ cup plain whole-milk Greek yogurt

2 tablespoons red wine vinegar

2 tablespoons extra-virgin olive oil

1 tablespoon chopped fresh oregano

3 medium garlic cloves, finely grated

Kosher salt and ground black pepper

1¼-pound pork tenderloin, trimmed of silver skin, halved lengthwise and cut into 1-inch chunks

8 Campari or cocktail tomatoes (about 1½ inches) OR 1 medium zucchini, halved lengthwise and cut into ½-inch pieces OR a combination

Set a wire rack in a broiler-safe rimmed baking sheet and mist it with cooking spray. In a medium bowl, stir together the yogurt, vinegar, oil, oregano, garlic and 1 teaspoon each salt and pepper. Measure ¼ cup of the mixture into a small bowl and stir in 1 tablespoon water; set aside for serving.

Add the pork to the medium bowl and mix until evenly coated. Thread the pork, alternating with the tomatoes, onto four 8- to 10-inch metal skewers. Place the skewers on the prepared rack, spacing them evenly apart. Let stand at room temperature while the broiler heats.

Heat the broiler with a rack about 4 inches from the element. Broil the skewers until lightly charred, 4 to 6 minutes. Remove from the oven, flip and broil until charred on the second sides, another 4 to 6 minutes. Serve with the yogurt sauce.

Optional garnish: Lemon wedges

Maple and Miso–Glazed Broiled Tofu

Start to finish: 45 minutes
Servings: 4

In this sweet-spicy tofu dish, **a mixture of maple syrup, Sriracha, miso and sesame oil does triple-duty—first as a marinade for the tofu, then as a basting liquid and finally, thinned with a little water, as an umami-rich serving sauce.** Pressing the planks of tofu yields a firmer texture in the finished dish, while allowing them to absorb more of the maple-miso mixture. Serve on greens, such as watercress or shredded cabbage, or with braised or stir-fried bok choy, or use as a topping for rice bowls.

Two 14-ounce containers firm OR
extra-firm tofu, drained, each cut lengthwise
into 4 planks of even thickness

3 tablespoons maple syrup

3 tablespoons white OR red miso

1½ tablespoons Sriracha OR chili-garlic sauce

1 tablespoon toasted sesame oil,
plus more to serve

1 tablespoon finely grated fresh ginger

Line a rimmed baking sheet with a double layer of paper towels. Lay the tofu planks in a single layer and cover with additional paper towels. Top with another baking sheet, then place cans or jars on top to weigh it down. Let stand for 30 minutes. Meanwhile, in a small bowl, stir together the maple syrup, miso, Sriracha, sesame oil and ginger.

Uncover the tofu; reserve the top baking sheet. Set a wire rack in the reserved baking sheet and mist it with cooking spray. Pat the tofu planks dry with fresh paper towels, then place on the prepared rack, spaced evenly apart. Liberally brush the tofu on all sides with some of the maple mixture; let stand while the broiler heats.

Heat the broiler with a rack about 6 inches from the heating element. Broil the tofu until just beginning to brown, 4 to 5 minutes. Using tongs, flip the tofu; broil until well browned and lightly charred, 5 to 7 minutes.

Transfer to a platter. Add water to the remaining maple mixture, 1 teaspoon at a time, until it has the consistency of heavy cream. Drizzle over the tofu followed by additional sesame oil.

Optional garnish: Toasted sesame seeds OR chopped toasted walnuts OR thinly sliced scallions OR chili crisp OR shichimi togarashi OR a combination

Ginger-Lime Grilled Snapper with Herb Sauce

Start to finish: 25 minutes
Servings: 4

In this weeknight-friendly main, the fish is cooked on a stovetop grill pan. **A zesty puree of cilantro, scallions, ginger and lime comes together quickly in a blender and boosts flavor from start to finish.** Some of it is rubbed on the fillets before cooking to season them and help the flesh caramelize as it browns. The rest is served alongside, providing a bright contrast to the smoky fish. Choose a firm-fleshed fish, such as snapper, mahi mahi or mackerel, that will hold up well during grilling. Coconut or turmeric rice is an especially good side.

1½ cups lightly packed fresh cilantro

1 bunch scallions, roughly chopped

3 tablespoons neutral oil, plus more
for the grill pan

2 tablespoons roughly chopped fresh ginger

1 tablespoon grated lime zest, plus
3 tablespoons lime juice, plus lime wedges,
to serve

Kosher salt and ground black pepper

Four 6-ounce snapper fillets OR mahi mahi
fillets OR swordfish steaks (about 1 inch thick),
patted dry

In a blender, combine the cilantro, scallions, oil, ginger, lime zest and juice and ¼ teaspoon each salt and pepper. Blend on high until smooth, about 1 minute, scraping the jar as needed. Measure ¼ cup of the puree into a wide, shallow dish; transfer the remainder to a small bowl and reserve. Add the fish to the dish, rub the puree into all sides and season with salt.

Heat a 12-inch grill pan over high until water flicked onto the surface immediately sizzles and evaporates. Using a heat safe brush, lightly brush the pan with oil, then place the fillets flesh side down in the pan. Cook until the fish releases easily, 2 to 3 minutes. Using a thin metal spatula, flip the fillets and cook, turning as needed, until the flesh flakes easily, 4 to 6 minutes. Serve with the reserved puree and lime wedges.

Optional garnish: Thinly sliced Fresno OR serrano chilies

Roasts and Traybakes

Tandoori-Inspired Chicken and Cauliflower Traybake

Start to finish: 55 minutes (20 minutes active)
Servings: 4

Indian tandoori chicken inspired this six-ingredient meal on a baking sheet. **We cut slashes into bone-in chicken parts to allow the seasonings to really work their way into the meat.** The technique is true to classic tandoori chicken. Yogurt not only tenderizes the chicken, it gets the seasonings to stick and assists with browning. Garam masala is warm and sweet, whereas curry powder is savory and earthy; use whichever you prefer or have. Serve with basmati rice and/or warm naan.

1 cup plain whole-milk yogurt, divided

4 tablespoons neutral oil, divided

1 tablespoon finely grated fresh ginger
OR 4 medium garlic cloves, finely grated
OR both

2 tablespoons sweet paprika

1½ tablespoons garam masala
OR curry powder

Kosher salt and ground black pepper

3 pounds bone-in, skin-on chicken thighs
OR chicken leg quarters, trimmed and patted dry

2-pound head cauliflower, trimmed and cut into 1-inch florets

In a large bowl, whisk together ½ cup yogurt, 2 tablespoons oil, the ginger, paprika, garam masala, 2½ teaspoons salt and ¼ teaspoon pepper. Measure 2 tablespoons of the mixture into a small bowl and stir in the remaining ½ cup yogurt; cover and refrigerate until ready to serve.

Using a sharp knife, cut parallel slashes, spaced about 1 inch apart, in the skin side of each piece of chicken, cutting all the way to the bone. Add the chicken to the yogurt mixture in the large bowl and turn to coat, rubbing the yogurt into the slashes. Transfer the chicken skin-side up to the center of a rimmed baking sheet, arranging the pieces in a single layer; let stand at room temperature for about 30 minutes; wipe out the bowl.

In the same bowl, toss the cauliflower with the remaining 2 tablespoons oil, ½ teaspoon salt and ¼ teaspoon pepper. Transfer to the baking sheet in an even layer around the chicken. Let stand at room temperature while the oven heats.

Heat the oven to 475°F with a rack in the middle position. Roast until the thickest part of the largest thigh or leg quarter reaches 175°F, 30 to 35 minutes. Transfer the chicken and cauliflower to a platter and serve with the yogurt sauce.

Optional garnish: Chopped fresh cilantro OR lemon wedges OR both

Slow-Roasted Fish with Lemon Grass and Sambal

Start to finish: 40 minutes (10 minutes active)
Servings: 4 to 6

We bake fish fillets at a low temperature to keep them tender and moist in this vibrant and spicy slow-roast. Sambal oelek—a tangy Indonesian chili sauce—forms the base of the marinade, which we enhance with lemon grass, shallot and turmeric. Look for sambal oelek in the international aisle of the supermarket; if not available, chili-garlic sauce is a good stand-in. Be sure to use a skin-on fillet (or fillets): the skin holds the flesh together, ensuring the delicate cooked fish can be easily transferred from baking sheet to platter. Serve over steamed jasmine rice, sprinkled with fresh cilantro leaves.

¼ cup neutral oil

2 stalks fresh lemon grass, trimmed to the bottom 6 inches, dry outer layers discarded, roughly chopped

1 medium shallot, roughly chopped

2 tablespoons sambal oelek OR chili-garlic sauce

1 tablespoon packed brown sugar

¾ teaspoon ground turmeric

Kosher salt and ground black pepper

One 2-pound or two 1-pound skin-on red snapper OR fluke OR haddock fillet(s)

Heat the oven to 275°F with a rack in the lower-middle position. In a blender, combine the oil, lemon grass, shallot, sambal oelek, sugar, turmeric, 1 teaspoon salt and ¼ teaspoon pepper. Pulse a few times, then blend on high, scraping the blender jar as needed, until the paste is as smooth as possible, about 1 minute.

Place the fish skin side down on a rimmed baking sheet. Brush the paste evenly onto the flesh side of the fillet(s), then bake until the flesh flakes easily, about 30 minutes.

Remove the baking sheet from the oven. Using a thin metal spatula, transfer the fillet(s) to a serving platter.

Optional garnish: Lime wedges OR fresh cilantro leaves OR both

Roasted Winter Squash with Lime, Chili and Cilantro

Start to finish: 50 minutes (15 minutes active)
Servings: 4

Roasted squash shines when we use spicy, tangy ingredients to banish one-note flavors. Lime, garlic and chilies add kick; brown sugar creates a glaze-like coating with molasses notes that enhance the earthy-sweet squash. **We season the squash in stages, tossing the vegetable wedges with seasoning glaze as they go into the oven and then adding more glaze after about 25 minutes to keep the seasonings fresh and bright.** Kabocha is a Japanese pumpkin with mottled green edible skin and dense, slightly starchy orange flesh. Acorn squash, with thin skin that doesn't require peeling, also is a terrific option.

¼ cup extra-virgin olive oil

1 tablespoon grated lime zest, plus
¼ cup lime juice, plus lime wedges, to serve

¼ cup packed brown sugar

2½-pound kabocha squash OR two
1¼-pound acorn squashes, halved lengthwise, seeded and sliced into 1-inch-thick wedges

Kosher salt and ground black pepper

2 medium garlic cloves, thinly sliced

1 or 2 serrano OR Fresno chilies, stemmed and sliced into thin rings

⅓ cup lightly packed fresh cilantro

Heat the oven to 400°F with a rack in the upper-middle position. In a small bowl, whisk together the oil, lime juice and sugar until the sugar dissolves. On a rimmed baking sheet, toss the squash with half of this mixture, 2 teaspoons salt and ½ teaspoon pepper. Arrange the pieces cut side down and roast until browned on the bottom, 25 to 30 minutes.

Using a wide metal spatula, flip each piece, drizzle with the remaining oil mixture and sprinkle with the garlic and chili(es). Roast until the squash is deeply caramelized and a skewer inserted into the largest piece meets no resistance, 10 to 15 minutes. Transfer to a platter, pouring over any juices. Top with the lime zest and cilantro and serve with lime wedges.

Optional garnish: Flaky salt OR toasted pumpkin seeds OR plain, whole-milk yogurt OR a combination

Chow Mein Traybake with Broccoli and Bell Peppers

Start to finish: 40 minutes
Servings: 4

Inspired by a recipe in Hetty McKinnon's cookbook "To Asia, With Love," we created this oven-only noodle dish, but we took some liberties, swapping instant ramen for the thin Chinese egg noodles customarily used to make chow mein. The ramen doesn't require actual cooking—it needs only to hydrate in boiling water for a few minutes. **We skip the splatter and stirring of stovetop cooking by using a baking sheet and a hot oven to oven-fry the noodles alongside broccoli and sweet bell peppers.** To finish, we toss everything with a simple blend of oyster sauce, hoisin sauce and garlic (or ginger), which brings delicious umami, saltiness and sweetness.

3 tablespoons soy sauce

2 teaspoons oyster sauce

2 medium garlic cloves, finely grated OR 2 teaspoons finely grated fresh ginger OR both

Kosher salt and ground black pepper

Three 3-ounce packages instant ramen noodles, seasoning packets discarded

3 cups boiling water

5 tablespoons neutral oil, divided

12 ounces broccoli crowns, cut into 1½-inch florets

2 medium red bell peppers, stemmed, seeded and sliced into ¼-inch strips

Heat the oven to 500°F with a rack in the middle position. In a small bowl, stir together the soy sauce, oyster sauce, garlic, ¾ teaspoon pepper and 3 tablespoons water; set aside.

Place the noodles in a large heatproof bowl, pour in the boiling water and stir. Let stand, stirring once or twice, until the noodles are pliable, about 6 minutes, then drain. Toss with 3 tablespoons oil, then set aside.

Meanwhile, generously mist a rimmed baking sheet with cooking spray. On the baking sheet, toss the broccoli with 1 tablespoon of the remaining oil, then distribute in an even layer. Roast until just starting to soften, about 4 minutes.

Using a spatula, push the broccoli to one end of the baking sheet. Pile the bell peppers onto the center, drizzle with the remaining 1 tablespoon oil and toss. Push the peppers to the opposite end of the baking sheet. Add the noodles to the center in an even layer. Roast until the broccoli is lightly charred, the peppers are tender and the noodles begin to crisp, 10 to 12 minutes.

Remove from the oven and drizzle the noodles and vegetables with the soy sauce mixture. Using tongs, toss well. Taste and season with salt and pepper.

Optional garnish: Thinly sliced scallions OR chili-garlic sauce OR toasted sesame seeds OR a combination

SAY CHEESE FOR CRISPER VEGETABLES

Elevating the weeknight winner of roasted vegetables can be as easy as adding cheese, especially when you borrow the Italian technique of baking it until crispy-chewy and lightly browned.

We were inspired by frico, a traditional dish from the Friuli region of Northern Italy. Frico, a kind of vegetable pancake, normally is made with potatoes and cheese, the latter being sprinkled onto the former toward the end of cooking. This adds savory richness as well as a satisfying chewy and crisp texture to the vegetable.

For our take, we roast Yukon Gold potato wedges, then sprinkle them with grated Gouda (manchego also works). We also apply the technique to butternut squash; its earthy sweetness pairs beautifully with salty-savory Parmesan.

And for a really interesting combination we borrow another Italian dish—panzanella, the bread and tomato salad. We toast bread alongside fresh fennel, sprinkling on grated pecorino Romano half-way through. Fresh tomatoes, salted so they're not too watery, are tossed in at the end for a standout dish.

RECIPES FROM TOP

| Parmesan-Roasted Butternut Squash | Roasted Potatoes with Gouda and Thyme | Panzanella with Tomatoes and Roasted Fennel |

Roasted Potatoes with Gouda and Thyme

Start to finish: 45 minutes (15 minutes active)
Servings: 4 to 6

Cheese baked until crisp enhances a simple roast of potatoes and shallots, adding texture and savory richness. Aged Gouda has rich, nutty, butterscotchy notes; manchego is similarly nutty but with some tanginess and subtle sharpness. Both are delicious here, so use whichever you favor. A sturdy wide metal spatula is the best way to get all the crispy, cheesy bits off of the baking sheet and onto your serving platter.

2 pounds medium Yukon Gold potatoes, not peeled, cut into ½-inch wedges

3 medium shallots, root end intact, halved lengthwise

6 medium garlic cloves, peeled and halved lengthwise

⅓ cup extra-virgin olive oil

Kosher salt and ground black pepper

4 ounces aged Gouda OR manchego cheese, finely grated (2 cups)

1 tablespoon fresh thyme, chopped

Heat the oven to 450°F with a rack in the middle position. On a rimmed baking sheet, toss together the potatoes, shallots, garlic, oil, and ½ teaspoon each salt and pepper, then distribute in an even layer. Roast until the potatoes begin to soften, about 20 minutes. Meanwhile, in a small bowl, toss together the cheese and thyme; set aside.

Remove the baking sheet from the oven. Sprinkle half of the cheese mixture over the vegetables, then, using a wide metal spatula, scrape up and turn the vegetables while incorporating the cheese; redistribute in an even layer. Evenly sprinkle on the remaining cheese mixture. Roast until the potatoes are well browned and tender and the cheese has crisped, another 10 to

15 minutes. Taste and season with salt and pepper. Using the spatula, transfer the vegetables to a platter.

Parmesan-Roasted Butternut Squash

Start to finish: 50 minutes (15 minutes active)
Servings: 4 to 6

Inspired by classic Italian pasta with pumpkin, we pair the earthy sweetness of butternut squash with warm nutmeg, woodsy herbs and salty-savory Parmesan. **The cheese is sprinkled on midway through roasting so it browns and crisps in the oven, adding layers of rich, toasty flavor to the dish.** Produced in northern Italy, Grana Padano is a grating cheese similar to Parmesan, but typically is less expensive, and a good option in this dish. This is delicious with roast chicken or pork, or toss the cooled squash with sturdy greens along with a vinaigrette to make an autumnal salad.

2-pound butternut squash, peeled, seeded and cut into 1-inch chunks

¼ cup extra-virgin olive oil

1½ teaspoons freshly grated nutmeg, divided

Kosher salt and ground black pepper

2 ounces Parmesan OR Grana Padano cheese, finely grated (1 cup)

1 tablespoon finely chopped fresh sage

1 tablespoon finely chopped fresh rosemary

Heat the oven to 450°F with a rack in the middle position. On a rimmed baking sheet, toss together the squash, oil, 1 teaspoon nutmeg, and ½ teaspoon each salt and pepper, then distribute in an even layer. Roast until the squash begins to soften, about 15 minutes.

Remove the baking sheet from the oven. Sprinkle the cheese over the squash, then, using a wide metal spatula, scrape up and flip the squash while incorporating the cheese. Redistribute in an even layer. Roast until the cheese is browned and a skewer inserted into the squash meets no resistance, 15 to 20 minutes. Sprinkle on the remaining ½ teaspoon nutmeg, the sage and rosemary; toss. Taste and season with salt and pepper. Using the spatula, transfer the squash to a platter.

Optional garnish: Toasted sliced almonds OR chopped toasted hazelnuts OR chopped toasted pumpkin seeds

Panzanella with Tomatoes and Roasted Fennel

Start to finish: 40 minutes
Servings: 4 to 6

Classic panzanella is a rustic Italian salad that pairs crusty bread with summer vegetables and fresh herbs, all dressed with olive oil and vinegar. For this version, we toast bread, torn into pieces, with wedges of fresh fennel and sprinkle on some grated pecorino (or Parmesan) midway through. **The browned cheese adds nutty-savory flavors and crisp texture. We also salt and drain the tomatoes to extract excess moisture that otherwise would dilute the salad and make it watery.**

8 ounces Campari or cocktail tomatoes, cored and cut into ½-inch wedges OR 1 pint cherry or grape tomatoes, halved

Kosher salt and ground black pepper

8 ounces country-style bread, torn into bite-size pieces (about 8 cups)

1 large fennel bulb, trimmed, cored and cut in ¼-inch wedges

5 tablespoons extra-virgin olive oil, divided, plus more to serve

2 ounces pecorino Romano OR Parmesan cheese, finely grated (1 cup)

3 tablespoons red wine vinegar OR white balsamic vinegar

1 cup lightly packed fresh flat-leaf parsley OR fresh basil

Heat the oven to 450°F with a rack in the middle position. In a colander set over a large bowl, toss the tomatoes with ½ teaspoon salt; set aside, tossing a few times to encourage the liquid to drain.

On a rimmed baking sheet, combine the bread and fennel. Drizzle with 4 tablespoons oil and sprinkle with ¼ teaspoon each salt and pepper; toss to coat, then distribute in an even layer. Roast until the fennel begins to soften, about 10 minutes.

Remove the baking sheet from the oven. Sprinkle the cheese over the bread mixture, then, using a wide metal spatula, scrape up and flip the mixture while mixing in the cheese. Redistribute in an even layer. Roast until the bread is browned and crisp and the fennel is tender and browned at the edges, another 10 to 15 minutes. Cool until barely warm, about 10 minutes.

Discard the tomato juices in the bowl, then transfer the tomatoes to the bowl. Add the remaining 1 tablespoon oil, the vinegar, parsley and ½ teaspoon pepper; toss. Add the bread-fennel mixture and toss again. Taste and season with salt and pepper. Transfer to a serving dish and drizzle with additional oil.

Optional garnish: Fresh mozzarella cheese, cut or torn into bite-size pieces OR bocconcini OR crumbled feta cheese

Sausage Traybake with Apples and Onions

Start to finish: 40 minutes (15 minutes active)
Servings: 4 to 6

Wide, low-sided baking sheets are ideal for oven-easy dinners; they facilitate heat circulation for better and faster browning. We pair savory sausages with sweet apples and onions, which get a flavor boost from spicy mustard; a glug of hard apple cider or beer is used to deglaze the baking sheet. We love the double dose of apple flavor from cider, though a crisp lager or malty amber beer also is delicious; if you prefer, use low-sodium chicken broth instead. Select apples with a firm texture yet thin skin that stays tender during roasting. Honeycrisp and Gala are good options.

2 medium red OR yellow onions, halved and sliced about ½ inch thick

1 tablespoon torn fresh sage OR 2 teaspoons fresh thyme, plus chopped sage or thyme to serve

2 tablespoons extra-virgin olive oil

Kosher salt and ground black pepper

1¼ pounds firm apples, quartered lengthwise and cored (see headnote)

1½ pounds kielbasa OR bratwurst OR sweet or hot Italian sausages, poked in several places with a paring knife

¼ cup hard apple cider OR beer OR broth (see headnote)

2 tablespoons whole-grain mustard OR Dijon mustard, plus more to serve

Heat the oven to 450°F with a rack in the middle position. On a rimmed baking sheet, toss together the onions, torn sage, oil and ½ teaspoon each salt and pepper; distribute in an even layer. Roast until the onions begin to soften and brown, about 10 minutes.

Remove from the oven and stir the onions. Add the apples and arrange the sausages on top. Roast until the centers of the sausages reach 160°F and the onions and apples are tender and lightly browned, 15 to 20 minutes.

Transfer the sausages and apples to a platter, leaving the onions in the pan. Pour the cider over the onions and stir, scraping up any browned bits. Stir in the mustard, then taste and season with salt and pepper. Transfer the onion mixture to the platter, spooning it around the sausages and apples. Sprinkle with chopped sage and serve with additional mustard.

Optional garnish: Chopped fresh dill OR pickled peppers OR both

Skillet-Roasted Chicken with Bread and Kale Salad

Start to finish: 1 hour 40 minutes (45 minutes active)
Servings: 4

This recipe was inspired by the late Judy Rodgers' wood oven-roasted chicken that has been on the menu at San Francisco's Zuni Cafe since 1987 and is a favorite to this day. We keep the dish one-pan easy by using a 12-inch skillet. The cooking starts on the stovetop and finishes in the oven, so make sure your pan is safe for use in a 475°F oven. The chicken is flipped twice during roasting. To do this, use a sturdy pair of tongs to grasp the bird by the backbone, insert one arm of the tongs into the cavity, then grip the chicken and flip it. **To boost flavor, we slip herb sprigs under the skin so they stay in place during roasting and flipping.** To promote crisp, browned skin, pat the bird dry before seasoning. And take advantage of all those wonderful pan drippings for the bread salad—they're the key to its rich, deep flavor.

Kosher salt and ground black pepper

3½- to 4-pound whole chicken, patted dry

6 thyme sprigs OR oregano sprigs

¼ cup plus 1 teaspoon extra-virgin olive oil, divided

8 ounces crusty bread, torn into large bite-size pieces (about 5 cups)

¼ cup golden raisins OR dried cherries, chopped

8 ounces baby kale OR frisée OR radicchio OR a combination, torn or cut into bite-size pieces (about 4 cups lightly packed)

¼ cup Peppadew peppers OR pickled sweet cherry peppers, thinly sliced, plus 2 tablespoons brine

Heat the oven to 475°F with a rack in the middle position. In a small bowl, stir together 1 tablespoon salt and 1 teaspoon pepper. Loosen the skin from the meat on the breast and thighs of the chicken. Slip the thyme sprigs under the skin. Sprinkle the salt-pepper mixture all over the chicken and in the cavity; set aside.

In a 12-inch oven-safe skillet over medium-high, heat ¼ cup oil until shimmering. Add the bread and cook, stirring occasionally, until golden brown, 3 to 5 minutes. Transfer to a large bowl, then toss in the raisins and ¼ cup water; set aside.

In the same skillet over medium, heat the remaining 1 teaspoon oil until shimmering. Place the chicken breast up in the skillet and transfer to the oven; roast for 15 minutes.

Remove the skillet from the oven (the handle will be hot). Using tongs, flip the chicken breast down, then roast for another 15 minutes. Remove the skillet from the oven once again and transfer the chicken to a large plate. Add the bread mixture to the skillet and toss to combine with any pan drippings. Set the chicken breast up on top of the bread. Roast until golden brown and the thickest part of the breast reaches 160°F, another 12 to 18 minutes.

Remove the skillet from the oven; the handle will be hot. Tilt the chicken so the juices run out of the cavity and into the skillet, then transfer the chicken to a cutting board. Let rest for 10 minutes.

Meanwhile, add the kale and peppers plus their brine to the skillet; toss with the bread. Taste and season with salt and pepper, then transfer to a platter. Carve the chicken, removing and discarding the thyme sprigs, and place the pieces on top of the salad. Drizzle with the accumulated juices.

Chicken with Avocado-Cilantro Sauce

Start to finish: 45 minutes (20 minutes active)
Servings: 4

Chicken roasted golden brown pairs perfectly with velvety avocado. **We let a bold and creamy sauce do the work for us, which keeps the roasting simple; we season the chicken with nothing but salt and pepper.** For our sauce we took inspiration from Venezuelan guasacaca, made from avocados, herbs and mild green chili, and a standard accompaniment to grilled meat.

3 pounds bone-in, skin-on chicken thighs OR breasts OR a combination, trimmed and patted dry

4 tablespoons extra-virgin olive oil, divided

Kosher salt and ground black pepper

2 ripe avocados, halved, pitted and peeled

1½ cups lightly packed cilantro OR flat-leaf parsley, plus extra chopped, to serve

1 jalapeño chili, stemmed and seeded

½ medium white onion, roughly chopped

3 tablespoons white vinegar

Heat the oven to 450°F with a rack in the middle position. On a rimmed baking sheet, toss the chicken with 2 tablespoons oil, then season with salt and pepper. Arrange skin side up and roast until the thickest part of the breast (if using) reaches about 160°F and the thickest part of the largest thigh/leg (if using) reaches about 175°F, 30 to 40 minutes. Remove from the oven and let rest for 10 minutes.

Meanwhile, in a food processor, combine the avocados, cilantro, jalapeño, onion, vinegar, the remaining 2 tablespoons oil and ¼ teaspoon each salt and pepper. Process until smooth, 1 to 2 minutes. Transfer the chicken to a platter and pour over any accumulated juices. Sprinkle with chopped cilantro and serve with the sauce.

Optional garnish: Lime wedges OR crumbled queso fresco OR chopped pickled jalapeños OR a combination

Harissa-Roasted Salmon with Lemon, Olive and Parsley Relish

Start to finish: 50 minutes (15 minutes active)
Servings: 4

Harissa, the North African spice paste we consider a pantry staple, adds flavor to salmon fillets along with garlic and lemon juice. After roasting, we serve the fillets with a simple three-ingredient relish made by combining parsley, lemon zest and chopped green (or black) olives. **We use the bold, zingy intensity of the herbal garnish to balance the fattiness of the salmon.** Serve with couscous alongside, and perhaps a cucumber or tomato salad.

3 tablespoons harissa paste

2 tablespoons extra-virgin olive oil, divided

3 medium garlic cloves, finely grated

1 tablespoon grated lemon zest, plus 2 teaspoons lemon juice, plus lemon wedges to serve

Kosher salt

Four 6-ounce center-cut skin-on salmon fillets (each 1 to 1¼ inches thick), patted dry

½ cup lightly packed fresh flat-leaf parsley OR cilantro, roughly chopped

½ cup pitted green OR black olives, roughly chopped

Set a wire rack in a rimmed baking sheet and mist it with cooking spray. In a small bowl, stir together the harissa, 1 tablespoon oil, garlic, the lemon juice and 1 teaspoon salt. Place the salmon skin side down on the rack. Rub the harissa mixture onto the top and sides of the fillets. Let stand at room temperature while the oven heats.

Heat the oven to 450°F with a rack in the middle position. Meanwhile, in a small bowl, stir together the parsley, olives, the remaining 1 tablespoon oil, the lemon zest and ¼ teaspoon salt.

Roast the salmon until the flesh flakes easily and the harissa mixture has deepened in color, 12 to 14 minutes. Serve the fillets with the parsley-olive mixture and lemon wedges.

Meatball Traybake
with Spicy Tomato Sauce

Start to finish: 1 hour (20 minutes active)
Servings: 4

A go-to pantry flavor solution does double duty when we add it to both meatballs and sauce. Depending on your mood and what you have on hand, give the dish a Mexican flair with smoky-spicy chipotle chilies in adobo, or use the spice paste harissa for a taste of North Africa. **We roast cherry tomatoes until they burst—their juices mingle with the seasonings to form a luscious sauce.** Then we nestle in the meatballs and roast everything in the same pan. Serve with crusty bread for dipping in the sauce. Refrigerate the meatballs before cooking; this firms them up so they'll hold their shape as they roast.

2 pints cherry OR grape tomatoes

6 medium garlic cloves, 4 cloves smashed and peeled, 2 cloves finely grated, reserved separately

¼ cup extra-virgin olive oil

2 medium chipotle chilies in adobo sauce, chopped, plus 2 teaspoons adobo sauce, divided OR 1 tablespoon plus 2 teaspoons harissa paste, divided

Kosher salt and ground black pepper

⅓ cup panko breadcrumbs

1 pound 90 percent lean ground beef OR ground lamb

Chopped fresh cilantro OR flat-leaf parsley, to serve

Heat the oven to 425°F with a rack in the middle position. In a 9-by-13-inch baking dish, toss together the tomatoes, smashed garlic, oil, chipotle chilies (or 1 tablespoon harissa), ¼ teaspoon each salt and pepper and ¼ cup water. Bake, uncovered, until the tomatoes have broken down, 30 to 35 minutes; stir once about halfway through.

Meanwhile, in a medium bowl, combine the panko and ½ cup water. Let stand until the panko softens, about 5 minutes, then use your hands to mash to a smooth paste. Add the beef, grated garlic, adobo sauce (or 2 teaspoons harissa) and ½ teaspoon each salt and pepper; mix thoroughly with your hands. Divide into 12 portions, rolling them into smooth balls. Place on a large plate and refrigerate until ready to use.

Remove the baking dish from the oven and nestle the meatballs in the tomato sauce. Bake, uncovered, until the meatballs are browned and the centers reach 160°F, about 15 minutes. Taste and season the sauce with salt and pepper. Sprinkle with cilantro.

Optional garnish: Crumbled cotija OR feta cheese

SPICED AND SPATCHCOCKED

As alluring as it can be, a perfectly roasted whole chicken can be a bit of a disappointment—hard to cook evenly and often turning out dry and bland. Enter two of our tried-and-trusted techniques, spatchcocking and seasoning under the skin.

Spatchcocking, or butterflying, the bird involves cutting out the backbone—a good pair of kitchen shears is all you need— and pressing the bird flat. That solves the problem of uneven cooking, putting breasts and thighs on the same plane so they cook in about the same time.

Meanwhile, we turn the skin from liability to asset. We make a seasoning paste that relies on a few high-impact ingredients and slide it right under the skin. The spices and herbs come into direct contact with the meat, which means better absorption, and the skin helps keep the seasonings in place.

Our trio of seasoning mixtures features a spicy-sweet mix of Korean gochujang and honey; a blend of miso, tomato paste and Parmesan that we, rightly, dub the "umami bomb;" and a cilantro, coriander and pickled jalapeño combination inspired by Yemen's pesto-like zhoug.

RECIPES FROM TOP

| Umami-Bomb Spatchcocked Roasted Chicken | Spatchcocked Roasted Chicken with Gochujang Butter | Spatchcocked Roasted Chicken with Cilantro, Coriander and Pickled Jalapeños |

Umami-Bomb Spatchcocked Roasted Chicken

Start to finish: 1 hour (15 minutes active)
Servings: 4

We combined a few of our favorite umami-rich ingredients to create a seasoning mixture for a spatchcocked chicken. Applied under the skin, directly onto the meat, the roasted bird is jam-packed with deep, complex flavors. Miso lends a salty-sweet taste and Parmesan cheese brings nuttiness; tomato paste adds concentrated sweet tomato flavor, while garlic contributes another layer of complexity. Use either red or white miso; white miso is mellower than the saltier, more assertive red miso. A simple tossed salad and crusty bread make good accompaniments.

4 tablespoons salted butter, room temperature

3 tablespoons white miso OR red miso

2 tablespoons finely grated Parmesan cheese

3 medium garlic cloves, finely grated

1 tablespoon tomato paste

Kosher salt and ground black pepper

4-pound whole chicken

Heat the oven to 425°F with a rack in the middle position. Set a wire rack in a rimmed baking sheet. In a small bowl, stir together the butter, miso, Parmesan, garlic, tomato paste and ½ teaspoon pepper; set aside.

Place the chicken breast down on a cutting board. Using sturdy kitchen shears, cut along both sides of the backbone, end to end; remove the backbone and discard. Spread open the chicken, then turn it breast up. Using the heel of your hand, press down firmly on the thickest part of the breast until the wishbone snaps.

Season the underside of the chicken with salt, then place it breast up on the wire rack. With your fingers, carefully loosen the skin from the meat on the breast and thighs. Using a spoon, distribute the butter mixture under the skin in those areas, then massage the skin to evenly spread the mixture and rub it into the flesh. Season the skin side with salt, then tuck the wing tips to the back.

Roast until well browned and the thighs reach 175°F, about 40 minutes. Let the chicken rest for about 10 minutes, then carve.

Spatchcocked Roasted Chicken with Gochujang Butter

Start to finish: 1 hour (15 minutes active)
Servings: 4

Our Korean-inspired seasoning paste elevates roast chicken with spicy-sweet flavor. The blend includes softened butter, gochujang and honey, plus fresh ginger and garlic, which mellow and sweeten as they cook. **We smear the mixture under the bird's skin, directly onto the meat, so it takes on the bold flavors.** Gochujang, one of our pantry staples, is a fermented chili paste commonly used in Korean cooking; it is loaded with spiciness, a hint of sweetness and lots of umami. You'll find it in the international section of the supermarket or in Asian grocery stores. Serve with steamed rice.

4 tablespoons salted butter, room temperature

¼ cup gochujang

4 teaspoons finely grated fresh ginger

3 medium garlic cloves, finely grated

1 tablespoon honey

Kosher salt

4-pound whole chicken

Heat the oven to 425°F with a rack in the middle position. Set a wire rack in a rimmed baking sheet. In a small bowl, stir together the butter, gochujang, ginger, garlic, honey and ½ teaspoon salt; set aside.

Place the chicken breast down on a cutting board. Using sturdy kitchen shears, cut along both sides of the backbone, end to end; remove the backbone and discard. Spread open the chicken, then turn it breast up. Using the heel of your hand, press down firmly on the thickest part of the breast until the wishbone snaps.

Season the underside of the chicken with salt, then place it breast up on the wire rack. With your fingers, carefully loosen the skin from the meat on the breast and thighs. Using a spoon, distribute the butter mixture under the skin in those areas, then massage the skin to evenly spread the mixture and rub it into the flesh. Season the skin side with salt, then tuck the wing tips to the back.

Roast until well browned and the thighs reach 175°F, about 40 minutes. Let the chicken rest for about 10 minutes, then carve.

Spatchcocked Roasted Chicken with Cilantro, Coriander and Pickled Jalapeños

Start to finish: 1 hour (20 minutes active)
Servings: 4

The seasoning for this roast chicken, applied under the skin directly onto the meat for maximum flavor, was inspired by zhoug, the zesty, pesto-like condiment said to have originated in Yemen. Lots of fresh cilantro adds herbaceousness; you can swap in parsley instead or combine the two herbs. In place of the traditional fresh chilies, we bump up the flavor with pickled jalapeños. Ground coriander brings citrusy notes to the mix (cardamom also works well). Accompany with pearl couscous or boiled or roasted potatoes.

½ cup lightly packed fresh cilantro OR fresh flat-leaf parsley OR a combination, finely chopped

¼ cup extra-virgin olive oil

3 tablespoons pickled jalapeños, finely chopped

2 teaspoons grated lemon zest, plus lemon wedges to serve

1 teaspoon ground coriander OR ground cardamom OR a combination

Kosher salt and ground black pepper

4-pound whole chicken

Heat the oven to 425°F with a rack in the middle position. Set a wire rack in a rimmed baking sheet. In a small bowl, stir together the cilantro, oil, jalapeños, lemon zest, coriander, ½ teaspoon salt and ¼ teaspoon pepper; set aside.

Place the chicken breast down on a cutting board. Using sturdy kitchen shears, cut along both sides of the backbone, end to end; remove the backbone and discard. Spread open the chicken, then turn it breast up. Using the heel of your hand, press down firmly on the thickest part of the breast until the wishbone snaps.

Season the underside of the chicken with salt, then place it breast up on the wire rack. With your fingers, carefully loosen the skin from the meat on the breast and thighs. Using a spoon, distribute the cilantro mixture under the skin in those areas, then massage the skin to evenly spread the mixture and rub it into the flesh. Season the skin side with salt, then tuck the wing tips to the back.

Roast until well browned and the thighs reach 175°F, about 40 minutes. Let the chicken rest for about 10 minutes, then carve. Serve with lemon wedges.

Pan-Roasted Pork Tenderloin and Fennel with Coriander and Orange

Start to finish: 50 minutes
Servings: 6 to 8

The seasonings in the Greek sausage loukaniko—garlic, orange and coriander—inspired this weeknight-friendly dish. We first season pork with a mixture of grated garlic, orange zest and crushed coriander seeds. **To ensure good caramelization on the outside and perfectly done meat on the inside, we sear the meat on the stovetop, then finish roasting it in the oven** along with fresh fennel (or leeks). A pan sauce made with more garlic, orange zest and orange juice adds another layer of complexity. You will need an oven-safe 12-inch skillet for this recipe.

5 tablespoons extra-virgin olive oil, divided, plus more to serve

5 medium garlic cloves, finely grated, divided

2 tablespoons grated orange zest, divided, plus ¼ cup orange juice, plus orange wedges to serve

1 tablespoon coriander seeds, lightly crushed OR 2 teaspoons dried oregano OR both

Kosher salt and ground black pepper

Two 1- to 1¼-pound pork tenderloins, trimmed of silver skin and halved crosswise

2 medium fennel bulbs, trimmed, cored and cut into ½-inch wedges OR 4 medium leeks, white and light green parts sliced 1 inch thick, rinsed and dried

1 tablespoon red wine vinegar

Heat the oven to 450°F with a rack in the middle position. In a small bowl, stir together 3 tablespoons oil, three-quarters of the garlic, 1 tablespoon orange zest, the coriander, 1 teaspoon salt and ¾ teaspoon pepper. Rub all over the pork.

In an oven-safe 12-inch skillet over medium-high, heat the remaining 2 tablespoons oil until barely smoking. Add the pork and cook, turning occasionally, until lightly browned on all sides, about 4 minutes. Transfer to a plate. In the same skillet over medium-high, combine the fennel and 2 tablespoons water. Cook, scraping up any browned bits, until lightly browned, 3 to 4 minutes. Set the pork on the fennel, then transfer the skillet to the oven. Roast until the center of the thickest part of the pork reaches 135°F or is just slightly pink when cut into, 9 to 12 minutes.

Remove the skillet from the oven (the handle will be hot), transfer the pork to a cutting board and tent with foil. To the fennel mixture in the pan, add the remaining garlic and 1 tablespoon orange zest, the orange juice and ½ cup water. Bring to a simmer over medium-high and cook, stirring, until the fennel is tender and the sauce is lightly thickened, 4 to 6 minutes. Off heat, stir in the vinegar, then taste and season with salt and pepper. Transfer to a serving dish. Slice the pork and arrange on top. Drizzle with additional oil and serve with orange wedges.

Optional garnish: Chopped fresh oregano OR flaky salt OR both

Chicken Traybake with Poblano Chilies, Tomatoes and Onions

Start to finish: 45 minutes (20 minutes active)
Servings: 4 to 6

Family-friendly chicken fajitas inspired this easy dinner on a baking sheet. **We add the ingredients in stages to ensure each cooks perfectly. First, we cook earthy poblano chilies and onions until tender. Then sweet-tart tomatoes join the mix, followed by boneless chicken parts, which need only a quick-roast to cook through.** Tangy tomatillos can be substituted for tomatoes, bringing more bright acidity. For a low-effort taco night, serve with warm tortillas and an array of condiments.

3 tablespoons extra-virgin olive oil

2 medium garlic cloves, finely grated

1 tablespoon chili powder OR 2 teaspoons ground cumin plus ¼ teaspoon cayenne

Kosher salt and ground black pepper

1½ pounds boneless, skinless chicken breasts OR thighs, trimmed

2 medium red OR white onions, peeled and cut into 1-inch wedges

2 poblano chilies, stemmed, seeded and cut into 1- to 1½-inch strips

1 pint grape OR cherry tomatoes OR 4 medium tomatillos (about 8 ounces), husked, cored and halved

Heat the oven to 500°F with a rack in the middle position. In a medium bowl, stir together the oil, garlic, chili powder, 1¼ teaspoons salt and ½ teaspoon pepper. Measure 2 tablespoons of the oil-spice mixture into a wide, shallow dish; add the chicken and turn to coat, rubbing in the seasonings; set aside.

To the remaining oil-spice mixture, add the onions and chilies. Toss, then distribute evenly on a rimmed baking sheet. Roast until the vegetables begin to brown and soften, 8 to 10 minutes. Remove the baking sheet from the oven, stir in the tomatoes and place the chicken on top. Roast until the thickest part of the breasts (if using) reaches 160°F and the thickest part of the largest thigh (if using) reaches 175°F, another 15 to 20 minutes.

Transfer the chicken to a cutting board and let rest for 5 minutes. Meanwhile, transfer the vegetables and any accumulated juices to a platter. Thinly slice the chicken, then taste and season with salt and pepper and transfer to the platter.

Optional garnish: Mexican crema OR sour cream OR hot sauce OR lime wedges OR a combination

Honey-Miso Salmon
and Broccolini Traybake

Start to finish: 30 minutes
Servings: 4

Miso, soy sauce and honey make a savory-sweet, umami-rich marinade for meaty, fat-rich salmon. Some of the mixture is set aside and combined with orange juice and zest, creating a savory-sweet sauce for drizzling over the finished dish. While the fish marinates, the Broccolini gets a head start on roasting. Then once the quick-cooking salmon is added, the traybake is nearly done. Serve with steamed rice, and perhaps a leafy green salad alongside.

2 tablespoons white OR red miso

2 tablespoons soy sauce

2 tablespoons honey

3 tablespoons neutral oil, divided

Four 6-ounce center-cut salmon fillets
(1 to 1¼ inches thick), patted dry

1 tablespoon grated orange zest, plus
2 tablespoons orange juice

1 pound Broccolini, trimmed OR broccoli
crowns, cut into 1-inch florets

Kosher salt and ground black pepper

Heat the oven to 425°F with a rack in the middle position. In a small bowl, whisk together the miso, soy sauce, honey and 1 tablespoon oil. Transfer half of the mixture to a wide, shallow dish; add the salmon skin-side up and set aside. Stir the orange zest and juice into the mixture remaining in the bowl; set aside.

On a rimmed baking sheet, toss the Broccolini with the remaining 2 tablespoons oil and ½ teaspoon each salt and pepper. Distribute in an even layer, then roast until beginning to brown at the edges, about 15 minutes.

Remove the baking sheet from the oven. Using a wide metal spatula, scrape up and flip the Broccolini, pushing it to the edges. Add the salmon, skin-side down, to the center of the baking sheet. Roast until the fish flakes easily and the Broccolini is lightly charred and tender-crisp, 7 to 10 minutes. Transfer to a platter and drizzle with the miso-orange sauce.

Optional garnish: Toasted sesame oil OR toasted sesame seeds OR sliced scallions OR red pepper flakes OR a combination

Lacquered Pork Ribs with Hoisin, Honey and Five-Spice

Start to finish: 2¼ hours (30 minutes active), plus resting
Servings: 4

These addictive, salty-sweet pork ribs were inspired by char siu, a popular style of Cantonese barbecued meat often made with long, thin strips of pork shoulder. To season racks of baby back ribs, we combine hoisin, honey, soy sauce, fresh ginger and five-spice powder. Part of the mix goes onto the ribs before they go into the oven; the rest is reserved for glazing during cooking. **Brushing ribs with a glazing mixture at 30-minute intervals builds layers of caramelization, resulting in a lacquered finish.**

½ cup hoisin sauce

¼ cup honey

1 tablespoon soy sauce

1 tablespoon finely grated fresh ginger
OR 3 medium garlic cloves, finely grated
OR both

1½ teaspoons Chinese five-spice powder

Kosher salt and ground black pepper

Two 3- to 3½-pound racks baby back pork ribs

Heat the oven to 325°F with a rack in the middle position. Set a wire rack in a rimmed baking sheet. In a small bowl, whisk together the hoisin, honey, soy sauce, ginger, five-spice, 1 teaspoon salt and ¾ teaspoon pepper. Measure ⅓ cup of the mixture into another small bowl and set aside for glazing. Pour the remainder onto the ribs, rubbing to coat both sides.

Place the ribs meaty side up on the prepared rack. Bake, brushing the surface of the rib racks with about 1 tablespoon of the glaze mixture about every 30 minutes, until well browned and a skewer inserted between the bones meets no resistance, 2 to 2½ hours. Transfer the rib racks to a cutting board and let rest for about 20 minutes. Cut the ribs between the bones and transfer to a platter.

Optional garnish: Toasted sesame seeds OR thinly sliced scallions OR both

Mojo Chicken and Sweet Potato Traybake

Start to finish: 45 minutes
Servings: 4 to 6

Latin American mojo is a punchy sauce/marinade starring citrus juice or vinegar, herbs and lots of garlic. It's often used to season meat, but is also a popular accompaniment to fried plantains or yuca. We turn those flavors into a bold, citrusy garlic-herb paste. **We double down on the seasoning paste, using some of it as a marinade and the rest as a bright finishing sauce.**

1 bunch cilantro, chopped, stems and leaves reserved separately

10 medium garlic cloves, smashed and peeled

3 tablespoons extra-virgin olive oil, divided

2 teaspoons grated orange zest, plus 4 tablespoons orange juice, divided

1 tablespoon dried oregano

Kosher salt and ground black pepper

3 pounds bone-in, skin-on chicken breasts OR thighs, trimmed and patted dry

1½ pounds medium sweet potatoes, peeled and cut into ½-inch wedges

In a food processor, combine the cilantro stems, garlic, 2 tablespoons oil, 2 tablespoons orange juice, oregano, 2 teaspoons salt and 1 teaspoon pepper. Process to a coarse paste, about 30 seconds. Measure 1 tablespoon of the mixture into a small bowl, then stir in the orange zest and remaining 2 tablespoons juice; set aside. Transfer the remainder to a large bowl and add the chicken. Rub the mixture into the chicken; let stand at room temperature while the oven heats.

Heat the oven to 475°F with a rack in the middle position. Transfer the chicken skin side up and in a single layer to the center of a rimmed baking sheet. In the now-empty bowl, toss together the sweet potatoes and remaining 1 tablespoon oil, then distribute evenly around the chicken. Roast until the thickest part of the breasts (if using) reaches 160°F and the thickest part of the largest thigh/leg (if using) reaches 175°F, 30 to 35 minutes.

Transfer the chicken to a platter. Push the potatoes to the perimeter of the baking sheet and add the reserved cilantro-orange mixture and half of the cilantro leaves to the clearing. Scrape up any browned bits, then stir to combine with the potatoes. Transfer the potatoes to the platter with the chicken and spoon any juices over the top. Sprinkle with the remaining cilantro leaves.

Gochujang-Glazed Tofu and Bok Choy Traybake

Start to finish: 45 minutes (25 minutes active)
Servings: 4

This salty-sweet and subtly spicy traybake takes inspiration from the Korean gochujang-glazed tofu dish, dubu gangjeong. To start, **we bake cornstarch-coated tofu in a ripping-hot oven to give it a crisp crust and flavorful browning.** We then brush it with a gochujang-honey glaze, which concentrates and caramelizes. Leafy green baby bok choy joins the tofu midway through, its tender-crisp stems and lightly charred leaves offering lots of textural and flavor contrast to the tofu. Steaming-hot rice is a perfect match for this well-seasoned traybake.

2 tablespoons neutral oil

2 tablespoons gochujang

2 tablespoons honey

2 tablespoons toasted sesame oil, divided, plus more to serve

Kosher salt and ground black pepper

¼ cup cornstarch

14-ounce container firm OR extra-firm tofu, drained, patted dry and cut into ½-inch planks

12 ounces baby bok choy, halved lengthwise and patted dry OR green beans, trimmed

Heat the oven to 475°F with a rack in the upper-middle position. Brush a rimmed baking sheet with the neutral oil. In a small bowl, whisk together the gochujang, honey, 1 tablespoon sesame oil, ½ teaspoon salt and ¼ teaspoon pepper; set aside.

Put the cornstarch in a wide, shallow dish; add the tofu and turn to coat. Place the tofu in the center of the prepared baking sheet, shaking off the excess starch and spacing the planks about ½ inch apart. Bake until the tofu is lightly browned and releases easily from the baking sheet, 15 to 18 minutes. Meanwhile, in a medium bowl, toss the bok choy with the remaining 1 tablespoon sesame oil and ¼ teaspoon each salt and pepper.

Remove the baking sheet from the oven and lightly brush the tops and sides of the tofu with some of the gochujang mixture. Using a thin metal spatula, flip the tofu, then lightly brush with gochujang mixture. Arrange the bok choy around the tofu. Bake until the tofu and bok choy are lightly browned, about 10 minutes.

Flip the tofu and bok choy, then once again lightly brush the tofu with gochujang mixture. Bake until the tofu is well browned, about 5 minutes. Remove from the oven and brush the tofu with any remaining gochujang mixture. Transfer to a platter and drizzle with additional sesame oil.

Optional garnish: Thinly sliced chives OR scallions OR toasted sesame seeds OR furikake OR crumbled nori snacks

Slow-Roasted Pork Shoulder with Fennel, Garlic and Rosemary

Start to finish: 4¾ hours (20 minutes active)
Servings: 8 to 10

This recipe takes inspiration from porchetta, a Tuscan-style pork roast seasoned with garlic, herbs and spices. We make a simple seasoning paste and rub the mixture into shallow cuts in the meat's fat so it clings to the roast. **Roasting meat on a baking sheet, rather than in a roasting pan, promotes better air circulation, accelerating cooking and boosting browning.** Use the time while the meat rests to throw together a zingy-fresh parsley-caper sauce that's a perfect foil to the richness of the meat.

3 tablespoons fennel seeds

½ cup extra-virgin olive oil, divided

⅔ cup lightly packed fresh rosemary

9 medium garlic cloves, 8 smashed and peeled, 1 finely grated, reserved separately

Kosher salt and ground black pepper

5-pound boneless pork shoulder roast, untrimmed

2 cups lightly packed fresh, flat-leaf parsley, chopped

¼ cup drained capers, plus 3 tablespoons caper brine

Heat the oven to 300°F with a rack in the middle position. In a food processor, process the fennel seeds to a mixture of finely ground and coarsely cracked seeds, about 2 minutes. Add ¼ cup oil, the rosemary, smashed garlic cloves, 1 tablespoon salt and 2 teaspoons pepper. Process to form a paste, about 30 seconds, scraping the bowl as needed.

With a knife, score a crosshatch pattern into the surface fat on top of the roast. Using your hands, rub the paste onto all sides of the roast and into the cuts. Place the pork fat side up on a rimmed baking sheet and roast until the center reaches 195°F, about 4 hours.

When the roast is done, tent with foil and let rest for about 15 minutes. Meanwhile, in a small bowl, stir together the remaining ¼ cup oil, grated garlic, parsley, capers and brine and ¼ teaspoon pepper. Transfer the roast to a cutting board. Cut into slices, then transfer to a platter. Serve with the sauce.

Crisped Chickpea and Cauliflower Traybake with Lemon-Garlic Yogurt

Start to finish: 35 minutes
Servings: 4

Contrasting flavors and textures make an easy tray-bake special. Cauliflower takes on light charring and becomes supple and tender while chickpeas roast alongside, turning toasty and crisp. A lemony, garlicky yogurt sauce ties everything together, and **a spice blend does double duty, seasoning the cauliflower-chickpea mixture as well as the sauce.** Curry powder lends a golden hue and an earthy spiciness; baharat, a Middle Eastern seasoning mix, leans toward warm, nutty, smoky-sweet notes.

¼ cup plus 1 tablespoon extra-virgin olive oil, divided

3 teaspoons curry powder OR baharat, divided

Kosher salt and ground black pepper

2½- to 3-pound head cauliflower, trimmed and cut into 1-inch florets

15½-ounce can chickpeas, rinsed and drained

⅓ cup plain whole-milk yogurt

1 tablespoon grated lemon zest, plus 2 tablespoons lemon juice, plus lemon wedges, to serve

1 medium garlic clove, finely grated

Heat the oven to 425°F with a rack in the middle position. In a large bowl, stir together ¼ cup oil, 2 teaspoons curry powder, 1 teaspoon salt and ½ teaspoon pepper. Add the cauliflower and chickpeas; toss to coat, rubbing the seasonings in. Transfer to a rimmed baking sheet in an even layer. Roast until the cauliflower is fully tender and lightly charred and the chickpeas have crisped, 50 to 60 minutes, stirring after 20 and 40 minutes.

Meanwhile, in a small bowl, stir together the yogurt, lemon zest and juice, garlic, the remaining 1 tablespoon oil, the remaining 1 teaspoon curry powder and ¼ teaspoon of salt.

Transfer the cauliflower-chickpea mixture to a serving dish, then taste and season with salt and pepper. Spoon on the yogurt sauce or serve the sauce on the side, along with lemon wedges.

Optional garnish: Pomegranate molasses OR thinly sliced fresh mint OR chopped fresh cilantro OR Aleppo pepper OR a combination

Index

bulgur
   caramelized onion, 119
   pilaf with, 103
   salad with, 95
   with tomato and mint, 110
burgers
   Cuban-spiced, 33
   pita, with crisped cheese, 23
butter
   beef rice bowl with, 123
   carrots roasted with, 45
   chicken with gochujang, 330–31
   corn sautéed with, 143
   pasta with, 148–49, 184, 211
   pork chops with browned, 153
   scallops with browned, 135
   tomato sauce with browned,
      192–93
   udon noodles with, 220
   vinaigrette with browned, 58

C

cabbage
   chicken yakisoba with, 237
   slaw with, 70
   See also kimchi
capers
   escarole and fennel salad with,
      46
   sauces with, 268, 344
   scallops with, 135
caraway seeds
   beet salad with, 55
   Hungarian potatoes with, 73
   tarka with, 160
carrots
   butter-roasted, 45
   five-spice stir-fried, 243
   rice with, 92
   salads with, 47, 50
   soups with, 139, 150
cashews
   coconut rice with, 117
   salads with, 47, 65
cauliflower
   with chili crisp sauce, 297

crisped chickpeas and, 345
   mustard-roasted, 84
   pasta sauce with, 197
   sweet-and-sour, 240
   tagine (stew) with, 141
   tandoori-inspired chicken and,
      309
celery
   farro with, 115
   salads with, 51, 77
celery root, barley pilaf with, 105
cheese
   creamy pasta sauce with, 197
   gemelli and peas with ricotta,
      204
   inverted pizzas with, 29, 30
   kimchi grilled, 35
   panini with provolone, 19
   pita burgers with, 23
   polenta with, 98–99
   potatoes with Gouda, 318
   quesadillas with crisped, 37
   salads with, 125, 199
   tartines with Gruyère, 10
   Tex-Mex migas with jack, 133
   zucchini with lemony ricotta,
      279
cheese, feta
   baked, 284
   Brussels sprouts with, 291
   farro with, 115
   salads with, 25, 41
cheese, mozzarella
   orecchiette with, 149
   pizzadilla with, 11
   pour-in-the-pan pizza with,
      4–5
cheese, Parmesan
   broccolini salad with, 63
   broccoli rabe and sausage with,
      157
   butternut squash with, 318–19
   eggs in purgatory with, 167
   farfalle pesto with, 185
   fettucine Alfredo with, 211

greens and crisped bread with,
      137
   oven-baked eggs with, 285
   pasta breadcrumbs with, 213
   penne carbonara with, 205
   spatchcocked chicken with, 330
   white bean soup with, 145
cheese, pecorino Romano
   panzanella with, 319
   pasta sauce with, 204–5, 215
   tortellini with, 207
chicken
   with avocado-cilantro sauce,
      324
   berbere-spiced skewers of, 287
   butter and lemon pasta with, 184
   with chilies, tomatoes, and
      onions, 335
   curry with tomatoes and yogurt,
      175
   fried rice with, 116
   gochujang, 225
   harissa-spiced, 263
   mojo, sweet potatoes and, 341
   orange-miso, 246
   rice bowl with, 122–23
   salad with zucchini and, 51
   shiitake-scallion, 173
   Sichuan pepper, 230–31
   skillet-roasted, 323
   spatchcocked roasted, 328–31
   tandoori-inspired, 309
   Thai asparagus and, 227
   tomato masala pasta with,
      148–49
   West African peanut, 169
   yakisoba, 237
chickpea flour flatbread, 25
chickpeas
   rice and, 113
   salad with, 43
   soup with, 151
   tagine (stew) with, 141
   traybake with crisped, 345
chili crisp, cauliflower with, 297

Acknowledgments

Writing a cookbook is a daunting endeavor, requiring the bringing together of numerous and disparate talents to achieve one well-conceived concept, from recipe conception and development through photography, editing and design. At Milk Street, many hands and minds make this possible.

In particular, I want to acknowledge J.M. Hirsch, our tireless editorial director; Michelle Locke, our relentlessly organized books editor; our exacting food editors Dawn Yanagihara and Bianca Borges; Matthew Card, creative director of recipes; and associate editor, Ari Smolin, for leading the charge on conceiving, developing, writing and editing all of this.

Also, Jennifer Baldino Cox, our art director, and the entire design team who captured a fresh look for Milk Street's evolving brand. Special thanks to Erik Bernstein, photographer (and props stylist); Erika Joyce, food stylist; and Gary Tooth, book designer.

Our talented kitchen crew, including our kitchen director, Wes Martin; Diane Unger, recipe development director; Courtney Hill, assistant recipe development director; and our recipe developers and research team, including Rose Hattabaugh, Malcolm Jackson, Dimitri Demopoulos, Elizabeth Mindreau, Kevin Clark, Hector Taborda and Andrew Jennings. Deborah Broide, Milk Street director of media relations, has done a spectacular job of sharing with the world all we do at Milk Street.

We also have a couple of folks to thank who work outside of 177 Milk Street. Michael Szczerban, editor, and everyone at Little, Brown and Company have been superb and inspired partners in this project. And my long-standing book agent, David Black, has been instrumental in bringing this project to life both with his knowledge of publishing and his friendship and support. Thank you, David!

And, last but not least, to all of you who have supported the Milk Street project. Each and every one of you has a seat at the Milk Street table.

Christopher Kimball

About the Author

Christopher Kimball is founder of Christopher Kimball's Milk Street, a food media company dedicated to changing the way we cook. It produces the bimonthly *Christopher Kimball's Milk Street Magazine*, as well as *Christopher Kimball's Milk Street Radio*, a weekly public radio show and podcast heard on more than 220 stations nationwide. It also produces the public television show *Christopher Kimball's Milk Street*, as well as two shows produced in partnership with Roku, *Milk Street Cooking School* and *My Family Recipe*. Kimball founded *Cook's Magazine* in 1980 and served as publisher and editorial director through 1989. He re-launched it as *Cook's Illustrated* in 1993. Through 2016, Kimball was host and executive producer of *America's Test Kitchen* and *Cook's Country*. He also hosted *America's Test Kitchen* radio show on public radio. Kimball is the author of several books, including *Fannie's Last Supper*.

Christopher Kimball's Milk Street is located at 177 Milk Street in downtown Boston and is dedicated to changing the way America cooks, with new flavor combinations and techniques learned around the world. It is home to Milk Street TV, a three-time Emmy Award–winning public television show, a James Beard Award–winning bimonthly magazine, an award-winning radio show and podcast, a cooking school and an online store with more than 1,700 kitchen tools and ingredients. Milk Street's cookbooks include *Milk Street Cookish*, the IACP-winning *Milk Street Vegetables*, and the James Beard–winning *Milk Street Tuesday Nights*. Milk Street also invests in nonprofit outreach, partnering with FoodCorps, the Big Sister Association of Greater Boston and the Boys & Girls Clubs of Dorchester.